Building Low-Code Applications with Mendix

Discover best practices and expert techniques to simplify enterprise web development

Bryan Kenneweg

Imran Kasam

Micah McMullen

BIRMINGHAM—MUMBAI

Building Low-Code Applications with Mendix

Copyright © 2021 Packt Publishing

Group Product Manager: Ashwin Nair

Publishing Product Manager: Pavan Ramchandani

Senior Editor: Senior Editor

Content Development Editor: Rakhi Patel

Technical Editor: Deepesh Patel

Copy Editor: Safis Editing

Project Coordinator: Kinjal Bari

Proofreader: Safis Editing

Indexer: Pratik Shirodkar

Production Designer: Vijay Kamble

First published: February 2021

Production reference: 1240221

Published by Packt Publishing Ltd.

Livery Place

35 Livery Street

Birmingham

B3 2PB, UK.

ISBN 978-1-80020-142-2

www.packt.com

To my darling, lovely wife, Ashley, the smartest, funniest best friend I have in this world, who picks me up when I need it, as well as keeping my feet on the ground when I deserve it, thank you for your endless love and motivation. To those who took a chance on me, giving me the opportunity to grow to where I am in life, thank you.

– Bryan Kenneweg

To my beautiful and supportive wife, Clarissa, thank you for being my sounding board, my idea consultant, and my hype woman. Your love keeps me striving to be a better person. To my mentor and co-host, Stephen Ledwith, thank you for the opportunities to learn and grow from my mistakes and for constantly guiding me up to the next level. To everyone who forced me to question my current position in life, which gave me the wherewithal to take the risk to move forward, thank you.

– Imran Kasam

To my incredible wife, Elizabeth, thank you for your unending support and love. Your joy and passion for life make me a better, happier person every day. Thank you for all that you do! To my boys, thank you for challenging me every day to be a kinder, more patient, and loving father and human. Your ability to provide an unending amount of craziness and pure joy is what keeps me going. Love you!

– Micah McMullen

Foreword

A Journey in Low-Code

I would be lying if I told you I discovered low-code in 2014. The truth is, low-code discovered me. After spending countless hours in the **traditional software development life cycle (SDLC)**, I knew there had to be a better way. Fortunately, the convergence of three undeniable emerging trends sent me on a journey that is still unraveling. The trends are 1) the cloud, 2) mobile, and 3) low-/no-code. My world has never been the same. Amazon released AWS in 2006, Apple announced the iPhone in 2007, and Mendix announced the first low-code app platform in 2005.

The authors of this book have collectively worked on some of the largest ongoing low-code implementations in the world. From banking to insurance, government to manufacturing, construction to logistics, real estate to manufacturing, and everything in between. Our paths have crossed traversing the globe to assist customers, attend Mendix World, and share best practices. With *Building Low-Code Applications with Mendix*, you will receive a crash course in modeling high-quality, scalable, and reliable applications. This book covers the essence of what you need to get familiar with low-code and how to use it in practice.

In their presentations and examples, Imran, Micah, and Bryan demonstrate how easy it is to create an account, get familiar with the development tools, understand the core components of low-code, and how to extend solutions via REST integrations. After you complete Imran, Micah, and Bryan's book, you'll understand how to architect a data model, build reusable microflows, and extend your applications with REST services. Mastering this material transforms the recipient of the knowledge from a casually informed to a capable full-stack rapid application developer.

Mastery of these powerful tools will unlock a wide range of cloud-native, device-agnostic applications.

Beyond developing solutions for desktops and smartphones, you'll begin to appreciate how to leverage the Mendix platform to transform the way your organization thinks about IT projects and innovation. The Mendix community is an ever growing ecosystem, and this is a great book to get you up to speed with low-code in 2021 and beyond.

Michael Guido

Chief Executive Officer, Kinetech

Michael Guido is the CEO of Kinetech, a low-code pioneer and Mendix partner. Michael is passionate about value creation, advising/collaborating with clients, architecting solutions, and leading teams to solve strategic and operational challenges across a range of industries in both the public and private sector. Prior to cofounding Kinetech, Michael worked as a strategy and systems integration consultant at Accenture before becoming the #2 USA business engineering consultant at Mendix. Michael holds a Bachelor of Science in systems engineering and a double minor in mathematics and business from the University of Virginia.

Contributors

About the authors

Bryan Kenneweg is a Mendix Expert certified developer, as well as a software engineer team lead at eXp Realty. He has worked as a consultant at TimeSeries and as a freelance developer. Bryan enjoys finding solutions for organizations to be more successful, a nice pint, and his family.

Imran Kasam is an independent Mendix architecture consultant who has been working with the platform since 2012. He is a Mendix Expert certified developer and Mendix MVP. Imran likes to help companies mature their engineering teams and software delivery practices. In his spare time, Imran records and produces a podcast with his mentor, called *The Architect and The Executive*.

Micah McMullen is a software engineer and team lead at eXp Realty. He has been working with Mendix since 2013 and is Expert certified. He enjoys solving complex business requirements with simple solutions. Outside of the office, Micah enjoys hiking, cycling, and spending time with his family.

About the reviewer

After joining Mendix in 2010 in the Mendix project department, **Rene van Hofwegen** worked as a consultant on several Mendix projects. Rene shifted his focus to Mendix Academy at the start of 2011, starting with hosting and developing Mendix training courses, which extended toward the overall management of Mendix Academy.

In 2017, Rene left Mendix, leaving behind the Mendix training and certification program, as it still exists. After leaving Mendix, Rene kept contributing to the Mendix community as a Mendix trainer and coaching Mendix developers in Europe. In 2018, he was appointed Mendix MVP and received the Mendix Trainer certification.

In 2021, Rene founded the Low-Code Academy. He collaborates with Mendix, Mendix Academy, and several Mendix partners to provide the best low-code training and coaching.

Table of Contents

Section 2:
Building Your First App

5

Getting Started with Your Baseline App

6

Understanding Domain Model Basics

7

Understanding the Basics of Page Design

8
Getting to Know Microflows

Section 3:
Leveling Up Your App

9
Customizing Your App

10
Error Handling and Troubleshooting

11
Storing Data

12
Getting Some REST

13
A Review and What's Next

Other Books You May Enjoy

Index

Preface

Thank you for taking a look at *Building Low-Code Applications with Mendix*. You will take the first step in discovering what low-code is, the differences between platforms, the benefits, and what Mendix is all about. First off, low-code is exactly what it sounds like. It uses a visual platform instead of a traditional one, which allows you to build applications more rapidly by reducing the need for traditional code. Mendix is one of the leaders in this field, which we will be using throughout this book. We will take you through the basics of account creation and breaking down the interface. From there, you will be guided through app creation, all the way to storing data and creating REST services. By the end, you will have a strong understanding of Mendix basics, as well as a fully functioning application.

Who this book is for

This book is intended for anyone excited to learn more about low-code and the Mendix platform. The content of the book will appeal to students learning about software development and computer science as well as seasoned software engineers looking to broaden their knowledge and learn a new tool. While it would be helpful for the reader to have at least minimal knowledge of computer science and software development, it is certainly not a requirement. Anyone with passion and curiosity can build applications with Mendix and we're hoping to help you get started on that journey!

What this book covers

Chapter 1, Introducing Mendix, goes through what low-code is and introduces Mendix and its history.

Chapter 2, Getting to Know the Mendix Platform, walks you through the Mendix account creation process, as well as the features of the Mendix platform once created.

Chapter 3, Getting to Know Mendix Studio, concentrates on Mendix Studio, Mendix's low-code web platform.

Chapter 4, Getting to Know Studio Pro, deep dives into what Studio Pro is, how to use it, as well as understanding the interface.

Chapter 5, Getting Started with Your Baseline App, helps you familiarize yourself with the Developer Portal and build a baseline app in Mendix Studio Pro.

Chapter 6, Understanding Domain Model Basics, covers the Mendix domain model and starts you building one in Mendix Studio Pro.

Chapter 7, Understanding the Basics of Page Design, introduces pages, widgets, layouts, and the Atlas UI framework to build a user interface in Mendix Studio Pro.

Chapter 8, Getting to Know Microflows, covers microflows and how to use them to create application logic in Mendix Studio Pro.

Chapter 9, Customizing Your App, discusses functions, sub-microflows, and some additional ways to enhance your application and implement custom business logic.

Chapter 10, Error Handling and Troubleshooting, explores ways to be proactive about problems and errors, which are an inevitable part of software development, and arms you with the tools to be able to dig into problems when they do pop up.

Chapter 11, Storing Data, explores how to build out your application's database. We will accomplish this by discussing various ways to associate your entities and create rock-solid domain models.

Chapter 12, Getting Some REST, looks at how connected the world is these days and the importance of understanding how to create integrations with other applications and data sources. In this chapter, you will learn how to pull data from a third-party data source using a REST call.

Chapter 13, A Review and What's Next, wraps it all up by taking a look back at all the subjects and areas we covered throughout the book!

To get the most out of this book

Readers should have a basic understanding of object-oriented programming, either through experience with another language such as Java, PHP, JavaScript, and so on, or advanced usage of scripting in MS Office products or similar. Keep an open mind about the possibilities of low-code programming. Use the low-code platform to better understand and apply the concepts of object-oriented programming. Install Mendix Studio Pro and work along with the exercises in the book.

Software/Hardware covered in the book	OS Requirements
Mendix Studio Pro 8.11 or higher	Windows 7 (service pack 1 or higher), 8, or 10 64-bit

Any additional frameworks required by Mendix Studio Pro will be automatically installed when installing Mendix Studio Pro.

The screenshots and references used in this book are from version 8.18.1 of Mendix Studio Pro. Later versions of Mendix 8 will most likely be suitable to follow along in. There could be slight differences in UI/UX, but you should be able to still follow the exercises as outlined. Mendix 9 and beyond have a higher likelihood of having different layouts and design, but it is hard to say what those may be at the time of writing this book. Regardless, the principles and best practices described throughout the book do not change.

If you are using the digital version of this book, we advise you to type the code yourself or access the code via the GitHub repository (link available in the next section). Doing so will help you avoid any potential errors related to the copying and pasting of code.

Download the example code files

You can download the example code files for this book from your account at www. packt.com. If you purchased this book elsewhere, you can visit www.packtpub.com/ support and register to have the files emailed directly to you.

You can download the code files by following these steps:

1. Log in or register at www.packt.com.
2. Select the **Support** tab.
3. Click on **Code Downloads**.
4. Enter the name of the book in the **Search** box and follow the onscreen instructions.

Once the file is downloaded, please make sure that you unzip or extract the folder using the latest version of:

* WinRAR/7-Zip for Windows
* Zipeg/iZip/UnRarX for Mac
* 7-Zip/PeaZip for Linux

The code bundle for the book is also hosted on GitHub at https://github.com/ PacktPublishing/Building-Low-Code-Applications-with-Mendix. In case there's an update to the code, it will be updated on the existing GitHub repository.

We also have other code bundles from our rich catalog of books and videos available at https://github.com/PacktPublishing/. Check them out!

Download the color images

We also provide a PDF file that has color images of the screenshots/diagrams used in this book. You can download it here: `https://static.packt-cdn.com/downloads/9781800201422_ColorImages.pdf`.

Conventions used

There are a number of text conventions used throughout this book.

`Code in text`: Indicates code words in text, database table names, folder names, filenames, file extensions, pathnames, dummy URLs, user input, and Twitter handles. Here is an example: "Once you have made a successful request to `MovieDB`, copy the results."

A block of code is set as follows:

```
length(trim(replaceAll('This is my random string','random
string','')))
```

Bold: Indicates a new term, an important word, or words that you see onscreen. For example, words in menus or dialog boxes appear in the text like this. Here is an example: "Add a new JSON structure by right-clicking on the new module and selecting **Add other** and then **JSON structure**:"

> **Tips or important notes**
> Appear like this.

Get in touch

Feedback from our readers is always welcome.

General feedback: If you have questions about any aspect of this book, mention the book title in the subject of your message and email us at `customercare@packtpub.com`.

Errata: Although we have taken every care to ensure the accuracy of our content, mistakes do happen. If you have found a mistake in this book, we would be grateful if you would report this to us. Please visit `www.packtpub.com/support/errata`, selecting your book, clicking on the Errata Submission Form link, and entering the details.

Piracy: If you come across any illegal copies of our works in any form on the Internet, we would be grateful if you would provide us with the location address or website name. Please contact us at copyright@packt.com with a link to the material.

If you are interested in becoming an author: If there is a topic that you have expertise in and you are interested in either writing or contributing to a book, please visit authors.packtpub.com.

Reviews

Please leave a review. Once you have read and used this book, why not leave a review on the site that you purchased it from? Potential readers can then see and use your unbiased opinion to make purchase decisions, we at Packt can understand what you think about our products, and our authors can see your feedback on their book. Thank you!

For more information about Packt, please visit packt.com.

Section 1: The Basics

The objective of this section is to gain a basic knowledge and understanding of what Mendix is, the reasons why you would use Mendix, and the elements within Mendix, as well as the tools you need before you create your first application.

This section comprises the following chapters:

- *Chapter 1, Introducing Mendix*
- *Chapter 2, Getting to Know the Mendix Platform*
- *Chapter 3, Getting to Know Mendix Studio*
- *Chapter 4, Getting to Know Studio Pro*

1

Introducing Mendix

First off, hello, welcome, and thank you for taking the first step and joining us on this journey. This book has been co-written by current Mendix developers with over 20 years of experience. Low-code is an exciting and fresh field, and we are thrilled that you are taking the first step on your path of low-code, as well as Mendix.

This is what you should expect from this book:

- Learn what low-code is
- Learn what Mendix is
- Use Mendix features, including its Studio and Studio Pro platforms
- Create your own baseline app
- Gain knowledge of domain model basics
- Work with microflow basics
- Learn effective troubleshooting
- Become proficient at error handling
- Create REST APIs
- Use advanced microflows
- Learn what you need, as well as how to prepare for the Mendix Rapid Application Developer Certification exam

We will take you from point A all the way to Z, and by the end, you will have a strong understanding of what low-code is, what Mendix is, as well as low-code application development skills and experience. You will have created a functional application, and have all the skills needed to pursue the first level of certification through Mendix.

In this introductory chapter, we'll learn about how Mendix came into existence, and learn why so many companies have made the decision to implement low-code in their business. By the end of this chapter, you'll have learned why low-code is so different from traditional programming and will be prepared to start using Mendix yourself.

This chapter will cover the following topics:

- What is low-code?
- What is Mendix?

What is low-code?

The term "low-code" or "no-code" did not really exist until a couple of years ago, but the concept is hardly a new one. For a while now, in enterprises as well as in small businesses, there has been the concept of a "power user" or a well-known "citizen developer," or just business users (who usually have little to no traditional developer experience) who take it on themselves to improve processes and even go as far as building whole applications. To do so, they often explore technologies such as Visual Basic for Applications, Microsoft's now legacy, event-driven programming language. Low-code tools such as Mendix expand on that philosophy, from the most tech-savvy of super developers to any average person who sees a business problem or process that a simple app could improve and solve and sets out to build it themselves.

Let's touch base more on the visual aspect of low-code development. The use of visual modeling allows you to build apps more rapidly by reducing the need for traditional code. In addition, the use of the interface to assemble and configure applications enables developers of various degrees of experience to create web and mobile applications using drag-and-drop components as well as model-driven logic. This allows developers to skip all the infrastructure and re-implementation of patterns that can and usually slow them down. The following screenshot shows the difference between visual code and traditional code:

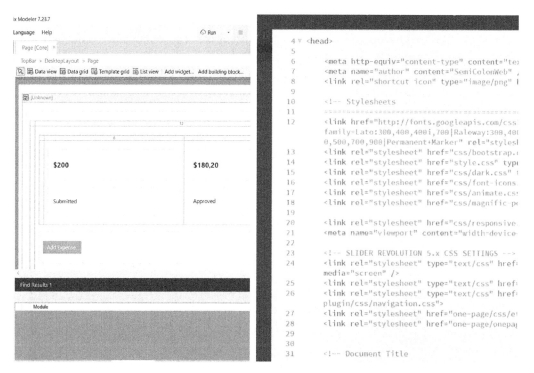

Figure 1.1 – Visual code versus traditional code

Now that we have a clear understanding of what low-code is, as well as how visual modeling plays into it, let's take a look at the platform piece that connects everything together. The growth of low- and no-code platforms has mushroomed exponentially due to a lack of skilled developers and the need to improve the turnaround time for projects so business process problems can be solved quickly. So, generally, a low-code platform is a visual development environment that allows developers, with any degree of experience, to drag and drop application components, connect them together, and create a mobile or web app.

With a platform like this, you don't need to code an application line by line. You get to draw it out, a lot like a flow chart. This makes developing powerful new applications extremely fast. Using this modular approach allows professional developers to quickly build applications by significantly reducing, or even relieving, the need to write traditional line-by-line code.

These platforms have also enabled anyone, from a **business analyst (BA)** all the way to business owners, to develop and test applications. This is because they have unlocked application development from having to know anything about traditional programming languages. All developers see is a user-friendly interface that allows components and third-party APIs to be hooked together and tested. You can see some examples in the following screenshot:

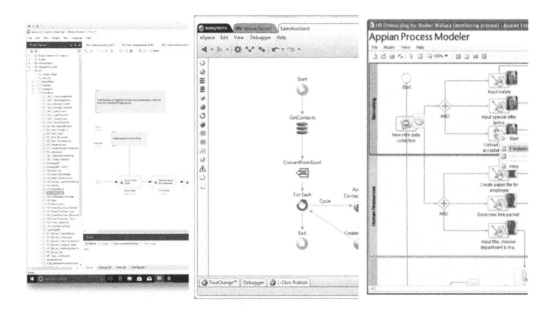

Figure 1.2 – Platform examples from left to right: Mendix, OutSystems, Appian

You now should be seeing why would you take the low-code route, and that these platforms are extremely powerful. According to Gartner:

"By 2024, low-code application development will be responsible for more than 65% of application development activity."

This is the reason why low-code and these platforms exist, and why there is always going to be the need to be able to rapidly develop low-code applications.

Now that we have established an understanding of what low-code is, let's learn what the Mendix platform is and how it relates to the use of low-code.

What is Mendix?

Now that you have learned what low-code is, as well as the different platforms there are, we will now go into more detail about the one we will be discussing in this book, Mendix. This is how the Mendix logo looks:

Figure 1.3 – Mendix logo

Mendix is a low-code platform, as well as being the leader in low-code development. It provides tools to build, test, and deploy applications.

A little background into Mendix's history: Founded in Rotterdam, the Netherlands, in 2005, Mendix has been building out the platform so that businesses can go live sooner and attain success faster. In addition, on October 1, 2018, Mendix was acquired by Siemens, the largest industrial manufacturing company in Europe. This allowed integrations and improvements to happen in a short period of time. You can see the entire Mendix team in the following photo:

Figure 1.4 – Original Mendix team members, 2007

I mentioned that Mendix is the leader of low-code. Here are some key points as to why it is used by so many companies:

- Cloud-native architecture

- Collaborative visual development

- Multi-channel user experiences

- Scale without redesign

- Able to deploy anywhere

This high-productivity platform allows the development of both mobile and web applications while keeping up the agile (like SCRUM) and DevOps best practices. Mendix even goes above and beyond, allowing business users to give direct feedback to the application, allowing important feedback to be directed to those developers who will be fixing or improving business processes.

While exploring the different low-code platforms and providers, there can be large, critical differences between collaboration and handling application life cycle management. The Gartner 2020 Magic Quadrant beautifully displays how Mendix is leading the way:

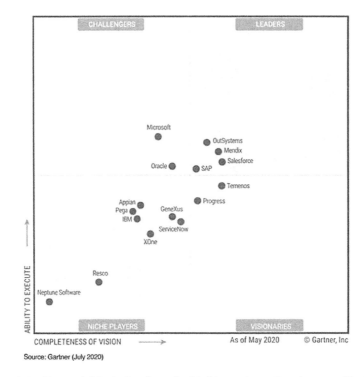

Figure 1.5 – Gartner's Magic Quadrant for Multiexperience Development Platforms

Mendix states (`https://www.mendix.com/resources/gartner-2020-mq-for-multiexperience-development-platforms/`):

> *"Mendix is the only Leader that supports all four mobile architectures,*
> *and the only one that supports the complete suite of mobile deployment*
> *options—web, PWA, hybrid, and native mobile apps—which enables our*
> *customers to leverage appropriate architecture to deliver the best mobile*
> *app for each use case".*

You might also be wondering who even uses Mendix. To name a few, ConocoPhillips, Ingersoll Rand, Chubb, Canada Post, New Balance, as well as eXp Realty. These businesses saw the need to transition to a low-code environment, as well as seeing how Mendix would help them achieve their goals – goals to modernize, to engage at an unprecedented level, to innovate, as well as to automate when possible.

Summary

In this chapter, we went into to what to expect from the book. We also then dived into what low-code is, how it differs from traditional programming, as well as low-code platforms. We then explained what Mendix is, the low-code platform that we will be using and discussing further in this book. We gave some details on the history, as well as what makes Mendix different from the other low-code platforms.

In the next chapter, we will further explore Mendix, and the many features it provides. We will take you through account creation and your account overview. We will then go into the Mendix Forum, the place where many developers go to get help or ask questions. Lastly, we will look at the Mendix App Store, where many developers, as well as Mendix itself, share free apps and widgets.

Knowledge check

Test your understanding of the concepts that were discussed in this chapter. Answers will be provided at the end of the *Knowledge check* in the next chapter.

1. The use of which of the following allows you to build apps more rapidly.

    a. Code

    b. Visual modeling

    c. Low-code

    d. A calculator

2. True or false: with Mendix, you don't need to code an application line by line.

   a. True

   b. False

3. Mendix was founded where?

   a. Austin, US

   b. Tokyo, JP

   c. Rotterdam, NL

   d. San Diego, US

4. Which of the following is NOT a reason why Mendix is used.

   a. Cloud-native architecture

   b. Ability to deploy anywhere

   c. Scale with redesign

   d. Multi-channel user experiences

5. What is Mendix?

   a. Mendix is a low-code platform.

   b. Mendix is a traditional coding language.

   c. Mendix is a code editor.

   d. Mendix is a type of fruit.

2
Getting to Know the Mendix Platform

In the previous chapter, we discussed low-code, as well as Mendix. Now that you have an understanding of both, in this chapter, we will walk you through the Mendix account creation process.

Once your account has been created, we will walk you through the available features. We will be exploring the Mendix community as well as the other options you will use once you create your account.

The main topics covered in this chapter are as follows:

- Creating an account
- Home page overview and breakdown
- Apps, people, and community
- Mendix Forum and docs
- Mendix App Store

Creating an account

Let's begin by creating an account.

To get started, go to www.mendix.com. This is the Mendix home page, but as a developer, you won't really be seeing this page; mainly, you will be logged into your developer portal, or even logged in directly to the modeler you are using. The following screenshot shows how the Mendix home page looks:

Figure 2.1 – Click "Start for free" to create your account on the Mendix home page

Now let's dive into registration. From the Mendix home page, we will start at the top right and click on **Start for free**. After clicking this, you will see the following page:

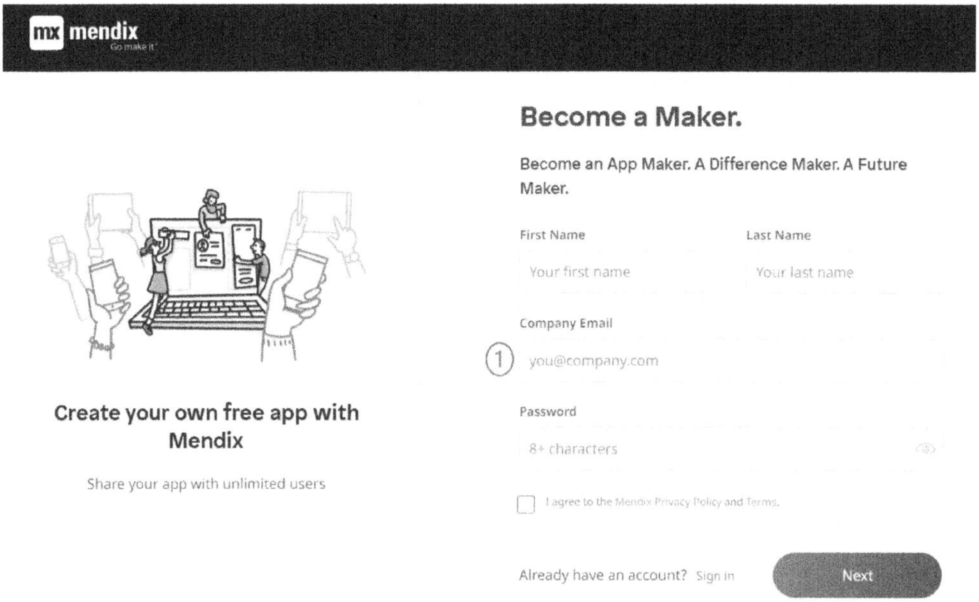

Figure 2.2 – First registration page

Once you land on this page, you will be asked for several pieces of information. Mendix asks for a company email. If you have a company email, school email, or even certain free emails (such as Zoho), that will be all that you need to meet the email requirements. This is because, based on the extension @exampleemail.com, you will be added to a company on the platform. Within this company collaboration, the sharing of company-related development assets and app node security rights can be managed. This makes it so that IT team within the company can support and control the Mendix app.

Next, you'll receive an email to confirm your signup:

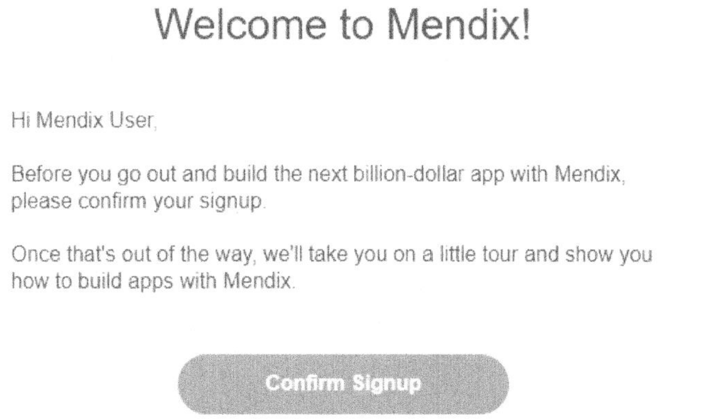

Figure 2.3 – Email that is sent from Mendix to finish up your activation

Once you confirm your signup, there will be several more additional questionnaires and, once completed, you will be presented with the Mendix home page.

Congratulations! You have made it through the registration process, and you are now a part of the Mendix community.

In the next section, we'll break down this entire home page.

Home page overview and breakdown

Mendix provides a lot of great resources and tools with your registration. In this section, we will take some time to explore what comes with your registration, and how it may benefit you in your future Mendix development. The following screenshot shows how the Mendix home page looks once we are registered:

Figure 2.4 – Mendix home page (after registration)

If we refer to the screenshot of the home page, we can see that we are met with a number of headings in the top section of the page. Let's quickly explore where each of these headings takes you:

- **People**: This is where you can connect with other Mendix developers.
- **Community**: This is where you can find blog posts, jobs, leaderboards, the Mendix shop, and more.
- **App Store**: Exactly what you think it is, it's a store where Mendix and fellow developers share their widgets and apps. You are also able to connect this to your app!
- **Academy**: This is where you can find some additional training and resources provided by Mendix, as well as live classes.
- **Forum**: This is where you go if you are having issues. You may search or even post questions to the many developers all over the world. In time, you may even assist new developers with their questions.
- **Docs**: In addition to its academy, Mendix also has page upon page of helpful documentation and best practices.

Now that you have a general overview of what the main tabs are about, let's take a closer look at each.

Apps, People, and Community

Now that you have your account created with Mendix, let's look at our first three tabs. First up, the **Apps** tab. In the following screenshot, you can see the different options under **Apps**:

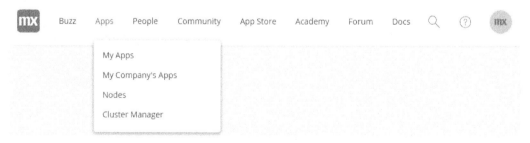

Figure 2.5 – Apps is where you can view your applications, as well as applications tied to your company, and/or alias

You may have noticed that we did not include **Apps** in our list. **Apps** is the section in which you can view company information and company applications. This is usually tied to the email you provided. This tab won't really be used in this book, however, we wanted to touch base on it.

Next, let's click the link for the **Community** section – it looks something like this:

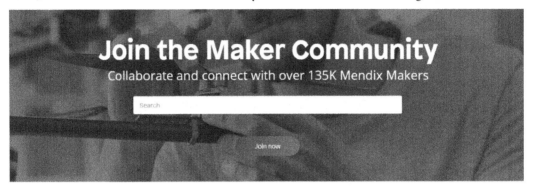

Figure 2.6 – The Mendix Community page allows you to connect with other Mendix developers

In the **People** tab, you can search for and explore all the public Mendix developer accounts. You can view their profiles and view what their rank is and what badges they have earned. You are also able to invite members to the platform:

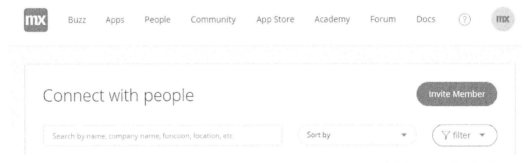

Figure 2.7 – The Mendix People tab allows you to search for and connect with fellow Mendix developers

Mendix is all about their community. With over 135,000 community members, you can view anything from job postings to forum postings as well as other community items. Mendix even has a store where you can redeem points that you earn by keeping active in the forums, and by simply developing.

Let's move on to other headings available from the Mendix home page.

Mendix Forum and Docs

The next feature Mendix provides for its users is its open **Forum**, as well as its **Docs** pages. These pages provide additional support as well as resources for your developing journey with Mendix. Simply put, if you have any issues or questions regarding problems you may be dealing with, the Mendix Forum is the place to submit those questions. Mendix has developers all over the world and, usually, you can expect to have your questions responded to within hours.

The Forum is also a great place to research and is a great resource to use if you stumble upon any bugs or issues, as there is a strong chance that someone has already posted the question and received a response. The following screenshot shows how the Mendix Forum home page looks:

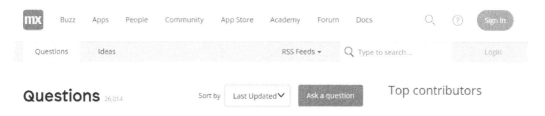

Figure 2.8 – Mendix Forum home page

One last point about the Mendix Forum is that you can also submit your ideas. While using Mendix, if you come across an issue with the platform, and if you have a great solution to fix it, you can post it, and even have your fix implemented in future releases.

Mendix **Docs** is a great and powerful dictionary for Mendix. If you are learning about a certain subject, and if you have some questions regarding it, going to Mendix Docs and doing a quick search is a great start. Following the Mendix principles of collaboration, Mendix Docs also allow you to contribute by providing, as well as improving, the current pages. This allows constant improvements and updates to be implemented. This is how the page looks:

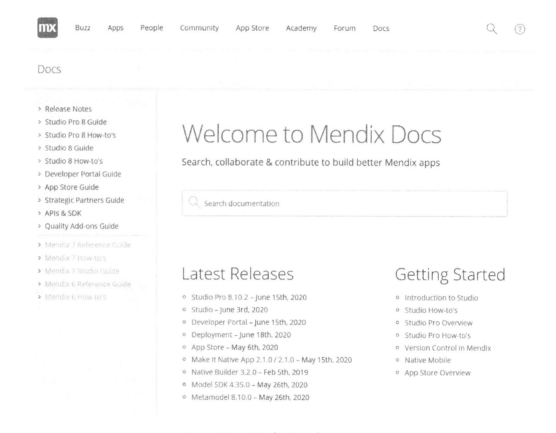

Figure 2.9 – Mendix Docs home page

With the ongoing updates and releases from Mendix, the **Docs** page is also the place to search for the current releases, as well as past releases. You can explore the versions and choose which one might be the best fit for the problem you, or your business, are trying to resolve.

Let's take a look at our final tab – the Mendix **App Store**.

Mendix App Store

Lastly, we are going to go over and explore the **App Store** tab. The following screenshot shows the Mendix App Store:

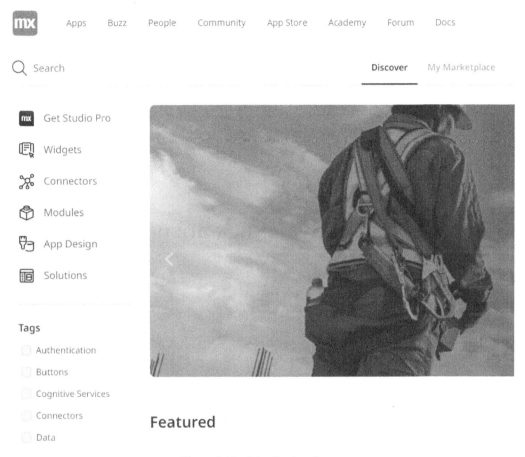

Figure 2.10 – Mendix App Store

The App Store, as a developer and user, is the place where you can easily add some more functionality to any of your apps, and with ease. Mendix provides this store where you can download either modules (functions and connectors) or widgets (frontend components) directly into your project, making integration a breeze. From this page, you can search for, rate, and download hundreds of apps that have been created by either the community or Mendix directly. The great thing about the Mendix community is hundreds of Mendix developers love to share the modules and widgets they have built to make your life as a developer easier.

Summary

In this chapter, we walked through the account creation process. Once registered, and once we'd landed on the home page, we started breaking down the features that a user receives once registered. We went over the basic home page layout and the navigation links at the top of the page.

Through the navigation, we explored the App Store, where you can connect with and download apps and widgets directly into your project. We explored the **Forum** and **Docs** pages. These pages provide a connection with the Mendix community, where you can ask questions and explore answers to any question you may have.

Now we have covered these basic fundamentals of getting Mendix set up and ready to go, we'll begin to dive deeper into Mendix development.

In the next chapter, we will start to explore the Mendix platform even further, and we will get to know Mendix Studio and Mendix Studio Pro.

Chapter 1 knowledge check answers

The following are the answers to the *Chapter 1, Introducing Mendix* knowledge check:

1. c
2. a
3. c
4. c
5. a

Chapter 2 knowledge check

1. What is the Mendix URL?

   a. Mendix.co

   b. Mendix.com

   c. Mendix.co.uk

   d. Mendix.net

2. Currently, you can use any email to register for a Mendix account.

    a. False

    b. True

3. Where would you go if you had questions or needed additional help?

    a. Buzz

    b. Community

    c. Forums

    d. Docs

4. You must pay to download apps in the App Store.

    a. False

    b. True

5. Where do you view blogs, jobs, and the leaderboards?

    a. Docs

    b. Community

    c. People

    d. Home

3
Getting to Know Mendix Studio

In the previous chapter, we walked you through getting your account set up, as well as the Mendix home page interface. In this chapter, we will be concentrating on Mendix Studio, Mendix's low-code web platform. By the end of this chapter, you will have a clear understanding of how to launch Mendix Studio, be familiar with the interface, and understand the reasons why you would use Mendix Studio.

The main topics this chapter covers are as follows:

- What is Mendix Studio?
- A breakdown of the UI and features
- Why would you use Mendix Studio?

What is Mendix Studio?

Mendix Studio is a browser tool that allows you to create fully functioning apps. You can view and edit apps without going into the extensive details that Studio Pro provides. With Studio, you also have the capability to collaborate with other team members that may be using Studio Pro at any time.

One of the most obvious benefits of using Studio is that you can run it in your browser without having to install any additional software on your PC. This allows you, the user, to dive right into your project almost anywhere and with just about any computer.

Using Mendix Studio

First, let's get you into Studio. We'll start by creating a blank app or using a template. To create an app, simply click on **Create App** on the home page at the top right. The following screenshot shows how to do this:

Figure 3.1 – Create App

Now that the app has been created, let's get you into Studio. To do so, click on the **Edit App** dropdown and select **Edit in Mendix Studio**. The option should look as in the following screenshot:

Figure 3.2 – Editing an app in Studio

Once clicked, you will be magically taken to your application in Studio view. Let's look at all of the tools and features in Mendix Studio and break them down.

A breakdown of the UI and features

Now that you know how to launch Mendix Studio, let's take you through the features and the UI of the modeler. By the end, you should have a clear understanding of what each button and feature does.

The following screenshot shows what you'll be met with upon opening the Mendix Studio UI:

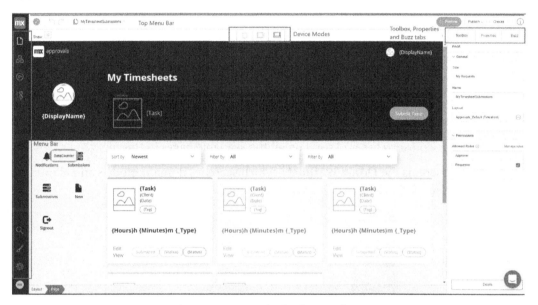

Figure 3.3 – Mendix Studio interface

The preceding screenshot shows an example of Studio as well as its components. The UI is extremely user-friendly and intuitive. The UI includes the following:

- A menu bar on the left
- A top menu bar
- Device modes
- The **Toolbox**, **Properties**, and **Buzz** tabs on the right

The following are the first three options that you will see on the top-left corner of Mendix Studio:

Figure 3.4 – The first three menu options

Let's look at the menu options on the left side, starting from top to bottom:

- The **Mendix logo** takes you back to the developer portal.

- The **page** icon searches and sorts on all the available pages in the app.

- The next icon is the **Domain Models**, which searches domain models and allows you to view and edit them on the current page:

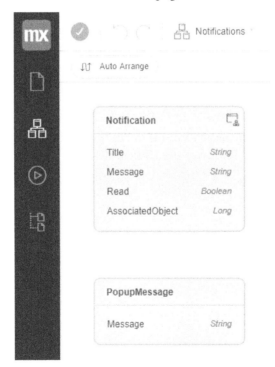

Figure 3.5 – Domain model page

- Then, the **Microflows** icon allows you to search for any microflows in the project.

Figure 3.6 – Navigation page

- The **Navigation Document** icon takes you to the navigation page, where you can add custom navigation to pages, or even run custom logic.

Figure 3.7 – Further menu options in Mendix

- The **search** icon allows you to search for certain microflows, pages, or even particular attributes and entities.

- The **Theme Customizer** allows you to customize the look and feel of your application. You can change colors or even upload existing themes and implement them into your app.

- Last is the **App Settings** icon. This is where you control user roles, page access, as well as microflow access (both by user roles). You also have the option to view, delete, and update existing widgets that may be pre-installed as well:

Figure 3.8 – Settings page

Moving on to the top menu bar, these navigation options are straightforward and mainly aimed toward actual navigation:

Figure 3.9 – Top menu bar

The top menu bar allows you to check Studio's internet connection, undo or redo recent changes, view your recent pages, preview or publish the application, and view any current errors in the app.

You can also view information using the **information** icon. You can find out what version is currently being used, check the documentation, ask the community if you are stumped or have any questions, or even get a refresher of what Mendix Studio has to offer.

Let's take a look at the right menu bar next.

The right menu bar has tons of controls for the current page/microflow you are working on. These tools include **Toolbox**, **Properties**, and **Buzz**. **Toolbox** shows tools that are currently available for the current editor. **Properties** shows the current properties tied to the currently selected item. Lastly, **Buzz** allows an app development team to leave comments on pages, microflows, and domain models so that your fellow developers on your team can communicate with each other.

Now that we have covered the basic features of the Mendix UI, let's move on to the question of why developers choose to use Mendix.

Why would you use Mendix Studio?

Now that you have gained some knowledge of what Mendix Studio is, as well as the UI and features of it, you may be asking, why would you use this platform? One of the biggest reasons why you would use Studio is that you are in a position where you need to demo certain features or want to make quick changes to your application and present those changes to the business or user. Mendix Studio would be a good option to make and demonstrate those changes:

Figure 3.10 – Anyone can be a developer with Studio

Mendix is also not only for developers but also for business analysts as well as product owners. Mendix prides itself on allowing citizen developers to be able to make changes to and develop applications. This is easily accomplished with Mendix Studio and its intuitive UI.

These changes allow anyone with any technical skill level to make changes and easily cooperate with developers on any project.

In short, Mendix is a highly accessible platform for people of any background.

Summary

In this chapter, we learned everything Mendix Studio. We walked through where to find and launch Studio. Once launched, we dissected the many features Studio has to offer. We browsed through the UI and provided details on what each button and option does.

Moving forward to the next chapter, we will explore the other platform that is used by the majority of Mendix developers, Studio Pro. We will explore what the platform is, how to download it, and look into the features.

Chapter 2 knowledge check answers

The following are the answers to the *Chapter 2, Getting to Know the Mendix Platform*, knowledge check questions:

1. b
2. a
3. c
4. a
5. b

Chapter 3 knowledge check

1. What is Mendix Studio?

   a. The Mendix page to find tips and tricks

   b. A downloadable tool that allows you to create fully functioning apps

   c. A browser tool that allows you to create fully functioning apps

   d. A browser tool that allows you to create themes

2. How do you launch Mendix Studio?

   a. By clicking **Create App**

   b. By clicking **Run**

   c. By clicking **Edit App** then **Run**

   d. By clicking **Edit App** then **Studio**

3. True or false: Studio is only available in the browser.

   a. True

   b. False

4
Getting to Know Studio Pro

Now that you have learned more about Mendix Studio in *Chapter 3, Getting to Know Mendix Studio*, we are going to take a look into Mendix Studio Pro. Studio Pro is the platform we will be using throughout this book as well as being the one that's currently used the most by Mendix developers.

The skills and knowledge gained in this chapter will be the foundation used moving forward.

The following topics will be covered in this chapter:

- What is Studio Pro?
- Downloading and launching Studio Pro
- UI breakdown

By the end of this chapter, you will have learned what Mendix's Studio Pro is, figured out how to download and launch the platform, understood the UI breakdown and important features, and why should you use Studio Pro.

What is Studio Pro?

So, what is Mendix Studio Pro? Mendix Studio Pro, just like Mendix Studio, is a powerful tool for creating applications. This visual, model-driven environment provides developers with everything they need to create complex and robust applications. With the "busy work" being removed from development, this allows you as the developer to add more value, while providing more flexibility for coding.

Mendix Studio Pro also allows users to model their applications by creating pages and adding logic and configurations. It also allows you to test your application's logic as well as deploying to your apps' environments.

Version control allows you to manage application development work on various development lines, as well as collaborating with Mendix Studio. Next, let's see how to download and launch Studio Pro.

Downloading and launching Studio Pro

Before we download Studio Pro, it is crucial to understand the system requirements. Mendix Studio Pro only supports 64-bit Windows 7, 8, and 10.

The following frameworks are installed (if necessary) automatically in addition to your Mendix Pro download:

- Microsoft .NET Framework 4.7.2

- Microsoft Visual C++ 2010 SP1 Redistributable Package

- Microsoft Visual C++ 2015 Redistributable Package

- AdoptOpenJDK 11 or Oracle JDK 11 (the former is installed automatically as of Mendix 8.0 if you do not have any JDK 11 installed)

To download Studio Pro, as a user, you have several options. One of the easiest ways to download is to edit the project that you want to work on. Simply log in to Mendix, click on a recent application you created, and click **Edit In Studio Pro**. When you click on **Edit In Studio Pro**, you will be presented with a popup. Click on **Open Mendix.VersionSelector** to be presented with version options as well as a download page:

Figure 4.1 – Version selector

If it is the first time you are opening a project, you will be presented with a page to download Mendix Studio Pro:

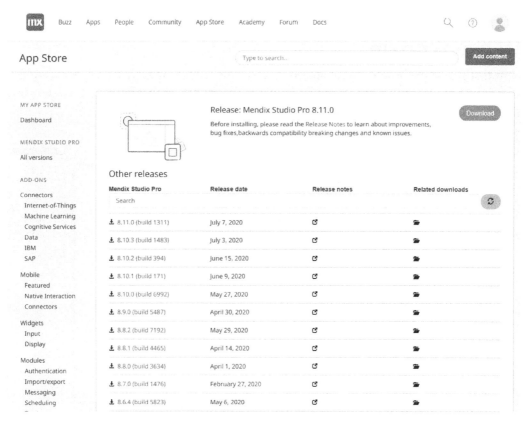

Figure 4.2 – Download page

This is the page where you are presented with the current, as well as older, versions of the Mendix platform. In addition, this is the other option in which you could directly download Studio Pro. In addition to downloads, you also can view the release notes associated with the release version. The release notes provide detailed information on what was improved, fixed, as well as added to Studio Pro.

Another option to download Studio Pro is directly in the App Store. In the App Store, click on **Get Studio Pro** and download it directly on the next page.

Once you click on **Download**, you will be prompted to go through a typical installation process. Once Studio Pro launches, you will be asked to provide your username and password. This will allow you to log in to your environment, as well as commit/retrieve any current updates. Next, let's understand the UI breakdown of Mendix Studio Pro.

UI breakdown

Now that you know how to install Studio Pro, we will be looking at the UI aspect, as well as pointing out the different features and options the modeler has to offer. In the following screenshot, you can see the entire Studio Pro interface:

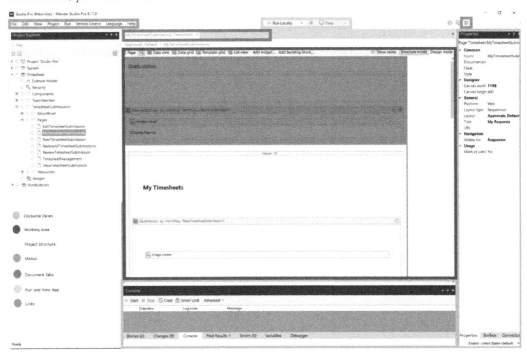

Figure 4.3 – Studio Pro interface

As you can see in *Figure 4.3*, we have broken down the home page for you to highlight the important sections. These sections include menus, run and view app links, links to the developer portal and App Store, project structure, working area, document tabs, and dockable panes. We will get into the how, what, and when to use these features in future chapters, so feel free to explore and get comfortable with the platform:

Figure 4.4 – Studio Pro top bar

The Studio Pro top bar contains the following items:

- Menus

- Buttons to run and view your application

- Links to the dev portal and App Store

In the top bar, you can view several menus such as **Edit**, **View**, and **Version Control**. Each item contains menu items that allow you to perform different actions, such as create a package, view any existing errors, and set preferences.

You can run and view your app in two different ways. The main way would be by clicking **Run Locally**. This allows you to run your app. The other option is **Run**. This runs your app in the free tier cloud environment, which is available to everyone. To view your local or cloud project, click **View**.

The top bar also includes some additional items:

- **File**: Allows you to manage documents and projects

- **Edit**: Allows you to perform editing functions such as search or copy within Studio Pro

- **View**: Allows you to choose how Studio Pro and dockable panes within Studio Pro are displayed

- **Project**: Contains project-wide settings

- **Run**: Contains actions for deploying and monitoring your app

- **Version Control**: Contains settings for version control

- **Language**: Contains language and translation settings

- **Help**: Allows you to view documentation, access the Mendix Forum, open the log file directory, or view information on the current information of Studio Pro

A **working area** is the current tab that you are working in. The area and the settings differ depending on the editor. This may be pages, microflows, domain model editors, and so on.

Document tabs, or just simple tabs, are just the current documents that are currently open. Like a web browser, you may have multiple tabs open, and you may close any extras that are not needed.

Dockable panes can be positioned around the current working area and contain different elements and settings. For example, you can view a list of errors, configure properties of a specific document or an element, or view the toolbox.

Dockable panes, by default, are where you will view any errors in your modeler/logic. We will go into more details in future chapters in regards to what this may look like, as well as how to troubleshoot:

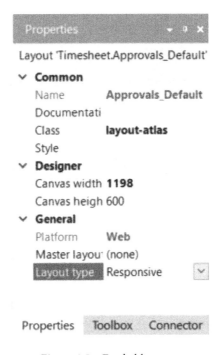

Figure 4.5 – Dockable panes

Properties shows the properties of the currently selected element. This is where a lot of editing in the modeler takes place. **Toolbox** shows the tools that could be used in the current editor. For example, on a page, you can insert all kinds of widgets (for example, a text box and data view) by dragging them from the toolbox to your form. **Connector** shows what elements can be connected to the currently selected element. For example, when a button is selected, the connector will show microflows that you can drag and drop onto the button to connect them.

The **project structure** shows the complete structure of the current project including all documents inside the model. Next, let's talk about the **Project Explorer** tab. The following screenshot shows how the **Project Explorer** tab looks:

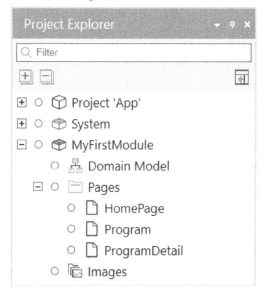

Figure 4.6 – Project Explorer

In **Project Explorer**, you can do the following:

- **Filter**: Enter the name of a module, folder, or document into the **Filter** field to filter documents of the project and highlight entered text within **Project Explorer**. When filtering by a module or folder name, all content of matching modules and/or folders is displayed.

- Open the document: Double-click the document to open it.

- Select the active document: Click the icon shown below the **Filter** field on the right side of **Project Explorer**. By default, the active document is always selected, so you can quickly see where the document you are editing is located. You can change this behavior in the **Edit | Preferences** dialog box.

- Expand all documents, which opens all the folders to view all pages, microflows, and other items.

- Collapse all documents, which closes all the folders.

- Perform actions specific to the selected folder: Right-click the selected folder to see what functions you can perform. The list of functions depends on the folder; for example, when right-clicking **MyFirstModule**, you can add pages, add microflows, rename items, export the module packages, copy/paste documents, and more.

Lastly, there is the console log, which by default is located at the bottom and is included as one of the many dockable panes. The console displays the output of the runtime when running your application locally.

Summary

In this chapter, we learned what Studio Pro is. We also took a look at how to launch Studio Pro, as well as where to download the platform from. Once downloaded, we explored the UI, as well as pointing out some important functionality and where to find them. After exploring the UI, we explored why you would use Studio Pro.

Moving forward, in the next chapter, we will move toward the test project. We will also see how to set up our environment correctly in detail, and break down Studio Pro further, and then provide more detail on what each action does. By learning these actions, you will know how to build the basics of a low-code application.

Chapter 3 knowledge check answers

The following are the answers to the *Chapter 3*, *Getting to Know Mendix Studio* knowledge check:

1. c

2. d

3. a

Chapter 4 knowledge check

1. What is Studio Pro?

   a. A better version of Studio

   b. A powerful traditional development tool

   c. A powerful model-driven environment

2. True or false: You can only download Studio Pro from the App Store.

3. How do you run your application in Studio Pro?

   a. **File | Run**.

   b. Set up your local environment details, then click on **Run Locally**.

   c. Click on **Run Locally**.

4. Where do you view errors in Studio Pro?

    a. **Properties**

    b. The working area

    c. In a dockable pane

Section 2: Building Your First App

In this part, you will be able to understand the basic fundamentals of the Mendix Modeler and master the best practices of Mendix app creation.

This section comprises the following chapters:

- *Chapter 5, Getting Started with Your Baseline App*
- *Chapter 6, Understanding Domain Model Basics*
- *Chapter 7, Understanding the Basics of Page Design*
- *Chapter 8, Getting to Know Microflows*

5

Getting Started with Your Baseline App

In the previous chapter, you were familiarized with Mendix and some of the related tools, such as Studio and Studio Pro. Now it is time to get down and get our hands dirty with apps in the cloud and in Studio Pro. In this chapter, we will explore how to manage apps in the Developer Portal and build and enhance our apps in Studio Pro using the App Store and custom content. In addition, we will take a look at the project settings, security, and a few of the most used preferences by pro Mendix developers.

In this chapter, we are going to cover the following main topics:

- Managing apps in the Developer Portal
- Using Mendix Studio Pro and the Mendix App Store
- Working with modules in your Mendix app
- Finding project settings, security settings, and preferences

Technical requirements

We will continue to use **Mendix Studio Pro** for the rest of the book. Please be sure you understand the system requirements and be sure to have it installed so you can follow along with the provided examples and sample project.

Mendix Studio Pro only supports 64-bit Windows 7, 8, and 10.

The following frameworks are automatically installed (if necessary):

- Microsoft .NET Framework 4.7.2

- Microsoft Visual C++ 2010 SP1 Redistributable Package

- Microsoft Visual C++ 2015 Redistributable Package

- AdoptOpenJDK 11 or Oracle JDK 11 (the former is installed automatically as of Mendix 8.0.0 if you do not have JDK 11 installed)

The sample project of this chapter can be found in `Chapter05` folder at `https://github.com/PacktPublishing/Building-Low-Code-Applications-with-Mendix`.

Managing apps in the Developer Portal

In *Chapter 2, Getting to Know the Mendix Platform*, we went over the Developer Portal and its major components. We will now go into more detail about the components involved in creating projects and collaborating with your team in an Agile environment.

Mendix projects, called apps, are available in the Developer Portal under the **Apps** main menu item:

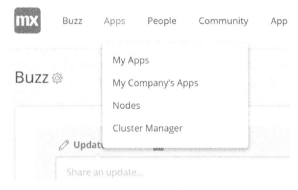

Figure 5.1 – Accessing Mendix apps

My Apps will take you to a list of projects you have created or to which you have been invited to collaborate. This is the landing page of the online Portal.

My Company's Apps will take you to a list of projects created by people within your organization.

Nodes will take you to a list of licensed nodes in the Mendix Cloud to which you have been invited.

Cluster Manager is where you manage any virtual private Kubernetes clusters registered in the Mendix Portal. We will not cover the cluster manager in this book.

Each app can have its own project team configured with roles such as **Product Owner**, **Business Engineer**, and **End User**. You can invite anyone to a project, regardless of whether they are in your organization. To access your app after being invited, the user will have to create a Mendix account, if they do not already have one (free to create at www. mendix.com with a business email address). Here is what the current set of default roles looks like in the Mendix Cloud:

ROLE ▲	PERMISSIONS
Application Operator	*Can view 'Overview, Capture, Develop, Feedback & Settings'* *Can view 'Deploy, Publish and Monitor'*
Business Engineer	*Can view 'Overview, Capture, Develop, Feedback & Settings'* *Can invite members* *Can edit 'Stories, Documents and Feedback'* *Can open app in Mendix Studio (Pro)* *Can view 'Deploy, Publish and Monitor'*
Guest	*Can view 'Overview, Capture, Develop, Feedback & Settings'*
Product Owner	*Can view 'Overview, Capture, Develop, Feedback & Settings'* *Can invite members* *Can edit 'Stories, Documents and Feedback'*
Scrum Master	*Can view 'Overview, Capture, Develop, Feedback & Settings'* *Can edit 'App settings'* *Can invite members* *Can edit 'Stories, Documents and Feedback'* *Can open app in Mendix Studio (Pro)* *Can view 'Deploy, Publish and Monitor'*

Figure 5.2 – Mendix Cloud Portal default user roles

Important note

To open an app in Mendix Studio or Studio Pro you must have **Business Engineer** or **Scrum Master** privileges. By default, the creator of an app will be assigned the role **Scrum Master**. The main difference between the default **Scrum Master** and **Business Engineer** roles is the ability to edit app settings. Be sure to give other developers you invite to your projects the role of **Business Engineer** unless you trust them to manipulate the app settings.

Now that you have seen some basics about where to find your Mendix apps, it is time to create a new project and write some user stories to start off your first development sprint.

Creating a new app and writing your first user stories

There are a few different ways to create a new Mendix app. You could create one locally from within Studio Pro. Mendix provides the team server, which acts as a repository for your model. It is not necessary to sync your app to the Mendix team server, but it is recommended to go down the route of using the Cloud Portal and team server to ensure your app has proper version control and reliable cloud storage. Mendix is also introducing support for GitHub; however, this book will focus on using the Mendix Cloud to create apps and manage repositories for your app models.

For the purpose of this book, you have been assigned requirements for a fictional video rental store called **Lackluster Video**. As you go through the rest of the chapters in this book, you will create an app to track inventory, customers, and rentals for the fictional business.

To start creating a new app, follow these steps:

1. Log in to the Mendix Developer Portal at `https://sprintr.home.mendix.com`.

2. From the top-right corner, click **Create App**.

> **Important note**
>
> **Starting your App**: There are a few places you can choose to start your app. You can use a blank app, you can upload a spreadsheet to create an app based on existing data, you can create an app based on app templates provided by Mendix, or you can create apps with custom app templates shared within your organization.

3. Hover your cursor over the **Blank App** icon and click **Select Template**:

Figure 5.3 – New app template selection

4.   On the next page, you will see a summary of the chosen app template along with its version, the corresponding Mendix version, and any tags on the app template. On this page, you may also find a gallery of images showing screen layout possibilities using the elements in the template. All basic apps come with Mendix's Atlas UI Resources:

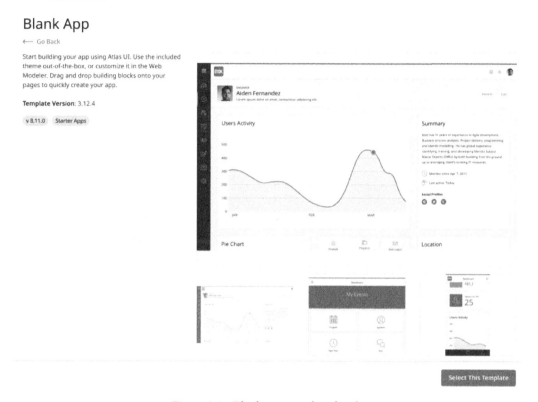

Figure 5.4 – Blank app template details

5.   From this page, you can choose **Select This Template** to continue or **Go Back** to choose another option. Click **Select This Template**.

6. On the proceeding pop-up window, you can customize your app. Give your app a name and choose an icon and color to customize it further. Name the app `Lackluster Video` and pick a color and icon of your choosing. Once the app has been named and customized, click **Create App**:

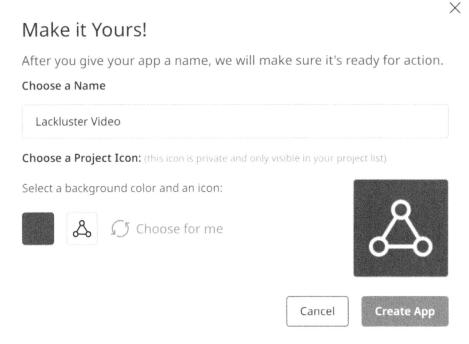

Figure 5.5 – Pop-up dialog for app customization

> **Important note**
> It will take a few minutes for your app to be provisioned in the cloud. Once this process is complete, you will be taken to the app team space. You can always find your apps by going to **Apps** in the main menu and choosing **My Apps**.

Once your new app has been provisioned, you will be taken to the app space in the cloud. Your **My Apps** page will also be updated with a tile for the new app. Click on the tile to get to the app team space in the cloud:

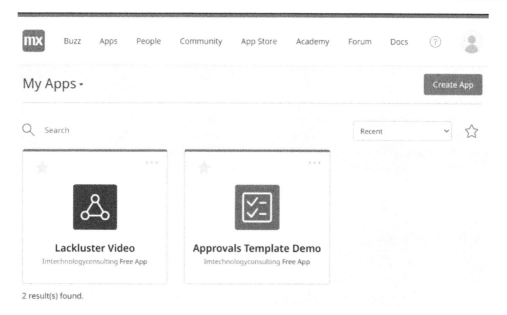

Figure 5.6 – My Apps in the Mendix Cloud

The left menu shows all the available options for managing an app in the Mendix Cloud. From this menu, you can access the features for the collaboration, development, deployment, and operation of your Mendix app along with the app settings. We will now go over a few important menu items you will need to be familiar with to properly build an app while embracing a proper software development methodology.

Embracing a development methodology

In an Agile environment, app features are usually described in terms of user stories and work is done on some type of SCRUM board, such as a Kanban board, in organized sprints. Mendix provides tools for managing your app's development life cycle with SCRUM tools in an Agile environment. To get to the storyboard, click **Stories** from the team space **COLLABORATE** menu:

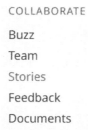

Figure 5.7 – COLLABORATE menu

Here, you can create stories and start to build a backlog of work that can be organized into sprints. Let's create one user story as an example. Later in the chapter, we will commit a change and tie it to this user story.

> **Important note**
> While it is not required to create user stories or sprints for the remainder of the work in this book, when working in a larger enterprise environment, it is recommended as a best practice to document development against written requirements and work in organized sprints.

To create a new user story in the **Stories** space, do the following:

1. Click **New Story**.

2. Title this user story `As a Developer, I would like to have access to the Mendix common functions library so that I can easily use standard functions in my app`.

3. The rest of the options can be left as the default. Click **Save**.

4. The **Stories** view for the **Lackluster Video** app should now show an empty sprint called **Get started** and a **Backlog** with one user story you created:

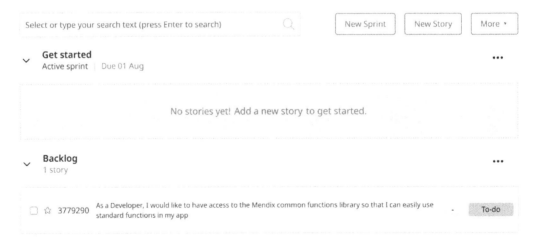

Figure 5.8 – View of the user story in Backlog

5. Go ahead and click and drag the story from the backlog into the active sprint. You will complete this story in the next section. The sprint view should look like this when you are done:

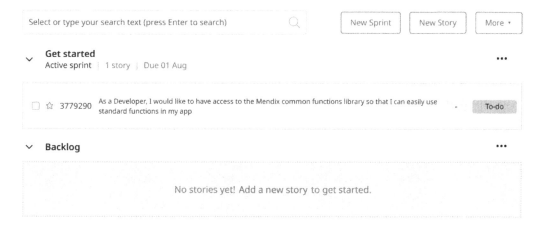

Figure 5.9 – View of the user story in Active sprint

The **Planning** section provides the Kanban board, **Burndown Chart**, and **Release Plan** for **Software Development Life Cycle (SDLC)** planning. Go ahead and move your user story to **Running** before you move into the next section by clicking the right arrow icon on the story card:

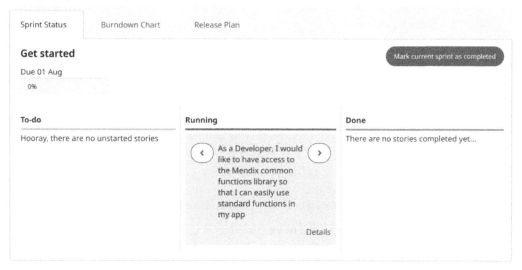

Figure 5.10 – Basic Scrum board in the Mendix Cloud

For more details on SCRUM and Agile processes or SDLC, please refer to other books on the subject, or check out Packt's *Agile Scrum Course: Scrum Fundamentals* at `https://subscription.packtpub.com/video/application-development/9781838644987`. For now, we will continue to invite other collaborators to our Mendix app.

Inviting collaborators to your Mendix app

Well done! You just created your very first Mendix Cloud app. You may not have a need for this quite yet, but we will quickly cover inviting collaborators to your project in the cloud before moving on to the real fun part of building your app!

> **Note**
>
> If you do not need to invite anyone to the project at this time, you may proceed with the next section, *Using Mendix Studio Pro and the Mendix App Store*.

To invite someone to collaborate on your Mendix Cloud app, you must do the following:

1. Log in to the Developer Portal.

2. Click **Apps | My Apps** to view a list of apps.

3. Click on the desired app from the list to view its team space.

4. From within the app team space, choose **Team** from the team space menu under **COLLABORATE**:

COLLABORATE

Buzz

Team

Stories

Feedback

Documents

Figure 5.11 – COLLABORATE menu

5. From the **App Team** page, click **Invite Member**.

6. Enter the email address(es) of anyone you want to invite and click **Add to invitee list**.

7. Select the desired role for each user, then click **Next**.

8. Add a personal message to the email invite, then click **Next**.

9. Finally, review the invite and confirm by clicking **Send Invitations**.

The user will receive an invite to their email inbox along with a pop-up invite the next time they log in to the Developer Portal. The user must accept the invite to join the project and be assigned any specific node permissions. Now, let's give the Cloud Portal a break and dive into Mendix Studio Pro to begin building our app!

Using Mendix Studio Pro and the Mendix App Store

Since we are working with Mendix Studio Pro, we will go through the process of signing into Mendix Studio Pro and opening our newly created app from there.

> **Important note**
>
> You can also open a project for editing in Mendix Studio Pro from the Mendix Developer Portal by clicking on **Edit in Studio Pro** from the app team space.

Opening your app in Mendix Studio Pro

The following steps will outline how to open your App in Mendix Studio Pro:

1. Launch Mendix Studio Pro from your computer.

> **Note**
>
> If you do not have Mendix Studio Pro installed on your computer, please refer to *Chapter 4, Getting to Know Studio Pro* for instructions on how to install it before continuing with this chapter.

2. Sign in to Mendix Studio Pro with your Mendix account or an available single sign-on account:

Figure 5.12 – Login screen for the Developer Portal in Studio Pro

After signing in, you will be placed on the **My Apps** page. You can create new apps and open existing apps from here. This page has quick links to places within the Mendix documentation as well as the App Store and Developer Portal. The **My Apps** page also has a list of recent projects for easy access.

3. From here, click **Open App**.

4. A pop-up window will appear with a radio button to select between a local or team server app. Select **Mendix Team Server**:

Figure 5.13 – Telling Studio Pro where to find your Mendix app

5. Choose the drop-down menu to select the **Lackluster Video** sample project created earlier:

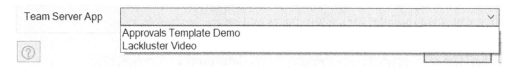

Figure 5.14 – Choosing which app to open

> **Important note**
> If you do not see the app in the list, ensure you are signed in to the team server by looking for your Mendix username in the upper-right corner and click **Refresh** to update the app list once you have signed in.

6. With the project selected from the drop-down list, you can now choose a development line (or branch line) to work from and tell Studio Pro where to store the project files on your local machine. For now, we will stick to the **Main Line** for development. You can choose your own location to store the project locally but do not rename the project folder. The automatic naming convention will help you keep better track of multiple development lines of the same project on your machine and will also allow you to be consistent with team members about what development line each person is working in:

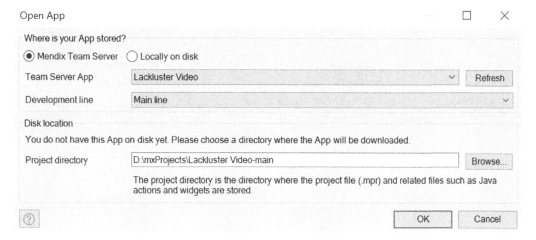

Figure 5.15 – Choosing the local project directory

7. With the **Team Server App**, **Development line**, and **Project directory** options selected, click **OK**.

The project files will be downloaded from the team server to a local directory and Studio Pro will launch the app for editing. Now that you have your app open in Studio Pro, you can easily add App Store content to your project right from within the project or start adding your own modules for custom pages and logic.

Installing a module from the Mendix App Store

In *Chapter 2*, *Getting to Know the Mendix Platform*, you learned about the Mendix App Store. In this section, you will learn how to import an App Store item into your app from within Studio Pro. The proper way to install any App Store content in your app is to connect to the App Store from within Studio Pro.

To connect to the App Store and download a module, do the following:

1. Click on the shopping cart icon in the upper-right corner of the Studio Pro window, next to your username:

Figure 5.16 – Shopping cart icon

2. You should see the App Store in the main window:

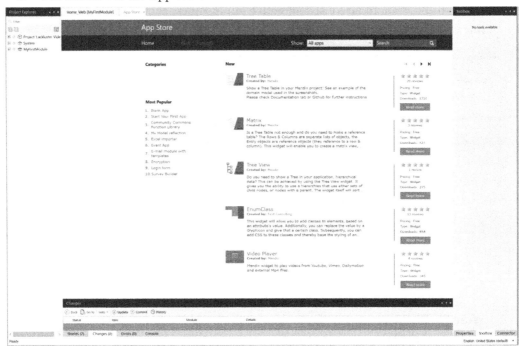

Figure 5.17 – Mendix App Store

3. Search for Community commons.

4. Select **Community Commons Function Library**:

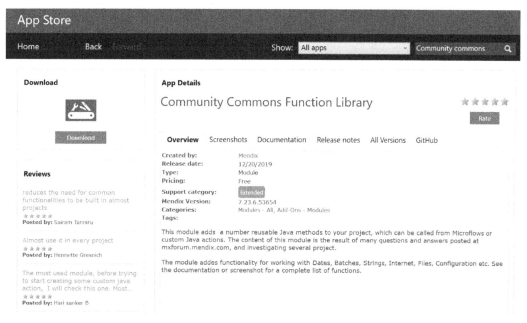

Figure 5.18 – Community Commons Function Library in the Mendix App Store

5. Click the green **Download** button.

6. When prompted, choose to install it as a new module and click **Import**:

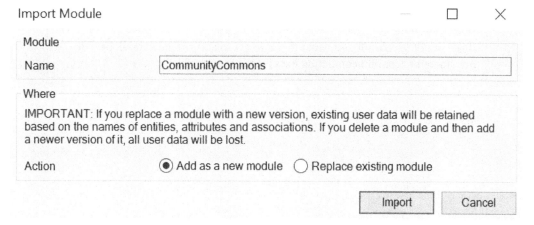

Figure 5.19 – Select Import when prompted

7. Your new module will be available under **Project | App Store modules**:

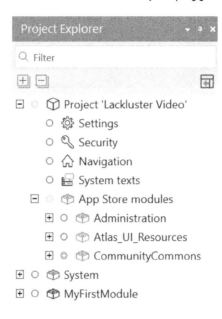

Figure 5.20 – Locating your new module

After installing a new module from the App Store, it is a good idea to ensure the app can still run with the new content. Running the app locally will essentially compile code from all the various modules and widgets into a local instance of the Mendix runtime. When you run the app, you will encounter any compile errors so you can fix them before you commit changes to the server.

> **Important note**
> It is best not to commit any errors to the server to ensure fellow developers do not attempt to commit conflicting fixes for the same problem.

Now we will run the app to ensure there are no errors, then commit all changes to the team server. To do this, complete the following steps:

1. Click **Run Locally** from the top bar of Mendix Studio Pro.

    You will see this confirmation message in the console log when the app has run successfully:

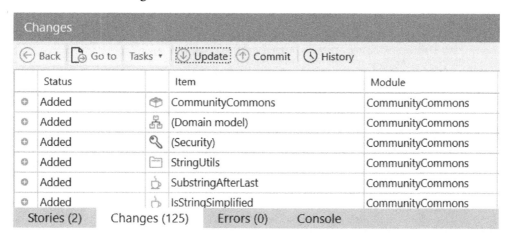

Figure 5.21 – Confirmation of the app running successfully

2. Click on the **Changes** tab and then click on **Commit**:

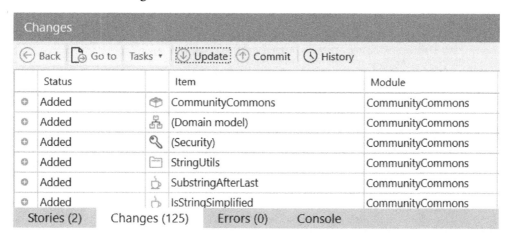

Figure 5.22 – Select Commit in the Changes tab

3. You will be prompted for a **Commit** message. Commit messages are important because they let other developers and managers know what changes went into this commit. Be as descriptive as possible when writing commit messages. To connect a commit to a user story in the Developer Portal, check the box next to that user story in the **Commit** window. Click **Refresh** to update the user story list if needed:

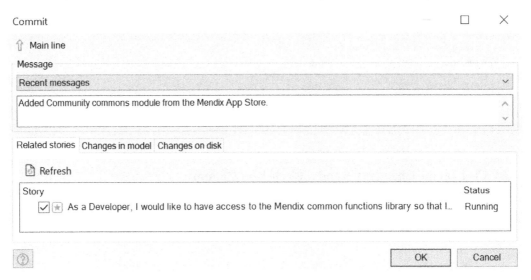

Figure 5.23 – Adding a Commit message

4. Click **OK**:

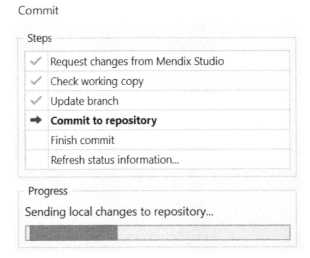

Figure 5.24 – Changes in the process of being committed

5. Once the changes have been committed, the **Changes** dock will show (**0**) unsaved changes.

6. Go to the **Planning** section of the Developer Portal on the web and move your user story to **Done**:

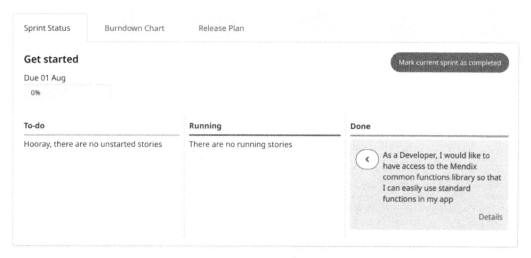

Figure 5.25 – Moving the user story to Done

You just created your first user story in the Developer Portal and installed some fresh App Store content into your Mendix app with Mendix Studio Pro. Now let me show you how to create your own modules for custom content.

Working with modules in your Mendix app

Not every function or feature you need in your app will be available in the Mendix App Store and it is also unlikely that a pre-built app template will serve the entire set of requirements for your project. When this happens, it is time to build some custom functionality into your Mendix app. To do this, you have to create your own modules and add elements to them. In this section, you will learn how to create a module and get a brief overview of the types of elements you can create within a module. You will also see how to organize your elements within the module. In later chapters, you will create some common module elements as we continue to build our video store app.

Creating a module

To create a custom module, follow these steps:

1. Right-click anywhere in the **Project Explorer** pane and click **Add module**:

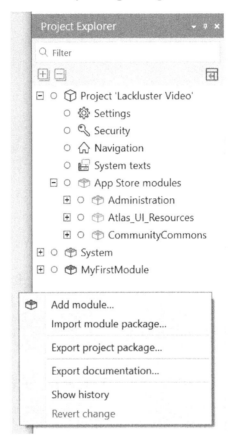

Figure 5.26 – Right-clicking on Project Explorer

2. On the subsequent pop-up window, give your new module a name. Call this one `VideoRentals`:

Figure 5.27 – Naming a new module

> **Important note**
> Module names should start with a letter and can only contain letters, digits, and underscores.

3. When the new module is created, it will have one element in it by default: the Domain Model. We will cover the Domain Model further in the next chapter.

Elements can be created within a module by right-clicking on the module to expose the context menu and selecting the element type to create. You can also delete or rename a module from the context menu. Here are the full options available:

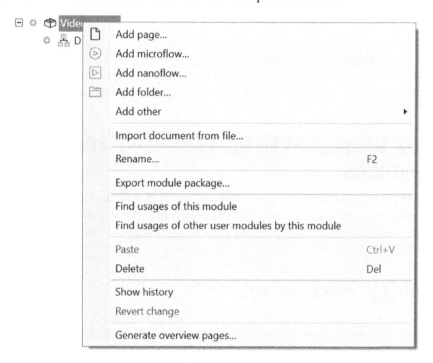

Figure 5.28 – Module right-click context menu

In the next section, you will explore deleting modules and adding elements to your modules.

Deleting a module

If you decide you no longer need a module or tried something from the App Store you ultimately do not want to keep, then you can delete modules from your app. To delete a module, right-click on the module to expose the context menu and click **Delete**. You cannot undo this action so be sure you really want to delete a module before you do.

Adding elements to modules

To add elements such as microflows, pages, and nanoflows to your module, right-click on the module to expose the context menu and select the item you would like to create. To expose a longer list of available items, choose the **Add Other** menu item.

As you start to create more elements in your custom modules, you can use folders to organize your elements and make the project easier to navigate in Studio Pro. Now that you have learned how to add App Store content and how to create custom modules in your app, let's look at the project settings and some common preferences.

Finding project settings, security settings, and preferences

There are other areas to consider when building your application, such as setting project security, managing your settings, and defining preferences for Studio Pro. In this section, you will see some common configurations used by professional Mendix developers in Studio Pro.

Managing project security

Project security relates to app security and what level of security you want enforced in your app. Mendix provides three options for app security. They are listed here as Mendix defines them:

- **Off** – No security is applied; users do not have to sign in and can access everything.

- **Prototype/Demo** – Security is applied to signing in, forms, and microflows. Configure administrator and anonymous access and define user roles and security for forms and microflows.

- **Production** – Full security is applied. Configure administrator and anonymous access and define user roles and security for forms, microflows, entities, and reports.

To access project security, click on **Security** from the **Project 'Lackluster Video'** navigation tree item in **Project Explorer**:

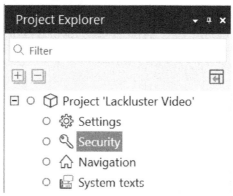

Figure 5.29 – Mendix Project Explorer

In **Prototype** and **Production** modes, you can set up policies for demo users in your free Cloud app or local environments and for anonymous user access. You can also set other security settings, such as password complexity requirements. For the purposes of our sample project, we will leave project security off for now.

> **Note**
>
> When running fully licensed apps for your organization in the Mendix Cloud, full Production security mode is required to ensure you are protecting your customers' data and privacy. Free-tier apps allow the option to run in **Security off** and **Demo** modes. When creating simple proofs of concept or experimenting with non-sensitive datasets, use your best judgment when implementing app security. Most larger organizations will have a standard security policy for apps in their ecosystem.

Maintaining project settings

To get to project settings, click **Settings** in the **Project 'Lackluster Video'** navigation item in **Project Explorer**. Here, you can manage advanced settings for the project, such as external databases, language support options, custom runtime settings, and more. These concepts are further explored in advanced modules in the Mendix Academy online. To keep things simple here, we will use the default settings in most cases and highlight any specific settings we need to adjust for our fictional video rental store.

Configuring project preferences

Project preferences can be found in the **Edit** menu under **Preferences**. Here, you can enable and disable Mendix Assist, the AI-assisted development process. You can also specify other settings such as the JDK (Java Development Kit) directory. At this level, most of these options will remain the default unless otherwise specified.

Summary

In this chapter, you learned how to create a project from the Developer Portal and open your project in Mendix Studio Pro to access the full features of the Mendix platform. You used the App Store to add common functions to your app so you can easily deliver readymade features to your app users. For the cases where App Store content is not available, you learned how to create your own modules so you can create custom features in your Mendix app. You also learned how to find project security, settings, and preferences in Mendix Studio Pro so you can gain full control of the development environment.

In the following chapter, you will further expand on your custom module by working with Domain Models, pages, and microflows in Mendix Studio Pro. This will give you power over the data, business logic, and presentation layers of your app.

Chapter 4 knowledge check answers

The following are the answers to *Chapter 4, Getting to Know Studio Pro* knowledge check:

1. c
2. False
3. c
4. c

Chapter 5 knowledge check

1. Where in the Cloud Portal would you go to view licensed nodes to which you have access?

    a. **Environments**

    b. **My Apps**

    c. **Nodes**

    d. **Cluster Manager**

2. Which statement best describes the **Planning** section of the Mendix Cloud Portal?

   a. Provides a kanban board, burndown chart, and release plan

   b. Allows you to invite others to collaborate on your app

   c. A wall feed of comments left by collaborators on the app

   d. A place to purchase third-party modules

3. Which Mendix product do you download and install locally in order to edit your Mendix app?

   a. Mendix Studio

   b. Mendix Web Modeler

   c. Mendix Studio Pro

   d. Mendix Code Editor

4. Where in Mendix Studio Pro do you see uncommitted work in your app?

   a. Variables

   b. Properties

   c. Changes

   d. Project Explorer

5. It is a good practice to commit errors in your Mendix app.

   a. True

   b. False

6. Where do you go to download third-party modules into your Mendix app?

   a. Mendix App Store

   b. Mendix Module Store

   c. Mendix Developer Pro Shop

   d. Mendix Community

7. Module names should start with a letter and can only contain letters, digits, and underscores.

    a. True

    b. False

8. Which security level applies full security to a Mendix app?

    a. Prototype

    b. Production

    c. Demo

    d. Secure Mode

6
Understanding Domain Model Basics

Welcome to the world of domain models! The **Domain Model** of the Mendix app represents the data layer of the application. When you are building an application, it is necessary to store the data for this application in some sort of structure. Mendix Studio Pro (and Studio) provides all the tools necessary to design the data structure of the app and display data in the app to your end users. Data could be things such as customer or order information and even an inventory of available videos to rent in the case of our fictional video store.

The domain model element of the module is where you visually design its data architecture. Modules can share data with each other in your Mendix app. The domain model consists of **entities**, which can be equated to tables in a relational database, and are also referred to as objects. These can also be referred to as transient objects in the case of entities that do not persist in the database. The domain model, or consumed data structure, also contains **attributes**, which are the columns with varying data types to hold data in the tables and can also be virtual attributes, which are calculated on the fly. The consumed data structure also contains **associations**, which show how the data objects relate to one another.

In this chapter, we will learn about the different entity types in a domain model. In addition, we will also explore attributes, data types, and associations in the Mendix domain model.

In this chapter, we are going to cover the following main topics:

- Understanding the different entity types in a Mendix domain model
- Working with attributes and getting to know data types
- Creating associations between entities to relate objects
- Designing a database for your Mendix app

By the end of this chapter, you will be able to design a basic Mendix domain model with entities, attributes, and even an association!

Technical requirements

The sample project of this chapter can be found in `Chapter06` folder at `https://github.com/PacktPublishing/Building-Low-Code-Applications-with-Mendix`.

Understanding the different entity types in a Mendix domain model

In this section, you will learn about the different entity types in a Mendix domain model. Terms such as persistable and non-persistable objects will be explained in detail. You will create entities and adjust common entity properties in your app's domain model. The data architecture of your app is important for ensuring that you are creating the right types of data objects to store information in a meaningful way.

In the *introductory* section of this chapter, entities were referred to as objects. These represent the objects from the real world in your application, such as customers or members, videos, and rentals. If you are coming from the **Structured Query Language (SQL)** world, you may refer to these as tables with records and use them as objects in your code when the record is consumed in your app. If you are coming from the business side, you may have represented an object of data in an Excel worksheet with columns or attributes, which describe these objects with pieces of data in the cells. A row of data is a single object from the table or class. We will talk more about attributes later in the chapter.

For now, it is good to understand that an entity represents a class or table of objects from the real world. A row of data is a single object, and it can have many attributes, or pieces of data, that describe it. Entities and their properties will be explained further through the exercise.

Creating an entity and setting entity properties

Entities are described by properties such as Name, Attributes, Access Rules, and more. We will now create an entity and then set some general properties. Later in the chapter, we will add attributes and other properties to your entity.

To create a new entity, perform the following steps:

1. Open Mendix Studio Pro.

2. Sign in to your Mendix cloud account if needed.

3. Open the **Lackluster Video** project created in *Chapter 5, Getting Started with Your Baseline App*.

4. Expand the **VideoRentals** module, as shown in the following screenshot:

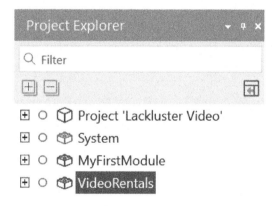

Figure 6.1 – Project Explorer with the VideoRentals module selected

5. Double-click on **Domain Model**:

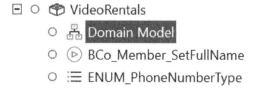

Figure 6.2 – VideoRentals module expanded in Project Explorer

6. Click on the **Entity** button from the **Domain Model** toolbar:

Figure 6.3 – Domain model toolbar in Mendix Studio Pro

7. Use a single left-click to drop the entity anywhere on the canvas to create a new one.

8. Double-click on the new entity to open the **Properties** window:

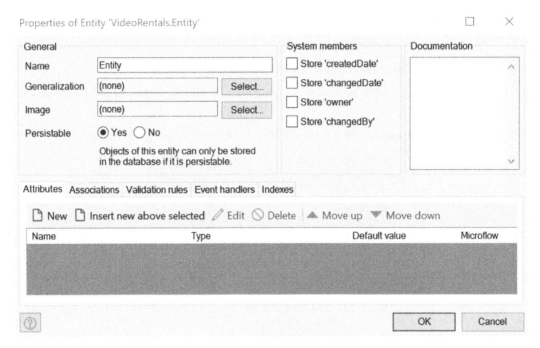

Figure 6.4 – The Entity Properties window in Mendix Studio Pro

The entity has many properties that can be manipulated from either the **Properties** window or from the **Properties** panel in Studio Pro. You can find a detailed description of these properties at `https://docs.mendix.com/refguide8/entities#properties`.

9. Enter the entity properties, as shown in the following screenshot:

Properties of Entity 'VideoRentals.Entity'   □   ✕

General			System members	Documentation
Name	Member		☑ Store 'createdDate'	Entity to hold the member object, a member is a person who can rent videos from the video rental store.
Generalization	(none)	Select..	☑ Store 'changedDate'	
Image	(none)	Select..	☑ Store 'owner'	
Persistable	⦿ Yes ◯ No		☑ Store 'changedBy'	
	Objects of this entity can only be stored in the database if it is persistable.			

Figure 6.5 – Completed member entity

10. Click **OK** to save your new entity.

The attributes will be added later in the chapter. For now, go ahead and click **OK** to save your new entity. Notice that the entity color is blue. This is because it is a persistable entity. A persistable entity will be stored in the application database for subsequent retrieval by the app. A non-persistable entity does not get stored in the database. We will not be working with non-persistable entities at this time, but keep in mind that they do not get stored in the database and will be created in memory.

These objects in the memory will get **garbage collected** when the user session ends and are not sufficient for storing information you may want to retrieve after the customer signs out of your app. Non-persistable entities are used to temporarily hold information to pass between microflows or to display on a page. These entities are colored orange in the domain model. The following screenshot shows what a persistable entity in the domain model looks like:

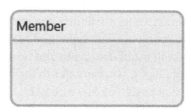

Member

Figure 6.6 – Persistable Member entity in the domain model

Now that you have created your new entity, it is time to populate it with attributes to describe it. In the next section, you will add some attributes to the **Member** entity and learn about the different data types available for creating attributes in the Mendix domain model.

Working with attributes and getting to know data types

In this section, you will get to know attribute and data types. You will also add a few attributes to the entity created in the previous section. You are now preparing your app to hold data you can later retrieve and manipulate. It is useful to understand how your app will store data. This data will be used in microflows in your app and also in pages to build user interfaces.

Attributes are pieces of information that describe an entity. An entity can have many attributes that describe various aspects of it. The member entity could have demographic information about the member, such as their name and location, or other important information pertaining to their membership, such as its status and start and end dates. Whether you come from the developer world or the business world, you can relate attribute types to the data types of SQL columns or Excel cells, respectively. This concept is explained further in this section.

Getting to know attribute types

Before creating any attributes, you should first understand attribute types. Objects are stored in the database in tables (called entities) as rows of information, represented by columns of data or attributes. Each column must be specified to hold a certain type of data. For instance, the `Member` entity represents the person who has joined the video rental club for movies. This person is a **member** of the video rental store and you abstract this object in your data layer with the `Member` entity.

The `Member` entity will have certain attributes, some of which relate to the attributes the person has in real life. The person likely has a name, which could be represented by a single string-type attribute called the `FullName` attribute, or two string-type attributes called `FirstName` and `LastName`. A string is a data type used to represent text information. Refer to the following table for a full list of data types and how they are used in the Mendix app. For a full list of available data types, you can refer to the Mendix online documentation at `https://docs.mendix.com/refguide/attributes#type`.

> **Important note**
>
> Notice that the attribute and entity names are given in **PascalCase**. It is highly recommended to follow a standard convention to name attributes, entities, and other elements in your application. This will increase the readability among developers as others collaborate on your project. You will also be able to understand the elements of someone else's project, assuming they have been following best practices. Check online on `Mendix.com` for the latest best practices and be sure to ask questions on the Mendix forum.

Now that you have got to know the various attribute types, it is time to start adding attributes to your entity.

Adding attributes to an entity in the domain model

To understand the concept of attribute types further, perform the following steps to add a few attributes to your Member entity:

1. In Mendix Studio Pro, open the **Lackluster Video** app. If the app is already open, you can skip to the next step:

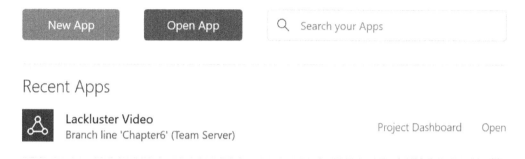

Figure 6.7 – Recent apps in Mendix Studio Pro

2. Navigate to **Domain Model** of the **Video Rental** module:

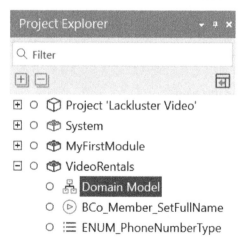

Figure 6.8 – Project Explorer in Studio Pro

3. Double-click on the Member entity.

4. Under the **Attributes** tab, click on **New**:

New   Insert new above selected   Edit   Delete   Move up   Move down

Figure 6.9 – Attribute menu in the Entity Properties dialog

5. Add the following attributes to your Member entity:

a) Enter the following values for **MemberId**:

- **Name**: MemberId
- **Documentation**: The member's unique identifier
- **Type: Autonumber**
- **Value: Stored**
- **Default value: 1**

b) Enter the following values for **FirstName**:

- **Name**: FirstName
- **Documentation**: The member's first name
- **Type: String**
- **Length: Limited**
- **Max length: 200**
- **Value: Stored**
- **Default Value**: *Leave this blank*

c) Enter the following values for **LastName**:

- **Name**: LastName
- **Documentation**: The member's last name
- **Type: String**
- **Length: Limited**
- **Max length: 200**
- **Value: Stored**
- **Default Value**: *Leave this blank*

d) Enter the following values for **FullName**:

- **Name**: FullName

- **Type: String**

- **Length: Limited**

- **Max length: 200**

- **Value: Stored**

- **Default Value**: *Leave this blank*

e) Enter the following values for **Active**:

- **Name**: Active

- **Documentation**: A Boolean to show whether the member is active or not

- **Type: Boolean**

- **Value: Stored**

- **Default Value: True**

The following screenshot shows the properties of the Member entity:

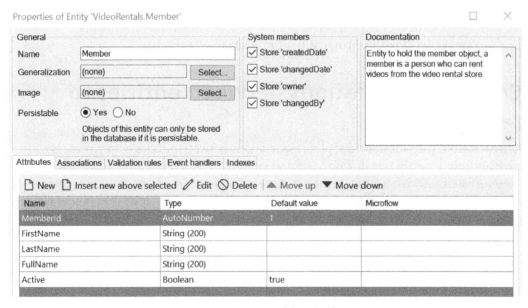

Figure 6.10 – Properties of the Member entity

> **Important note**
>
> A **calculated attribute**, also known as a **virtual attribute**, is the one that is not stored in the database but calculated on the fly when the object is loaded into the client. While this can be convenient for aggregating data in the moment, too many calculated attributes will lead to a diminished experience as more client resources will be needed to load pages in your app. This part of the book will focus on creating *persistable* entities with *stored* attributes.

Be sure to click **OK** in the **Entity Properties** window to save your entity with the new attributes. Your entity should look like the following diagram:

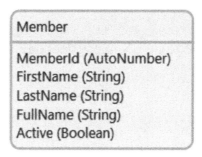

Figure 6.11 – Member entity with attributes

You now have your first entity in the **VideoRentals** domain model. This entity abstracts the member class of your application and has properties describing the member. In the next section, you will see how two entities can relate to one another.

Creating associations between entities to relate objects

In this section, you will start to explore associations between entities. Often there is a relationship between two different entities. Perhaps there are orders associated with inventory items or customers. Maybe you have multiple addresses or phone numbers associated with a single customer object. The way you look at the app's data model will help you understand how different entities are related.

Associations are used to represent the relationship between two entities. In Mendix Studio Pro, an association is drawn by clicking the edge of one entity and dragging a line to the edge of another entity or by editing the **Associations** tab of the **Entity** properties dialog window. Associations have a property known as **multiplicity**. This property describes the relationship between entities in terms of one-to-one, one-to-many, or many-to-many. Multiplicity is shown in Mendix with a **one (1)** or a **star (*)**.

The relationship between two entities can also be described as a parent-child relationship because one of the entities will own the relationship. An arrow on the line joining two entities will indicate the owner of the relationship. The arrow will point from the owner to the other entity. If both entities own the relationship, or in the case of a one-to-one (1-1) or many-to-many (*-*) relationship, there will be no arrow. Let's now take a closer look at associations and how to build them.

Adding an entity with associations

The video rental store wants to keep multiple phone numbers for each member. This way, there is more than one way to contact someone when the rental return is late. They specify many phone numbers but not how many, so it is not feasible to create an attribute for each phone number in the Member entity, since you do not know how many phone numbers the member might have.

Rather than creating many different phone number attributes in the Member entity, a better way to show this is to create a PhoneNumber entity with an enumeration attribute called PhoneNumberType (with values such as Cell, Home, and Work) and use an association to show a many-to-one relationship between PhoneNumber and Member.

Perform the following steps to create a PhoneNumber entity and associate it with your Member entity:

1. Open the **VideoRentals** domain model in Mendix Studio Pro.
2. Add a new entity to this domain model and name it as PhoneNumber. Then, open the **Entity Properties** window by double-clicking on the entity.

3. Give the entity the following properties (use default settings unless otherwise specified):

    •   Attribute 1:

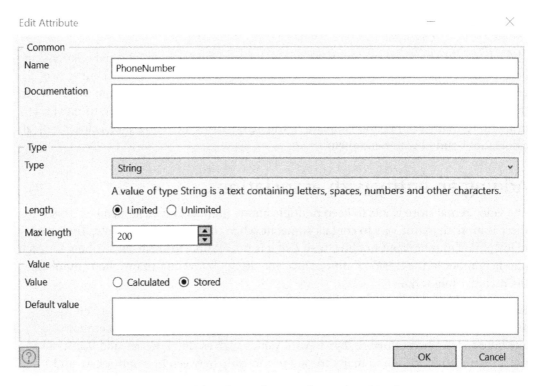

Figure 6.12 – The Edit Attribute window – PhoneNumber

- Attribute 2:

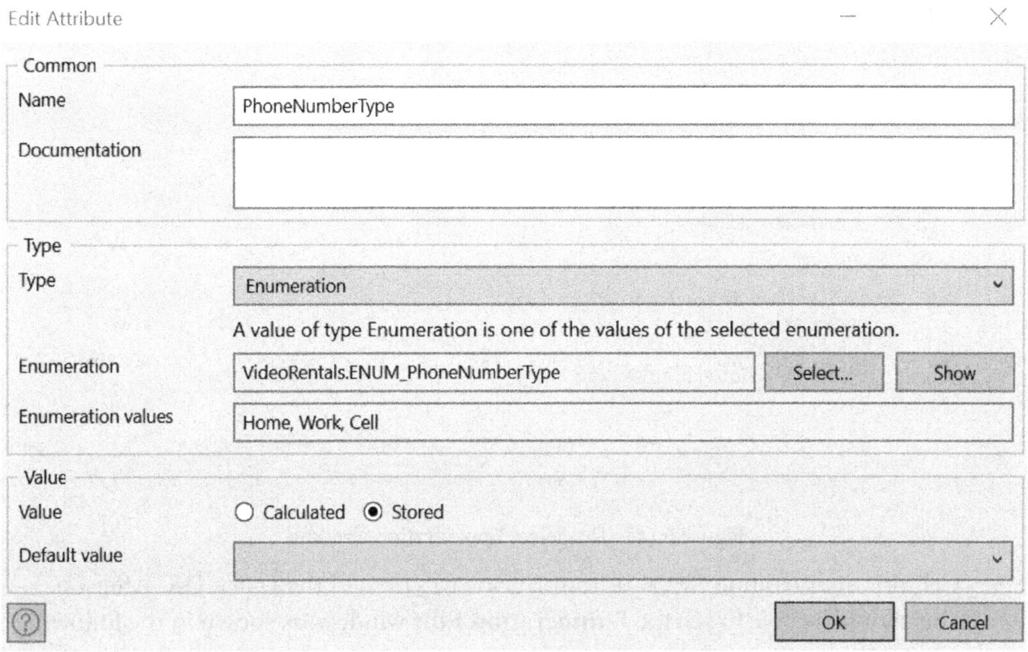

Figure 6.13 – The Edit Attribute window – PhoneNumberType

In the **Select Enumeration** dialog window, make certain that your **VideoRentals** module is highlighted, and then click the **New** button to create a new enumeration:

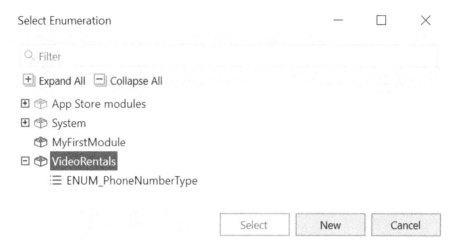

Figure 6.14 – The Select Enumeration window

4. Call this enumeration ENUM_PhoneNumberType and then click **OK**. After this, you should be able to see the **Enumeration Edit** window, as shown in the following screenshot:

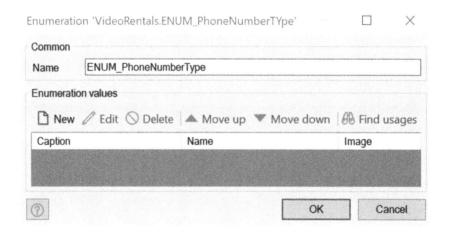

Figure 6.15 – The Enumeration Edit window

5. Click on **New** to add a new enumeration value.

6. In the **Caption** field, type Home. Notice that Mendix will autofill the **Name** field of **Enumeration values** as you type the caption. It is best to leave this value as it is to ensure that the app functions as you expect.

7. Repeat *steps 5-6* to create enumeration values for **Work** and **Cell**.

8. Once all the values have been created, click **OK** in the **Enumeration Edit** window to return to the **Add Attribute** window:

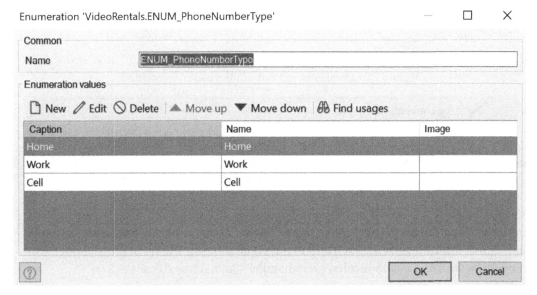

Figure 6.16 – The Enumeration Edit window with values

9. You can choose a default value or, for this enumeration attribute, leave it empty and then click **OK** to save the attribute.

10. Click **OK** to save the PhoneNumber entity.

11. Hover your cursor on the edge of the PhoneNumber entity and then click and drag a line over to the edge of the Member entity.

This will create a line with an arrow pointing from `PhoneNumber` to `Member`. On the `PhoneNumber` side, there is a star (*), and on the other side, there is a number one (**1**). This means that there can be phone numbers associated with one member and this is shown in the following diagram:

Figure 6.17 – Domain model with entities and an association

Naming conventions

There are many best practice naming conventions for elements in Mendix Studio Pro. When you allow Mendix to name elements for you, the name will most likely follow proper conventions. Unless there is a specific reason to rename things such as associations, it is always best to leave the name given as this lends easy readability for developers among Mendix apps.

In this section, you created a second entity with an enumeration attribute and associated this entity with your `Member` entity. In the next section, you will learn more about entity properties, such as validation rules, event handlers, and access rules.

Designing a database for your Mendix app

In addition to attributes and associations, there are also other entity properties to consider when designing the data layer of your Mendix application. These properties include event handlers, access rules, validation rules, and indexes. In this section, we will briefly go over these properties and how to set them in a Mendix entity. For more information on how these constructs work, it is recommended for you to read more about data architecture and database design. For now, we will cover a simple use case of each.

Using validation rules at the entity level

Validation rules are rules used to ensure that data being entered into the data field conforms to a desired standard. Rules can be about ensuring that a value stays unique, such as on object ID or an email address. Rules can also be about validating the length or format of the data as well as forcing the data to equal a specific value. Entity-level validation rules will be executed in addition to any form-level or microflow-level validation programmed into your application when a user attempts to save or commit an object to the database.

Now, you will add a simple validation rule to the `FirstName` attribute of the `Member` entity to make the `FirstName` attribute required. In the real world, you may perform this validation in a microflow, but for the purpose of this lesson, you will add validation to the entity directly.

> **Validation**
>
> Data validation can be performed at the entity level, on pages, or in microflows. It is important to follow the standard of your organization when deciding where to inject data validation into your Mendix application. For the latest best practices, be sure to check the Mendix online documentation (`https://docs.mendix.com/refguide/`) and the Mendix Forum (`https://forum.mendixcloud.com/`).

To add entity-level validation to a data attribute, perform the following steps:

1. Open the **Lackluster Video** application in Mendix Studio Pro and navigate to the **VideoRentals** module domain model.

2. Double-click the `Member` entity to open its **Entity Properties** window.

3. Click on the **Validation rules** tab.

4. Click **New**.

5. Choose the `FirstName` attribute.

6. Enter a friendly error message such as `First name is required`.

7. Enter the **Rule Type** as `Required`.

8. Click **OK** to save the rule. You will now see your new rule in the **Validation rules** tab.

9. Click **OK** to save the Member entity:

Figure 6.18 – Validation Rules tab with the first name required rule

Great work on creating a new validation rule! You can take a look at the following link and see what other types of validation rules are available in Mendix: https://docs.mendix.com/refguide/validation-rules#1-introduction.

Now that you have created a validation rule in your entity, it is time to move on to event handlers. In the next section, you will learn about event handlers and how to use them in your Mendix app.

Using event handlers in your domain model

Event handlers are used to trigger certain logic during database events. These events are before or after a create, commit, delete, or rollback of an object. During an event, a specified microflow, or piece of logic, will execute. This microflow can take the object in question as an input parameter and perform some logic either before or after the event takes place.

The microflow of a before commit event handler should return a Boolean value, which is True or False. You can choose to raise an error if False is returned from the microflow. This will ensure that the selected event does not occur if something goes wrong with your event handler. You can also ignore this by deselecting the option or always returning True in the processing microflow.

> **Infinite loops**
>
> Too many event handlers can lead to a sub-optimal database. The more logic executed when creating, saving, deleting, or rolling back an object, the more time it will take to complete the action. A microflow that executes before or after the commit of an object should never also commit the same object with events. This will create an infinite loop where the microflow keeps calling itself repeatedly with each commit. Use caution when creating event handlers.

You will now add an event handler to the Member entity. This event handler will calculate the contents of the FullName attribute whenever the Member entity is committed (or saved). Go through the following steps to understand further how event handlers work with entities.

To add an event handler to an entity, perform the following steps:

1. Open the **Lackluster Video** application in Mendix Studio Pro and navigate to the **VideoRentals** module domain model.

2. Double-click the Member entity to open its **Entity Properties** window.

3. Click on the **Event Handlers** tab.

4. Click **New**.

5. Enter the **Moment** value as **Before**, **Event** as **Commit**, and **Pass event object** as **Yes**.

6. Do the following for **Microflow**:

    a) Click **Select**.

    b) With **VideoRentals** selected in the pop-up window, click **New**.

    c) Name this microflow BCo_Member_SetFullName.

    d) Click **OK**.

7. Check the **Raise an error when the microflow returns false** box:

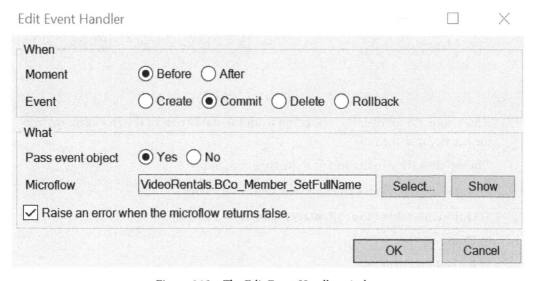

Figure 6.19 – The Edit Event Handler window

8. Click **OK**. You will now see the newly created event handler in the **Entity Properties** window:

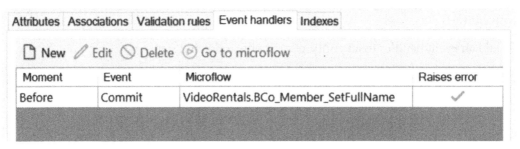

Figure 6.20 – Event handlers in the Entity Properties window

> **Microflows**
>
> Since Studio Pro created this microflow for you, it already has the basic elements such as input parameter, a start event, and an end event that returns a Boolean value. You will learn more about microflows and common microflow actions in *Chapter 8, Getting to Know Microflows*. For now, perform the following steps to add an action to calculate the full name for your member.

9. From **Project Explorer**, look for the newly created microflow, BCo_Member_ SetFullName, and double-click on this microflow to open it for editing.

10. Click the **Activity** icon from the toolbar:

Figure 6.21 – The Microflow toolbar in Studio Pro

11. Hover your cursor over the line going from the start event to the end event to drop the activity into the flow.

12. Double-click the activity to select the type of action.

13. Choose **Change Object** and enter the following values:

    a) **Object**: **Member (VideoRentals.Member)**

    b) **Commit**: **No**

    c) **Refresh in client**: **No**

14. Click **New** to add an attribute to change and add the following values to it:

a) **Member**: **FullName**

b) **Type**: **Set**

c) **Value**: $Member/FirstName+' '+$Member/LastName

15. Click **OK**:

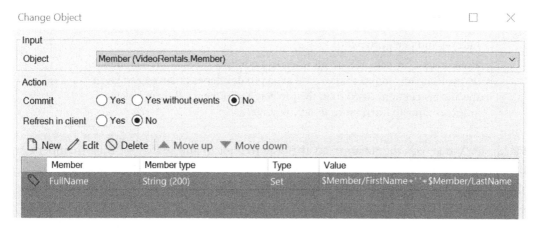

Figure 6.22 – The Change Object dialog for the member entity

While event handlers can be useful, they can also lead to poor performance if not used correctly. Be sure to really understand the use case before applying event handlers to your Mendix domain model. Experiment with the different event handler types to see how they cause your app to behave. Can you think of a use case of a before or after delete event handler?

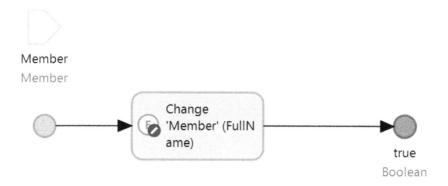

Figure 6.23 – Microflow: Bco_Member_SetFullName

In the next section, you will learn more about **indexes** on the Mendix entity.

Optimizing your database with indexes

Indexes are used to help improve the retrieval time of data within a database table. A cost of additional storage space and potentially slower write speeds comes with using indexes. While you may be able to improve read times by adding more indexes, the write time for the same table will decrease slightly as there is more overhead to maintain the index.

> **Indexes and performance**
>
> There is a performance trade-off when using indexes. It is not recommended that you add any indexes unless you are a pro developer or have been given specific instructions to do so in the project requirements. Research database indexes online to learn more about the subject.

Lackluster Video uses the `MemberId` attribute to refer to and search for their members in the application. There is a requirement to index the `MemberId` field to improve search speeds when looking up members by their `MemberId`.

To add an index to your `Member` entity, perform the following steps:

1. Open the **Lackluster Video** application in Mendix Studio Pro and navigate to the **VideoRentals** module domain model.

2. Double-click the `Member` entity to open its **Entity Properties** window.

3. Click on the `Indexes` tab.

4. Click **New**.

5. Click **Change Attributes**.

6. Select **MemberId** from the **Available attributes** section and move it to the **Index attributes** section by clicking the right arrow in the middle of the window:

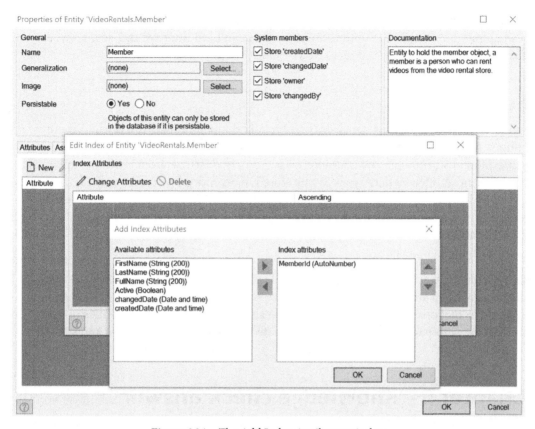

Figure 6.24 – The Add Index Attributes window

7. Click **OK** in the **Add Index Attributes** window.

8. Click **OK** in the **Edit Index** window.

    You will now see the new index on your entity.

9. Click **OK** to save the entity:

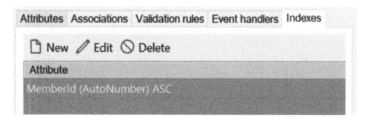

Figure 6.25 – Index tab of the Entity Properties window

Great work! You have now created your very first index on a Mendix entity. Be sure to read up on indexes to really understand how they can both improve and degrade your database performance depending on how you use them.

Summary

In this chapter, you learned the basics of a Mendix domain model. You learned about entities and how they are data objects to be used in the application to store data for later retrieval in business logic and user interfaces. You also learned about attributes and data types and how different data types can be stored in an entity. The pieces of data themselves are like cells in an Excel table, the columns are attributes, the worksheets are the entities, and each row is an object, or a record of data. Last but not least, you learned about associations and how to relate objects to one another along with learning about a few use cases for relating objects.

Congratulations! You now know how to create entities, how to modify entity properties, including adding attributes, and how to create associations to relate entities to one another. In the following chapters, you will be able to see your app and entities in action by working with pages and microflows to create the app's presentation and application layers.

Chapter 5 – Knowledge check answers

Here are the answers to the questions set in *Chapter 5, Getting Started with Your Baseline App*:

1. c
2. a
3. c
4. c
5. b
6. a
7. a
8. b

Chapter 6 – Knowledge check

1. What do you call the element in Mendix Studio Pro that represents the data layer in your Mendix app?

    a. Domain model

    b. Page

    c. Module

    d. Microflow

2. What do you call a data table in the Mendix domain model?

    a. Spreadsheet

    b. Entity

    c. Dataset

    d. Attribute

3. An attribute represents a column of data in an entity.

    a. True

    b. False

4. Which of the following are available data types in the Mendix domain model?

    a. Auto Number, Date and Time, Binary

    b. Binary, Short, Integer

    c. String, Double, Auto Number

    d. Array, Class, Date and Time

5. A calculated attribute is also known as a virtual attribute.

    a. True

    b. False

6. What color do persistent entities appear as in Mendix Studio Pro?

    a. Gold

    b. Purple

    c. Gray

    d. Blue

7. What is a relationship between two entities in the Mendix domain model called?

    a. Relation

    b. Association

    c. Multiplicity

    d. Entity property

8. What is a database element used to improve the retrieval time of data from within a table?

    a. Validation rule

    b. Event handler

    c. Index

    d. Enumeration

7
Understanding the Basics of Page Design

In the previous chapter, you learned the basics of the domain model and how to design the data architecture for your Mendix app. Now, we will look at one of the main elements that allows the Mendix developer to design the app's user interface: the page. We will cover the basics, such as creating and designing pages, and get into connecting data to your page and using widgets. Alongside this, we will also dive into the Atlas UI framework provided by Mendix to streamline the user experience design process and show you how to use various other design elements such as snippets and page templates.

In this chapter, we are going to cover the following main topics:

- Building user interfaces
- Understanding the Atlas UI framework
- Applying layouts, widgets, and building blocks
- Calling a page in your Mendix app

Technical requirements

The sample project of this chapter can be found in `Chapter07` folder at `https://github.com/PacktPublishing/Building-Low-Code-Applications-with-Mendix`.

Building user interfaces

Mendix provides the construct of the **page** to build the user interface of your application. This section will teach you about pages and how to build them. Pages are built with **layouts** and **widgets** in Studio Pro. Layouts are re-usable elements that can be applied to pages and provide common components to the page such as menus, headers, and footers. Widgets provide elements such as text boxes, sliders, and more to allow users to interact with your app's pages. **Atlas UI** provides page templates and other building blocks to give your pages a modern design with standard web elements.

As you go through the exercises in this chapter, you will create a page, learn about the Atlas UI building blocks and other widgets to design your page, and use buttons and navigation to call your page. These skills will help you to build robust user interfaces with the given elements in Mendix Studio Pro.

Creating a new page

In Mendix Studio Pro, there are a few ways to create a new page. The simplest way is to use the Project Explorer to choose a module and create a new page. The following exercise will walk you through the steps of creating a new page in Mendix Studio Pro.

To create a new page, follow these steps:

1. Open Studio Pro.
2. Sign in to your Mendix account.
3. Open the **Lackluster Video** project.
4. Expand the **VideoRentals** module.
5. Right-click on **VideoRentals**.

6. Click on **Add page…** to launch the **Create Page** screen:

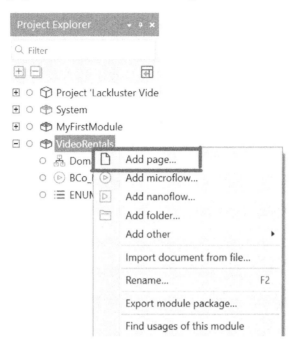

Figure 7.1: Module context menu

7. Create a page with the following configurations:

- **Responsive (Web)**
- **Page Name**: Member_Overview

- **Navigation Layout**: **Atlas_Default** (**Atlas_UI_Resources**)

- **Template**: **Blank**

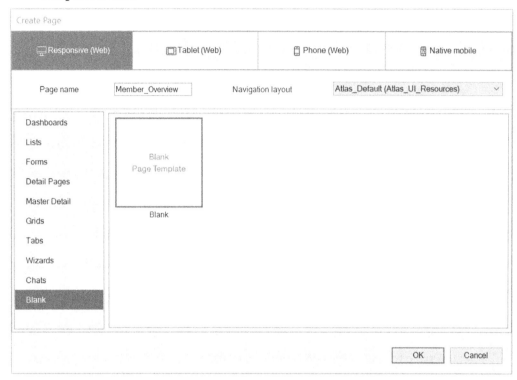

Figure 7.2: The Create Page screen with template options

8.   Click **OK**.

The **Create Page** screen is where you can choose what type of page to build. The set of tabs at the top allow you to switch between device types. The next row has fields to set the page name and navigation layout. Check the official documentation for naming convention best practices at `https://docs.mendix.com/howto/general/dev-best-practices`. The bottom section of this screen is where you can choose from preset or custom page templates. You will read more about page templates in the upcoming *Atlas UI* section.

After you have created a new page, you will be taken to this page in Mendix Pro Studio. Based on the chosen template, there will be some widgets already on the page. The grayed-out areas cannot be edited directly from the page editor. To modify those, you must edit the navigation layout itself. Be careful with editing navigation layouts as those changes will apply to every page using the layout. You will learn more about navigation layouts later in the chapter:

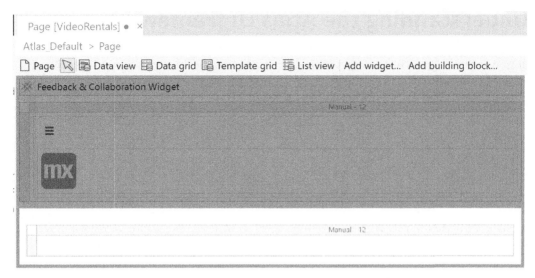

Figure 7.3 – New blank page with grayed-out layout area and editable main area

The main area of the page will be editable. The blank page template comes with a layout grid configured with a single row and a single column that is 12 columns wide. You can add any number of rows to the grid to expand the page vertically. You can add up to 12 columns to the layout grid, and the total width of all columns must not equal more than 12. The layout grid widget is built upon the 12-column layout principle. Any elements added to the page should be placed within this main layout grid. Layout grids can be nested to allow for more granular control of space on the page.

> **Tip**
> To delete a page or any element from Studio Pro, right-click on the element from the **Project Explorer** pane and click **Delete**, or simply select the element in the **Project Explorer** pane and press the *Delete* key on your keyboard. If you want to temporarily exclude an element from the project without deleting it, then choose **Exclude from Project** from the context menu.

Now that we know how to create a page, we will learn how to add some UI elements to bring your page to life in the next section.

Understanding the Atlas UI framework

Atlas UI is a design framework built by Mendix to give the same ease of use to UI/UX design as Studio Pro gives to app development. You can intuitively design your app's user interface with ready-to-use widgets, page templates, building blocks, and even entire app templates. Atlas UI was built on three design principles:

- Simplicity
- Harmony
- Flexibility

The full details of the Atlas UI framework and its available design devices can be found at `atlas.mendix.com`. You are also encouraged to explore the various templates available from the **Create Page** screen. For now, let's add a few common elements to our newly created `Member_Overview` page.

Applying layouts, widgets, and building blocks

Pages in a Mendix app are constructed with navigation layouts, widgets, and building blocks. In this section, you will get to know navigation layouts along with when and how to use them. Think of navigation layouts as the structure for the page. There are also many common widgets and not-so-common widgets available in Studio Pro and the Mendix App Store. You will learn how to add widgets to your page so you can display data and build some interaction for your end users. Last but not least is Atlas UI. This is Mendix's framework for building a robust UI with recognizable web elements such as dashboard tiles, headers, cards, and more. In the following exercises, you will learn about navigation layouts, add some common widgets to your page, and experiment with some Atlas UI building blocks.

Getting to know navigation layouts

Navigation layouts can be applied to many pages, and they control the common elements of the page, such as the main navigation menu, company branding, and the feedback widget. Using navigation layouts will ensure consistency across pages in your app. You can change the layout of a page from the page properties. For now, keep the navigation layout of your page as **Atlas Default**.

Using common widgets

In the page editor, in Studio Pro, there are a few ways to add a widget to your page. The toolbar in the editor window has quick selection options for the four main native data connector widgets, including the data view, data grid, template grid, and list view widgets. The **Add widget...** menu shows all the other native and app store-downloaded widgets available. The **Add building block...** menu gives a list of the Atlas UI building blocks available for use on the page.

Let's now add a data grid widget to this page so we can view the records in the Member entity created in the previous chapter.

To add a data grid to your page, do the following:

1. Open the **Lackluster Video** app in Mendix Studio Pro.

2. Expand the **Video Rentals** module.

3. Double-click the Member_Overview page.

4. Click the **Data grid** button from the **Page editor** toolbar:

Figure 7.4 – Page editor toolbar

5. Click on the screen in the middle of the layout grid on the page to drop the data grid onto the page.

6. Find and open the **Connector** panel:

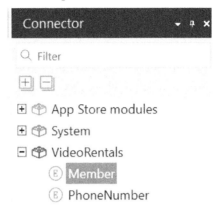

Figure 7.5 – Connector panel

7. Click and drag the **Member** entity onto the top portion of the selected data grid you placed on the page in *step 5*.

> **Important note**
>
> If the **Connector** panel is empty and says **Nothing to connect**, then make sure that the data grid is selected on the page. Some panels respond to the widget selection in the page editor.

8. On the **Data Source Options** dialog screen, make sure that the **Database** radio option is selected for **Type** and the box labeled **Automatically fill the contents of the data grid** is checked:

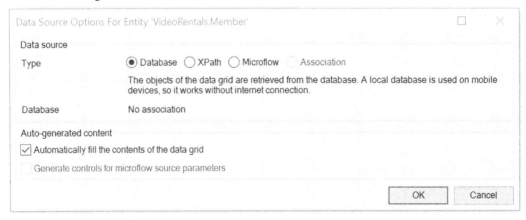

Figure 7.6 – Data source options dialog screen

9. Click **OK**.

Congratulations! You just placed your first widget onto a page in your Mendix app and connected it to a data source. There are a couple of things to notice here:

- The search fields and columns were automatically added to the page.

  This may or may not be desired depending on the size of the subject entity. Size in this case is based on the number of attributes in the entity. The requirement may only be to show certain attributes. You can leave the **Automatically fill the contents of the data grid** box unchecked. This will allow you to drag and drop only the attributes you want to display in the grid and allow the user to search. You can always edit the columns and search fields of the data grid after it has been created.

- There were two errors generated when the grid was created.

  These two errors have to do with the **New** and **Edit** buttons on the grid. Mendix places these two buttons on the grid upon creation, but there are no pages connected to these buttons.

One of the many benefits of working in Studio Pro is the ability to allow the modeler to do some of the work for you. In the previous step, when the data grid was added to the page with the **Automatically fill the contents of the data grid** box selected, you saw the grid get created with search fields and columns for display connected to attributes. This saved you from doing this manually, avoiding some steps.

Studio Pro can do more complex things than create columns and fields. It can even create entire pages for you! To fix the errors generated previously on the **New** and **Edit** buttons, complete the following exercise:

1. Right-click on the **New** button:

Figure 7.7: Data grid control bar with errors

2. Click **Generate Page**.

   Notice the new page already has a name: Member_NewEdit. This is automatically generated based on Mendix best practices.

3. Change **Navigation layout** to **PopupLayout (Atlas_UI_Resources)**.

4. Choose the **Form Vertical** layout.

5. Click **OK**.

Notice how both errors cleared up when this page was created. Double-click on the new page from **Project Explorer** to view it. Also, notice how Studio Pro automatically created a data view widget connected to the Member entity with all the attributes from the entity dropped into it. A data view widget is a page element you can use to view a single object, or record, from an entity from your domain model. There are also default **Save** and **Cancel** buttons on this widget. You can further customize this page from here by adding or removing widgets and buttons. For the purpose of this book, we will leave the page as is. In the next section, you will learn how to work with Atlas UI building blocks to build structure into your pages.

Creating with Atlas UI building blocks

Now that we have a page with some data connected, let's spruce up the page a bit with some design. To start, we will add a header section with a page title and subtitle. Complete the following exercise:

1. Open the **Lackluster Video** project in Mendix Studio Pro.

2. Open the Member_Overview page from the **VideoRentals** module.

3. Click **Add building block…**:

Figure 7.8 – Page editor toolbar

4. Choose **Hero Header 2** from the **Header** section.

5. Hover your mouse above the data grid added in the previous section but keep the cursor in the layout grid. This will highlight a box to indicate a spot where you can place the building block:

Figure 7.9 – Highlighted box to drop a building block or widget on a page

6. Click to drop the **Hero Header 2** building block onto the page. If you dropped the building block below the data grid, simply click and drag to reposition it at the top.

7. Your page should look like this:

Figure 7.10 – Member_overview page with Hero Header 2 building block showing default content

8. Double-click the text **Hero Header Title** text to edit it.

9. Change **Caption** to Members.

10. Change the **Render mode** to **Heading 3**.

11. Click **OK**.

12. Repeat *steps 8-9* for the subtitle. Change **Caption** to A list of video store members.

Now, since we want design elements to be useful to the visitor, let's also change the image to something more relevant by following these steps:

1. Double-click on the image above the title to edit it. Notice the options to modify the appearance, visibility, and click behavior of the image.

2. Click **Select** next to **Image** to find a new image.

3. Scroll down and choose the **illustration_users** image under **Atlas_UI_Resources. Native_Content**.

4. Click **OK**.

Now the header should look something like this:

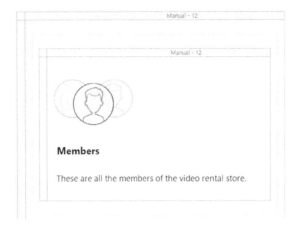

Figure 7.11 – Hero Header 2 with custom content

There you go! It is that easy to create robust user interfaces in Mendix Studio Pro. In this section, you learned how to build pages in Studio Pro. You used elements such as navigation layouts, widgets, and Atlas UI building blocks to design a robust user interface. In the next section, you will learn how to connect your page to the app's navigation and use microflows and buttons to call pages in your Mendix app.

Calling a page in your Mendix app

When you want to direct users around your app, you will guide them through pages. Your app's logic will determine which page to show and when to show it. If you are working with a UX designer, you may receive some mock-ups or a storyboard of the user flow through your app. Even if you aren't working with a designer, you still have to think about how your user will get from point A to point B, why they would even want to go there, and what they will see when they get there.

There are a few ways you may need to get a user to a page in your app. The user could be coming from the main menu, they could be clicking a button somewhere in your app, or they could have executed some function that resulted in the display of a certain page. The user will also have a home page to land on every time they log in or refresh the app. In this section, you will learn how to use the main navigation to build the app menu. You may have other ways to get to a page besides the main menu. The user can be shown links or buttons that can call a page directly or through a microflow, which will allow you to create or retrieve and pass data objects to the page. With the following exercises, you will learn how to connect a page to the app's main navigation and call the page from a button using a direct page call and how to use a microflow to call a page.

Understanding the main navigation

The main navigation for your Mendix app is located in the **Project** module in **Project Explorer**. To add a menu item, do the following:

1. Expand the **Project** module in **Project Explorer**:

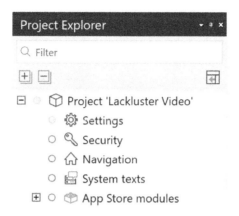

Figure 7.12 – Project module in Project Explorer

2. Double-click **Navigation**.

3. Click **New item** on the **Menu** bar in the middle of the screen:

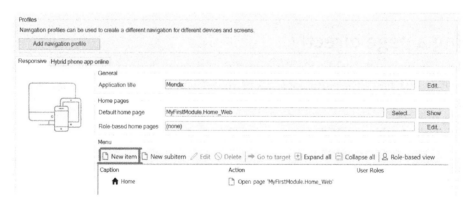

Figure 7.13 – Main app navigation editing

4. Use the following settings:

- **Caption**: Members

- **Icon**: **Glyphicon 'user'**

- **On click**: **Show a page**

- **Page**: `VideoRentals.Member_Overview`:

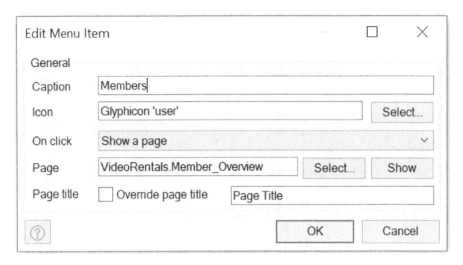

Figure 7.14 – Edit Menu Item dialog box

5.   Click **OK**.

There is now a navigation item for members. In the next section, you will learn how to call a page directly from a button widget.

Calling a page directly

In some cases, you will be able to call a page directly from a button or widget on another page. Not every page will go into the app's main navigation. Complete the following exercise to learn how to use a widget on a page to call a page in your app:

1.   With the **Lackluster Video** project open in Studio Pro, expand the `MyFirstModule` module.

2.   Double-click **Home_Web** (this is the home page of your Mendix app).

    If you are ever unsure of which page is the home page, you can always open the main navigation page to view the selected home page.

3.   Create two more columns in the lower layout grid by right-clicking on the column and choosing **Add column right**:

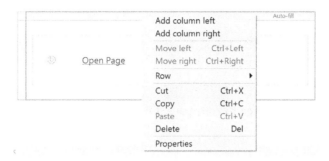

Figure 7.15 – Layout grid with column context menu

> **Important note**
> Create a consistent design. Remove the header on this page and change it to the **Hero Header 2** building block to match the other page you created in the *Creating a new page* section. Go back to the other steps if you are unsure of how to do this.

4. Click **Add building block…**.

5. Choose **Card Action**.

6. Drop the building block into the first column in the lower layout grid.

    This will generate two warnings since there are no on-click events defined for the elements of this building block:

Figure 7.16 – Card Action building block with default content showing warnings

7. Double-click on the **image** icon to edit it.

8. Click **Select** next to the **Icon** field.

9. Choose **Image**.

10. Select the same user illustration from the previous section and click **OK**.

11. Under **Events**, change the selection to **Show a page**.

12. Choose the Member_Overview page.

13. Click **OK**.

14. Double-click **Open Page**.

15. Change **Caption** to Members.

16. Follow *steps 11-12* for the **Events** section.

17. Click **OK** to be taken back to your page. Observe the modified tile:

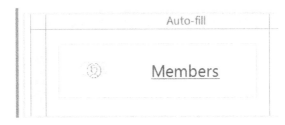

Figure 7.17: Card Action building block with custom content and warnings cleared

That was easy! Good job on adding and customizing another Atlas UI building block. Keep going to learn how to use a microflow to call a page in your Mendix app.

Calling a page from a microflow

Another way you may want to call a page is by using a microflow. Often, you will have some custom logic that results in showing a specific page to the end user. You may also have some use cases where you want to manipulate an object prior to showing the user a page to edit it. In the following exercise, we will explore the latter.

The requirement for adding new members to the video rental app states that there should be at least one phone number given for the member in order for them to be saved. You may have noticed in the *Creating with Atlas UI building blocks* section that there was no phone number field shown for the member on the auto-generated page.

The default **New** button and auto-generated page did not account for the PhoneNumber entity. So, the new page will only contain attributes from the Member entity.

In the following exercise, you will use a microflow to create the new PhoneNumber entity and pass it to a page for editing in the UI. First, you will have to modify the Member_ NewEdit page with the additional data grid for the PhoneNumber entity. Let's start with that.

To update the Member_NewEdit page, do the following:

1. Open the **Lackluster Video** project in Mendix Studio Pro and expand the **VideoRentals** module.

2. Double-click the Member NewEdit page from **Project Explorer** to open it for editing.

3. Choose **Data grid** from the page editor toolbar:

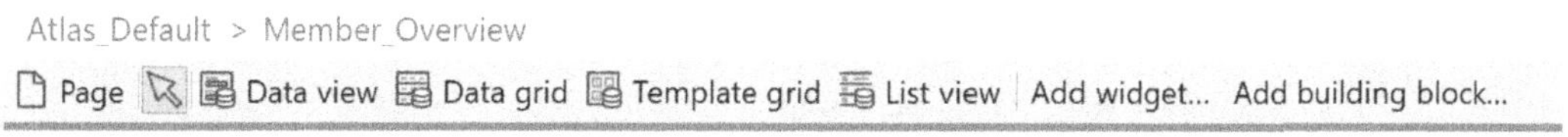

Atlas_Default > Member_Overview

🗋 Page ⬚ 🖥 Data view 🖥 Data grid 🖥 Template grid 🖥 List view │ Add widget... Add building block...

Figure 7.18 – Page editor toolbar

4. Drop this data view so it is nested in the member data view, below the **Active** radio buttons.

5. From the **Connector** panel, click the PhoneNumber entity, then drag and drop it onto the new data grid.

6. From the **Data Source Options** popup, choose **Type: Association**.

7. Click **OK**.

8.   Rearrange the columns to put the type attribute before the phone number attribute by dragging and dropping the column:

Figure 7.19 – Member_NewEdit with a nested PhoneNumber data grid

Now that you have modified the `Member_NewEdit` page to hold phone numbers, you will need to add a way for new phone numbers to be created. For this, you will use a custom action button connected to a microflow that will create the `PhoneNumber` object and pass it to a page for editing.

We will leverage Studio Pro as much as possible to build this microflow and generate the resulting `PhoneNumber_NewEdit` page. You will learn more about microflows in the next chapter, but for now, let's complete the following exercise to create a simple microflow to show a page.

To add a custom action button to the data grid, do the following:

1.   Right-click in the control bar of the data grid, then click **Add button** and **Action**:

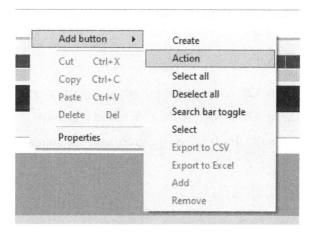

Figure 7.20 – Data grid control bar context menu

2.   Double-click the **Action** button to open its **Properties** dialog screen.

3.   Delete the caption and leave it empty.

4.   Select an option for **Icon**; choose the **Glyphicon Plus** sign.

5.   Change **On click** event to **Call a Microflow**.

6.   With the **VideoRentals** module selected on the proceeding **Select Microflow** popup, click **New**.

7.   Call this microflow `Act_PhoneNumber_Create`.

8.   Click **OK**.

9. Right click on the newly added **Action** button which has a + sign on it and choose **Go to on click microflow**.

Mendix creates a microflow with some input parameters. When an object is given as the input parameter, the microflow is expecting that object to be passed in when the microflow is invoked.

10. Given that you will be creating a new PhoneNumber object in your microflow, go ahead and delete the input parameter with the same name by selecting it and pressing *Delete* on your keyboard:

Figure 7.21 – Delete the PhoneNumber input parameter

11. Right-click in the microflow editor, then click **Add | Activity**.

12. Drag the activity on the line between the green and red dots so it snaps to the line:

Figure 7.22 – Microflow with the activity snapped to the center line

13. Double-click the activity to edit it.

14. Choose **Create Object**.

15. Click **Select** next to the **Entity** field.

16. Double-click PhoneNumber.

17. Click **New**.

18. For **Member**, choose **VideoRentals.PhoneNumber_Member (VideoRentals. Member)**.

19. Click **Generate**.

20. Select **Variable**.

21. Choose **Member** (`VideoRentals.Member`).

22. Click **OK** three times.

> **Associations**
>
> Setting the association is important to ensure that the phone number object is related to the right member object. If you do not set the associations properly, then you will create orphaned objects in the database and will need to clean them up periodically.

23. Follow steps *11-13* to add another activity after the first one and open it for editing.

24. Choose **Show Page**.

25. Click **OK**.

26. For **Object to pass**, select the `NewPhoneNumber` object.

27. Next to **Page**, click **Select**.

28. With the **VideoRentals** module selected, click **New**.

    Notice that this new page already has a name and appropriate layout.

29. Select the **Form Vertical** template and click **OK** twice.

Congratulations! You have learned how to use a microflow to display a page in your Mendix app.

In this section, you learned all about calling pages. Pages can be linked to the main menu or to buttons and links on other pages. Pages can also be called via microflow so you can manipulate some data before showing it on the page.

Summary

In this chapter, you learned how to create robust user interfaces. Studio Pro provides the construct of the page for you to display information to end users. The pages are designed using layouts, widgets, and Atlas UI building blocks in Mendix Studio Pro. You also learned how to call pages from the app main navigation, directly from page widgets, and with microflows. The exercises showed you how to apply these concepts to the example video store application. In the next chapter, you will go into more depth with microflows and learn how to validate data with custom save functions.

Chapter 6 knowledge check answers

The following are the answers to *Chapter 6, Understanding Domain Model Basics*, knowledge check:

1. a

2. b

3. a

4. a

5. a

6. d

7. b

8. c

Chapter 7 knowledge check

1. Which Mendix product provides page templates and other building blocks to give your app pages a modern design with standard web elements?

   a. Pages

   b. Widgets

   c. User experience

   d. Atlas UI

2. Mendix Studio Pro provides the ability to build responsive pages and device-specific pages:

   a. True

   b. False

3. Which screen in Studio Pro allows you to pick a page template and navigation layout for a new page?

   a. Properties

   b. Changes

   c. Create Page

   d. New Entity

4. How do you make changes to the grayed-out areas of a page in Studio Pro?

    a. Edit Navigation Layout

    b. Double-click on the gray area

    c. Edit Page Template

    d. Add Page

5. What must the total width of columns in a layout grid add up to?

    a. 10

    b. 9

    c. 12

    d. 6

6. To temporarily remove a page from a project without deleting it, you can use the Exclude from project feature of Studio Pro:

    a. True

    b. False

7. What three design principles was Atlas UI built upon?

    a. Ease of use, structure, widgets

    b. Simplicity, harmony, flexibility

    c. Harmony, ease of use, layouts

    d. Simplicity, flexibility, aesthetics

8. Navigation layouts can be applied to multiple pages in a Mendix app:

    a. True

    b. False

8

Getting to Know Microflows

Now that you have covered pages and domain models, which represent the presentation and data layers of your app, respectively, it is time to dive into the application or business logic of the Mendix app with **microflows**. Although Mendix Studio and Studio Pro come with many preset buttons that offer instant functionality to your app, you must learn how to use microflows if you want to extend this with any custom logic.

Think of microflows as visual representations of program code that would traditionally be text. Microflows are drawn like visual diagrams, with **activities** such as retrieving and manipulating data, creating and modifying variables, displaying pages to users, and more.

In this chapter, you will learn how to create microflows with proper naming conventions and how to call microflows from pages, as well as using microflows to show pages. You will also learn about the various elements used to build microflows and learn a bit about Mendix Assist, the AI-guided process for building microflows with best practices in mind.

In this chapter, we are going to cover the following main topics:

- Understanding common microflow elements
- Using decisions to navigate your application logic
- Putting annotations in your microflow
- Learning with Mendix Assist

By the end of this chapter, you will be able to create custom logic for your application using microflows in Studio Pro.

Technical requirements

The sample project of this chapter can be found in `Chapter08` folder at `https://github.com/PacktPublishing/Building-Low-Code-Applications-with-Mendix`.

Understanding common microflow elements

In previous chapters, you made some small microflows for your application while working with entities and pages. You used **activities** in those microflows to perform certain functions such as changing attributes on an object or showing a page. Microflow activities give Mendix developers a wide variety of preset functions to use in Mendix applications. For the more professional developers out there, Studio Pro can be extended with custom Java actions. You can read more about that in the full online Mendix documentation. For now, let's learn about some common microflow elements.

Controlling the flow with events

You may have noticed (if you were paying attention) that the microflows you worked with in previous chapters all started with a green dot and ended with a red dot. These dots are **events**. Microflows read left to right. Let me rephrase that: *good* microflows read left to right and top to bottom, the same way an artist would interpret the viewer's eye flow across a painting. The happy path generally flows left to right, with exceptions stemming downward to their own ends. Negative decisions will stem down and keep going to the right along the flow until their respective line meets another decision point, and the process continues until it all ends.

There are three types of events: **start**, **stop**, and **error**. All microflows must begin with a start event. You can add events (and other elements) to a microflow by using the toolbar at the top of the microflow editor or by right-clicking in the microflow window. The following screenshot shows a start event with a `Change` object activity:

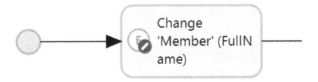

Figure 8.1 – Microflow start event and Change object activity

While there can only be one start event in a microflow, there can be multiple **end** events. The number of end events will depend on the number of decisions and alternate paths programmed into your flow. You can have regular end events or **error** events. Error events are the termination of error handling flows. Error handling is an advanced topic that you can read about in detail in the online Mendix documentation. For now, you can think of it as exception handling flows that can be configured for certain microflow elements, which may result in an error in their processing. In the following screenshot, you can see what a microflow toolbar looks like:

Figure 8.2 – Microflow toolbar

Now that you know how to start and stop your microflows, let's get started with working with objects and lists. In the next section, you will learn about microflow activities to manipulate data in your application logic.

Working with objects and lists

As you learned, entities in your domain model contain rows of data. Each row of data can be referred to as an **object** in your application. There are several microflow activities available for working with objects. The most common ones are **Retrieve**, **Change object**, **Create object**, **Commit object**, and **Delete object**. They do precisely what they are named. Rather than make you construct SQL queries to manipulate objects, the microflow allows a more visual approach to working with data. You can retrieve either an individual object or a list of objects. The following screenshot shows the **Object** and **List** microflow activities:

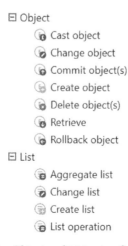

Figure 8.3 – Object and List microflow activities

Some common things you would do with data is to either change it or save it when it is changed by the user on one of your pages. In the following exercise, we will add custom logic to save a new member with its list of phone numbers when the user clicks **Save**.

You will do a few things to set up the scenario. In the previous chapter, we added a grid for phone numbers onto the `Member_NewEdit` page with a button to create a new phone number. You also created a page called `PhoneNumber_NewEdit`. First, we will make some changes to `PhoneNumber_NewEdit` and apply custom logic to the **Save** button. Let's do this by following these steps:

1. Open the **Lackluster Video** project in Mendix Studio Pro 8.

2. On your keyboard, press *Ctrl + G* to launch the **Go To** pop-up window.

3. Start typing in `PhoneNumber_NewEdit`. Once it has been selected, press *Enter* to be taken to this page.

4. Right-click on the green **Save** button and select **Edit On Click Action…**.

5. For the **On click** event, choose **Call a microflow** from the drop-down list. This will expand the **Edit Action** box with microflow selection options.

6. Next to **Microflow**, click **Select**.

7. With the **VideoRentals** module selected, click **New** from the bottom of the pop-up window.

8. Call the new microflow `Act_PhoneNumber_Save` and click **OK**.

9. Click **Show** next to **Select**, then click **OK** to close the **Edit Action** pop-up window.

    You will be taken to the newly created microflow with an **input parameter** built in.

    > **Input parameters**
    >
    > Input parameters are the given inputs for microflows. While they are not always required, the situation will dictate how many and what kinds of input parameters you need. The input parameter options are primitive data types, such as strings, integers, and Booleans, as well as Mendix objects and lists of objects. Read through the online documentation for the full list of available input parameter types.

You have now configured a button on a page to use a custom microflow. This microflow is empty. Notice in the **Errors** dock in Studio Pro how you have generated a new warning by creating this empty microflow with an input parameter that is not used yet. This warning will clear once we start putting some elements into the microflow. Also, take note of the start and end events automatically put into this new microflow. You will build your logic in between these points. In the following screenshot, we can see a microflow that has an input parameter and a start and end event:

Figure 8.4 – New microflow with input parameter indicating warning and start/stop events

The warning shown is because you have an object in the microflow that is not being used. This will get resolved as we add more activities and do something with this input parameter.

In the next exercise, you will add some activities to save the new phone number and close the `PhoneNumber_NewEdit` window. Let's do this by following these steps:

1. Your newly created microflow in Mendix Studio Pro called `Act_PhoneNumber_Save` will be open for editing.

2. Add a new activity and **select Type of Action** as **Commit Object**.

    You can click on the activity, drag it, and hover it over the line to link it into the flow.

3. Choose the `PhoneNumber` object from the dropdown to commit and choose **Yes** for **Refresh in client**:

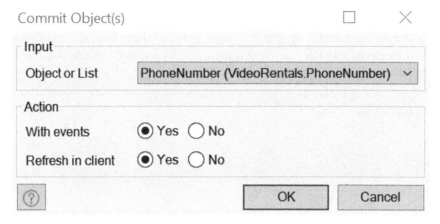

Figure 8.5 – Commit Object(s) dialog

4. Add a second new activity and **select Type of Action** as **Close page**.

This will close the currently open screen. In the case of this example, the `PhoneNumber_NewEdit` page will close to take the user back to the `Member_Edit` page.

This is what your completed microflow should look like:

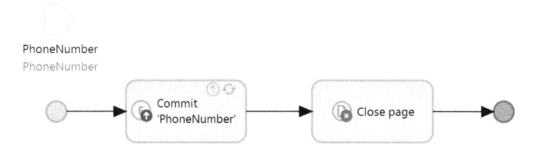

Figure 8.6 – Microflow: Act_PhoneNumber_Save

This set of exercises helped you set up a custom **Save** button for the phone number object associated with your video rental store member. In the next section, you will learn about decision logic and add some validation to your microflows.

Using decisions to navigate your application logic

Decisions will split or join flows of logic in your microflow. At a decision point, there is usually some sort of evaluation of a condition that could have multiple outcomes. It could be a true or false scenario or a possibility of options in an enumerated list. The outcome could even be the calculation of some complex expression. For now, you will learn how to use decision elements called **decision splits** to validate the data fields on your member and phone number objects. This will ensure that when members and phone numbers are saved, they will not have blank data fields.

Validating phone number on save

Follow these steps to add some validation logic to the `Act_PhoneNumber_Save` microflow:

1. Navigate to the `Act_PhoneNumber_Save` microflow in Mendix Studio Pro 8.

2. Right-click in the microflow.

3. Click **Add**.

4. Click **Activity**.

5. Double-click the activity.

6. Choose **select Type of Action: Create Variable**.

7. Drag the new **Create Variable** activity over the line to the left of the **Commit and Close page** activities. This should snap the **Decision** element into the flow. Drop it there.

8. Create a Boolean variable with the value and name as shown in the following screenshot:

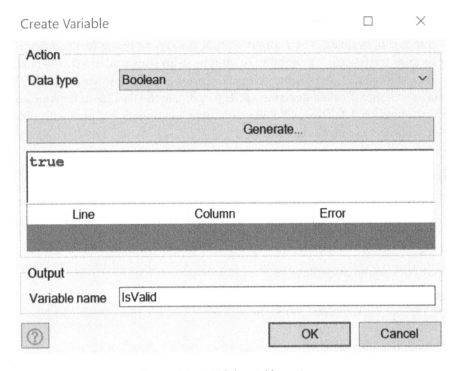

Figure 8.7 – IsValid variable settings

9. Click **OK**.

10. Right-click in the microflow.

11. Click **Add**.

12. Click **Decision**.

13. Drag the new **Decision** element (represented by a yellow diamond) immediately after the **Create Variable** activity to snap it into the flow.

14. Double-click the yellow diamond to open the **Decision** dialog and enter the following:

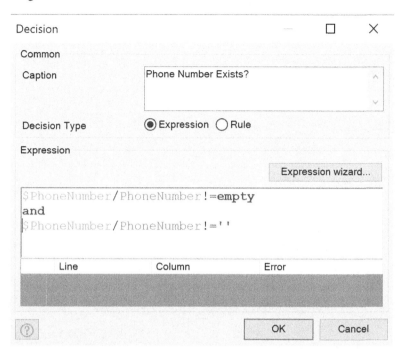

Figure 8.8 – Decision dialog in the microflow

15. Click **OK**.

> **Microflow expressions**
>
> While this book does not go too deep into microflow expressions, you can find more documentation about them online. Microflow expressions are XPath expressions used to calculate or validate certain conditions. Press *Ctrl + Enter* on your keyboard while in the expression editor to see a full list of available functions. Click the help icon on the bottom left of the **Decision** dialog to view the Mendix online documentation or press *F1* on your keyboard. The expression in *step 7* is a common one used to validate an empty string. In a later chapter, you will learn some more advanced functions around this concept.

16. Right-click on the now-red arrow coming out to the left of the yellow diamond and set the condition value to **true**.

17. Click the bottom of the yellow diamond and drag it down to add a new activity. Choose **Validation Feedback** and use the following settings:

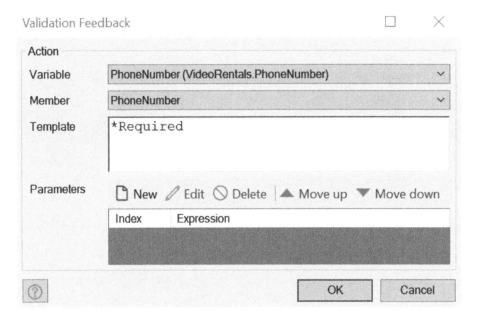

Figure 8.9 – Validation Feedback dialog in the microflow

18. Click **OK**.

19. Add another activity below the **Validation Feedback** activity and choose **Change Variable**.

20. Draw a line from the **Validation Feedback** activity to the **Change Variable** activity to add it to the sequence flow.

21. Change the IsValid variable and set it to false.

22. Draw a line from the right of the **Change Variable** activity back up to the main flow and use a merge element (red diamond). The microflow should look like this:

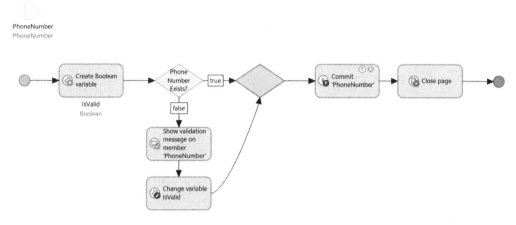

Figure 8.10 – Act_PhoneNumber_Save with validation

What this microflow is doing is using the **Decision** to validate the phone number attribute and ensure it is not empty. If it is empty, the expression will result in a `false` output, which will trigger the validation feedback message and end the flow without committing the object. If the expression returns `true`, then the microflow will continue and commit the object. Now, let's add another validation check for the PhoneNumberType attribute and then a final check on the IsValid attribute to determine whether or not to commit the object.

Validating PhoneNumberType on save

Follow these steps to validate PhoneNumberType in the Act_PhoneNumber_Save microflow:

1. Navigate to the Act_PhoneNumber_Save microflow in Mendix Studio Pro 8.
2. Right-click in the microflow.
3. Click **Add**.
4. Click **Decision**.
5. Drag the new **Decision** element before the **Commit Object** activity on the true path of the phone number empty check validation **Decision**.

This should snap the **Decision** element into the flow in between the first yellow diamond and the **Commit Object** activity. Drop it there.

6. Double-click the yellow diamond to open the **Decision** dialog and enter the following:

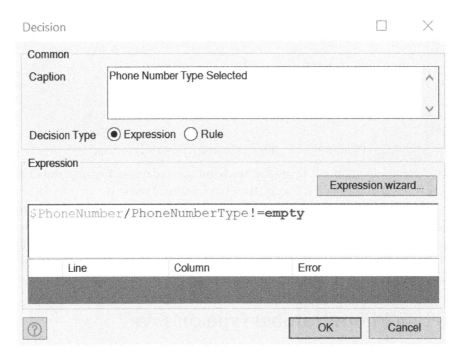

Figure 8.11 – Decision for phone number type validation

7. Click **OK**.

Notice that this one only required the empty check. This is because of the data type of this attribute. It is an enumeration instead of a string. To validate a null value, you only need to check for empty.

8. Right-click on the now-red arrow coming out to the left of the yellow diamond and set the condition value to **true**.

9. Draw a line from the bottom of the yellow diamond and add a new activity called **Validation Feedback** with the following settings:

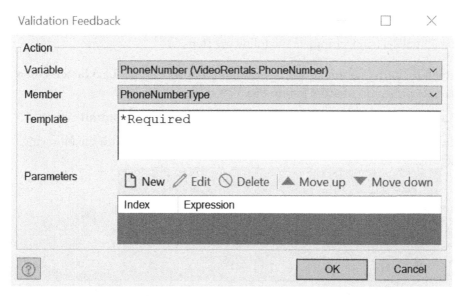

Figure 8.12 – Validation Feedback for the phone number type attribute

10. Click **OK**.

11. Draw a line from the bottom of the **Validation Feedback** activity and add another **Change Variable** activity to set `IsValid` to `false` and merge the flow back into the main path. Your microflow should look like this now:

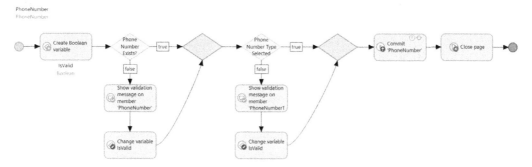

Figure 8.13 – The Act_PhoneNumber_Save microflow with null check validation on the phone number and phone number type attributes

If you are paying attention, you will notice that this microflow commits the object even when the validation check on each attribute returns a `false` output. The last thing needed here is one more split to check the value of the `IsValid` variable and determine whether to commit the object or not.

To add the final decision, complete the following steps:

1. Open the `Act_PhoneNumber_Save` microflow from the **Lackluster Video** sample project in Mendix Studio Pro.

2. Add a **Decision** to the main flow immediately before the **Commit** activity.

3. Double-click the yellow diamond to modify the **Decision** with the following settings:

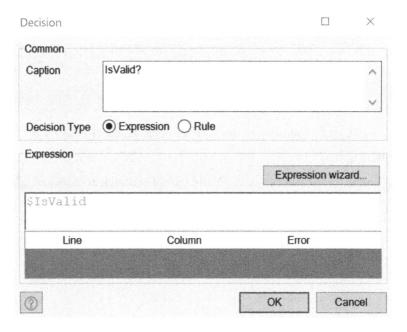

Figure 8.14 – Decision with a check on the IsValid variable

4. Click **OK**.

5. Set the condition on the flow coming out of the yellow diamond into the **Commit** activity to be **true**.

6. Draw a line out of the bottom of the yellow diamond and terminate the flow with an end event.

    Notice how Studio Pro will automatically set this as the **false** flow condition. This is because it is the final condition option available for the given expression.

Great work! Now you have a custom **Save** button that validates both fields of your object on save. You are well on your way to creating a solid application! In the next section, you will learn how to make your microflows even more defensible by adding some clarity in the form of annotations.

Putting annotations in your microflow

If you have ever worked with traditional coding stacks, you may have encountered long blocks of code with little to no explanation of what was going on. The same thing can happen in a microflow. The blocks need not belong, but with a series of blue rectangles, yellow diamonds, and green circles, you may think you are staring into a bowl of marshmallow cereal instead of a block of programming code.

Annotations are like comments and notations allowed in other programming languages. These blocks of text are ignored by the code compiler. They are there to allow developers to leave meaningful messages to one another about the programming logic. So, be sure to put them to good use!

Adding an annotation, or two...

In the following exercise, you will add some annotations to your custom save microflow, which will add some clarity for the next developer who looks at this project.

Follow these steps to add some annotations to `Act_PhoneNumber_Save`:

1. Navigate to `Act_PhoneNumber_Save` in Mendix Studio Pro.

2. Click the annotation icon in the microflow toolbar:

Figure 8.15 – Annotation icon in the microflow toolbar

3. Drop an annotation to the top of the screen, just right of the input parameter, and resize it so that it spans the entire flow. Give a general explanation of what this microflow does in this annotation.

4. Add a second annotation and drag a line from the annotation to each of the two yellow diamonds to connect the annotation specifically to those elements. The microflow should now look something like this:

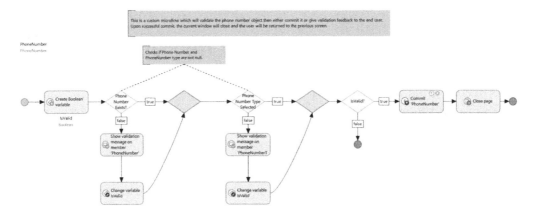

Figure 8.16 – The Act_PhoneNumber_Save microflow with annotations

Wow, look at that! A custom microflow with validation and annotations. You are well on your way to becoming a pro developer. This exercise demonstrated how annotations can be used in a generic way to describe a microflow and how to tie annotations to specific elements of the microflow for clarity. Now, let's learn one more thing about microflows and extract a sub-microflow out of this microflow to clean up the readability of the flow.

Extracting a sub-microflow

When building microflows, it is important to get the functionality right first. A feature of Mendix Studio Pro is the ability to extract a sub-microflow from a microflow. Studio Pro will automatically set the input and output parameters based on how objects are used in the microflow. There are limitations to this feature. For example, you cannot extract events (end and start events) and the set of microflow elements selected for extraction must end in a single flow.

For this exercise, you will extract the validation steps from the phone number and save the microflow into a validation sub-flow. To do this, complete the following steps:

1. Open the Act_PhoneNumber_Save microflow from the **Lackluster Video** sample project in Mendix Studio Pro.

2. Using your mouse, click in the upper-left corner of the microflow and drag the mouse toward the left and down to select the validation elements from the **Create Variable** activity through the last merge (red diamond) element.

Be sure to grab the annotation as well. The selected elements will look like this:

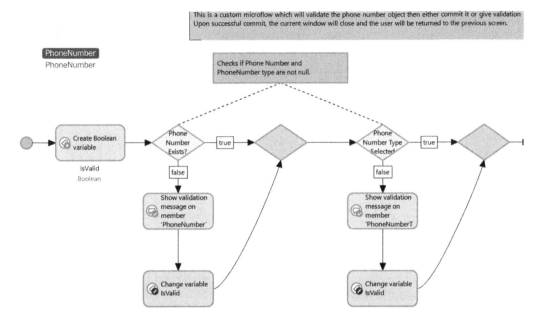

Figure 8.17 – Selected elements for the sub-microflow extraction

3. Right-click on one of the elements to expose the **Context** menu.

4. Choose **Extract submicroflow….**

5. On the popup, name the new sub-microflow Val_PhoneNumber.

6. Click **OK**.

Now, you have a custom save microflow with a validation sub-flow for PhoneNumber. You used Studio Pro to help you craft these microflows to ensure proper input and outputs. Using a sub-microflow, you added some readability to the microflow and created a reusable component in the case of a phone number that needed validation somewhere else in the app.

Repeat the previous exercises to create a custom save microflow with a validation sub-flow for the Member object and connect this custom microflow to the **Save** button on the Member_New page. The following screenshots show the completed microflows:

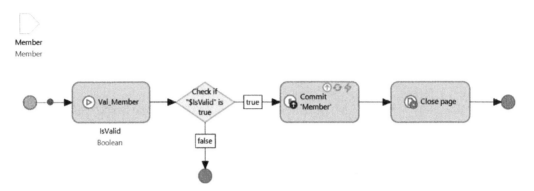

Figure 8.18 – The Act_Member_Save microflow

The following is the validation sub-microflow you extracted in the previous step. Notice how Studio Pro automatically created the input parameter, start and end events, and the output of the IsValid Boolean back to the parent flow:

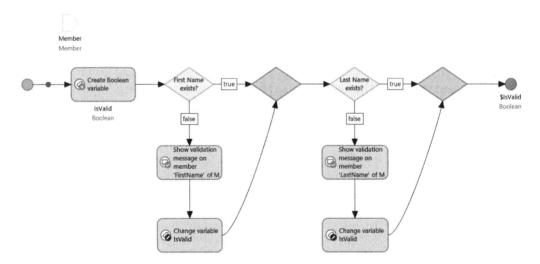

Figure 8.19 – The Val_Member microflow

In the next section, you will learn how to use Mendix Assist to create AI-driven microflows.

Learning with Mendix Assist

Mendix Assist is one of the latest tools in the ever-growing toolkit provided by Mendix to ease the development process. Mendix Assist is an AI-driven engine that helps the developer make decisions about programming. The data for the recommendations given by Mendix Assist comes from analyzing Mendix apps over the years and teaching the AI assistant Mendix best practices. You will notice blue dots appear on the flow and a little blue and white bow tie icon appear on activities:

Figure 8.20 – Mendix Assist icon in a microflow

You can engage Mendix Assist by clicking on these icons and looking at the recommended actions. Mendix Assist has a fairly high success rate with choosing the right option and the accuracy gets higher with each day and new sets of models to analyze. Here is what the selection menu looks like for Mendix Assist:

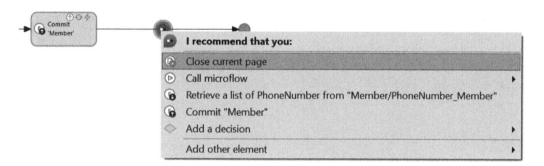

Figure 8.21 – Mendix Assist selection menu

If you do not see the Mendix Assist icons, check your modeler preferences. Follow these steps:

1. In Mendix Studio Pro, click on **Edit** then **Preferences**.

2. In the **General** tab, be sure to check whether the box next to **Enable Mendix Assist** is selected.

To learn more about Mendix Assist, be sure to view the full documentation available online as well as videos and announcements from Mendix, Mendix Academy, and annual events such as Mendix World.

Summary

In this chapter, you learned how to create custom logic with microflows in your Mendix app. You explored some common microflow activities and created a custom microflow with decision logic to validate your object on save. You also learned about annotations and how to add clarity to your microflows. Mendix Assist is a great tool to learn how to build microflows and ensure you are choosing the right actions in the right order.

After completing the exercises in this chapter, you now know how to create custom logic for your app to validate data and save objects. You also know how to extract a sub-microflow from your parent microflow, which lets Studio Pro do the heavy lifting on setting input and output parameters.

In the following chapters, you will learn how to customize your app and extend it with advanced concepts such as error handling and REST integrations.

Chapter 7 knowledge check answers

The following are the answers for the *Chapter 7, Understanding the Basics of Page Design,* knowledge check:

1. d
2. a
3. c
4. a
5. c
6. a
7. b
8. a

Chapter 8 knowledge check

1. What do you call the green dot at the beginning of a microflow?

    a. Enter event

    b. Start event

    c. Beginning event

    d. Opening event

2. What are the three types of events available in a microflow?

    a. Enter, end, pause

    b. Beginning, middle, end

    c. Start, stop, error

    d. Open, close, error

3. True or False: Objects can be retrieved in a microflow either individually or as a list of multiple objects?

    a. True

    b. False

4. Which object activity would you use to delete an object from the database?

    a. Delete object

    b. Remove object

    c. Erase object

    d. Commit object

5. Which microflow activity would you use to change the flow based on an expression or other calculated logic?

    a. Inheritance split

    b. Decision

    c. Flow changer

    d. Expression split

6. To return a message to the user for an attribute that fails validation, which microflow element is best suited?

    a. Error feedback

    b. Attribute feedback

    c. Validation feedback

    d. Message feedback

7. Which Mendix product is an AI-driven engine that helps the developer make decisions about programming?

    a. Mendix Assist

    b. Skynet

    c. Mendix Data Hub

    d. IBM Watson

8. True or False: It is best practice to prefix the name of Mendix microflows in Studio Pro with a meaningful prefix that gives some indication of the microflow's function?

    a. True

    b. False

Section 3: Leveling Up Your App

In this part, you will learn how to enhance your application with custom business logic and rules, defensively anticipate and troubleshoot when bad data shows its face, and, as it's a big world out there, connect to it!

This section comprises the following chapters:

- *Chapter 9, Customizing Your App*
- *Chapter 10, Error Handling and Troubleshooting*
- *Chapter 11, Storing Data*
- *Chapter 12, Getting Some REST*
- *Chapter 13, A Review and What's Next*

9
Customizing Your App

In this chapter, we will dive deeper beyond opening pages and saving records. We will take a closer look at adding custom business logic and rules to drive user experience and functionality. We will turn your user stories into working, navigable applications that take your development to the next level!

To help get us there, we will cover the following topics and concepts:

- Functions and expressions – We will discuss functions that will help us work with and manipulate string attributes, integers, enumerations, and DateTime attributes. We will also explore relational expressions that are used to work with multiple data points at the same time, for example, finding the delta between two integers.

- Sub-microflows – You may know what a microflow is, but what is a sub-microflow? In the previous chapter, we extracted a set of activities in a microflow to create a sub-microflow. But why was that necessary? In this chapter, we will find out exactly what sub-microflows are, how we should best use them, and why it's important to use them.

- Configurable settings – Being flexible with certain settings that are used in your application can become very important as requirements change over time. In this section, we will explore how to configure settings in the runtime so that calculations and business logic can be flexible and scalable as your application evolves.

- Java actions – Mendix offers an incredible amount of native functionality but sometimes it is necessary to extend an application's functionality beyond what is offered out of the box. Custom Java actions allow a greater level of customization and extendibility. In this section, we will talk about a few use cases and point you to some great resources.

After considering the topics and concepts listed, you will gain the following skills:

- Learn how and when to apply Mendix functions for various attribute types

- Understand what a sub-microflow is, when to leverage its power, and how to do it properly

- How and why to create configurable settings in your app and how to use them

Technical requirements

The sample project of this chapter can be found in `Chapter09` folder at `https://github.com/PacktPublishing/Building-Low-Code-Applications-with-Mendix`.

Having some fun with Mendix functions and expressions

Leveraging Mendix out-of-the-box functions and expressions is where you can really start to have some fun with your data and business logic. You will start to be able to build validations and business rules/logic and really customize the user's experience. You can essentially think of functions and expressions as ways to compare a given piece of data to another input or even itself, or perhaps manipulate it in some way.

There are a lot of functions and expressions that Mendix offers that may look similar to the ones you have seen in more traditional languages or perhaps in an application such as Microsoft Excel. Regardless, it's important to understand their intended use and syntax from within Studio Pro and how to interact with them while building out needed validation or rules in a microflow.

This section isn't intended to cover *every* function or expression Mendix has to offer. Rather, this is a look at some of the most commonly used functions and expressions and how to go about using them. For a complete listing of every available function and expression, please take a look at the reference guides provided by Mendix (`https://docs.mendix.com/refguide/expressions`). In this next section, we will specifically look at functions and expressions for strings, integers, DateTime, enumerations, and relational expressions.

In the following few examples, we will discuss briefly what each function does, show an abstract example, and then have an exercise where you will have an opportunity to jump into Studio Pro to try it out for yourself!

Understanding string functions

A string function is a way for the application's business logic to interact with strings. The functions can perform a wide array of logic to manipulate, alter, and extract values, combine multiple strings, and much more! Let's take a closer look at some of the more commonly used functions in the next sections.

toLowerCase and toUpperCase

These function calls perform an operation that does exactly what their names imply. When used, these will convert any string to either all uppercase or all lowercase, depending on which one was called. The following figure shows an example of these function calls:

Example	Returns
toLowerCase('hereIsaRANDOMString')	hereisarandomstring
toUpperCase('hereIsaRANDOMString')	HEREISARANDOMSTRING

Figure 9.1 – Example of toLowerCase and toUpperCase

These are useful when attempting to standardize data collected from users or when trying to compare separate values to see whether they are equal or not.

length

The `length` function will return the number of characters within the string passed to it. The following figure shows an example of this function:

Example	Returns
length('hereISaRANDOMString')	19

Figure 9.2 – Example of length

This function is used for ensuring user entry data meets a minimum number of characters or checking whether one string is larger/smaller than another one.

substring

The `substring` function will return a string from within the string that was passed into it. This seems confusing but it's really not. Check out the examples shown in *Figure 9.3*. For example, this function could be used in determining what the first initial of someone's first name is:

> **Important note**
>
> One word of caution: if you are attempting to use a starting point or a length that is greater than the actual length of the string, it will result in an error. This is definitely something to keep in mind if you plan on using this function.

Example	Returns
substring('Hello World',3)	'lo World'
substring('Hello World',7)	'orld'
substring('Hello World',0,5)	'Hello'
substring('Hello World',6,2)	'Wo'
substring('Hello World',27)	ERROR

Figure 9.3 – Examples of substring

There are two different variations of how this function can be used. The first two examples give a substring starting at a particular place and returning the rest of the string. The next two examples have a third parameter that indicates the length of the substring returned.

find

With this find function, you can essentially search a given string to see whether it contains a certain value. If that value is found, the function will return the starting location of that value from within the string. If the value is not found, a value of -1 will be returned. See the following figure for a few examples:

Example	Returns
find('Hello World', 'World')	6
find('Hello World', 'Goodbye')	-1
find('Hello World', 'o', 6)	7

Figure 9.4 – Examples of find

This function could be used for locating a value in a string or to check whether or not it exists at all. This function can be paired nicely with the substring function.

contains

The contains function checks whether the given string contains a particular value. This function is very similar to the find function previously described. However, the difference is this function returns a Boolean. This function checks whether a value is contained in a string by comparing two strings to each other:

Important note
This function is case sensitive!

Example	Returns
contains('Hello World', 'World')	true
contains('Hello World', 'world')	false
contains('Hello World', 'o')	true

Figure 9.5 – Examples of contains

replaceAll

The `replaceAll` function does exactly what the name implies. It will replace all occurrences of a particular value or expression contained within the string you are inspecting. This function has three parameters. The first is the string you wish to convert. The second is the value you wish to replace. The third is the value you wish to replace the second value with. Check out the following examples; it's not as complicated as it sounds!

> **Important note**
>
> `replaceAll` function is case sensitive!

Example	Returns
replaceAll('Hello World', 'World', 'Galaxy')	'Hello Galaxy'
replaceAll('Hello World', 'world', 'Galaxy')	'Hello World'
replaceAll('Hello World', 'Hello', '')	' World'
replaceAll('Hello World', 'l', '')	'Heo Word'

Figure 9.6 – Examples of replaceAll

Its possible use case is removing a specific character or characters from a string.

String concatenation (+)

You can think of this function as a way to add two or more strings together to form a new string.

Its possible use cases are concatenating a user's first and last name attributes to form a "full name" attribute and combining a user's street address with their city, state, and ZIP code to form a full address:

Example	Returns
'Hello' + 'World'	'HelloWorld'
'Hello' + ' ' + 'World'	'Hello World'
'Hello' + ' Big ' + 'World'	'Hello Big World'

Figure 9.7 – Examples of concatenation (+)

urlEncode/Decode

The `urlEncode` function essentially just makes the string you are encoding safe to include in a URL and formats it in a way that makes it acceptable to send over the internet. Without getting into the computer science behind it, this function basically just replaces "unsafe" **American Standard Code for Information Interchange (ASCII)** characters with % and then adds two hexadecimal digits afterward. `urlDecode` does the exact opposite of this. It takes the encoded value and converts it back into a readable-to-a-human structure. The following figure shows some examples:

Example	Returns
urlEncode('Hello World')	'Hello+World'
urlEncode('Hello, World!)	'Hello%2C+World%21'
urlDecode('Hello%2C+World%21')	'Hello, World!'

Figure 9.8 – Examples of urlEncode and urlDecode

It is used in a URL when consuming an API. It is particularly helpful when you are unsure of the value that will be used because, perhaps, it's from a user input screen.

parseInteger

This function will attempt to convert a given string to an integer.

Its possible use case could be when there is a string attribute in your database that actually contains an integer value. Perhaps this was something a user mistakenly entered or provided by an external resource. The string attribute may read as 100 but to the application, that's not a number. You cannot add other numbers to it, it's just a string that contains the characters 1, 0, and 0. So, to do anything "number-like" with that value, you first must convert it to an integer:

> **Important note**
> This function will attempt to convert the given string to an integer. However, if the string contains non-numeric characters, an error will result.

Example	Returns
parseInteger('100')	100
parseInteger('100S')	error

Figure 9.9 – Examples of parseInteger

trim

This function removes all the extra whitespaces at the beginning and the end of a string. This function is great to use when handling user input data. You can see some examples in the following figure:

Example	Returns
trim(' Hello World ')	'Hello World'
trim(' ')	''

Figure 9.10 – Examples of trim

It removes extra whitespaces so that you are sure your data starts and ends with characters.

Integer function calls

When working with integers, you will often need to perform various actions with them. For example, you may need to calculate the sum of two integers, convert an integer to a string value, or many other scenarios. In this section, we will look at a few commonly used functions that will allow you to work more fully with integers. Let's have a look!

Arithmetic/mathematical expressions

These common mathematical expressions are no different than what you learned in elementary or primary school: addition, subtraction, multiplication, and division. Despite their simplicity, do not underestimate their power!

- Addition is represented by +.

- Subtraction is represented by -.

- Multiplication is represented by *.

- Division is represented by *div* or :.

> **Important note**
>
> These mathematical expressions can be combined to form longer, algebraic-like expressions if needed. Please do keep in mind that the Studio Pro takes into account the standard mathematical order of operations. For example, multiplication is handled before addition, expressions contained inside parentheses will be prioritized, and so on.

Note in *Figure 9.11* a few examples of how the arithmetic expressions are used:

Example	Returns
3 + 5	8
10 − 4	6
3 * 4	12
12 div 4 OR 12 : 4	3
20 + 5 : 5	21
(20 + 5) : 5	5

Figure 9.11 – Examples of mathematical expressions (+ - * div :)

It can be used if you are looking for the sum of two attributes, determining spots left for a class, or any other place you may need to perform a mathematical operation.

max/min

The max and min functions perform the exact opposite operations of each other. max will return the largest number in a set of given numbers while min will, you guessed it, return the smallest number in a set of given numbers.

A possible use case is determining the highest or lowest scores on an exam or which course has the highest or lowest amount of registrants:

> **Important note**
>
> This function has the potential to return an integer or a decimal. It's best if you set the return value in a variable to use a decimal. Otherwise, you run the risk of an error if a decimal is returned and it tries to write to an integer attribute.

Example	Returns
max(1,2,5.9,2,7.3)	7.3
min(3,6,1,7,3)	1

Figure 9.12 – Example of max and min

round, floor, ceil

These expressions are combined here because they perform very similar operations. round will round a number to the nearest given decimal place. By default, with no additional parameters, it will round to the nearest whole number. floor will essentially round decimals down to the nearest whole number, while ceil will round everything up to the nearest whole number.

Possible use cases could be to determine how many cases of something should be placed (ceil), calculating payments that have a currency exchange in which the exchange rate goes out greater than to the hundredths decimal place. Using the round function will make it possible to pay your customer appropriately. In *Figure 9.13*, several examples are listed:

Example	Returns
round(2.2)	2
round(2.5)	3
round(4.67643, 2)	4.68
ceil(3.11)	4
floor(7.99999)	7

Figure 9.13 – Example of round, ceil, and floor

toString

This function attempts to convert an integer to a string.

A possible use case is adding the result of a mathematical expression to the end of a string attribute.

Note: You may consider wrapping this with an `if` statement when there is potential for the integer value to be empty. If the integer is empty, the `toString` function may return a blank or null value to the user, and adding a blank or null to the string wouldn't really be useful and may present an ugly-looking string to the end user:

Example	Returns
toString(1)	'1'

Figure 9.14 – Example of toString

Let's move on to our next function.

DateTime function calls

These functions allow you to interact with `DateTime` data. Often times when dealing with dates, you will need to calculate a particular number of days from the given date, subtract days, or compare two dates, for example. These functions will give you the power to do that! Let's take a look at a few of the commonly used functions.

addDays, addMonths, addYear, and so on

These commonly used `DateTime` functions will add a set number of days, months, years, and so on to a given date. The available units added range from milliseconds all the way up to years.

Its possible use cases are setting a rental return date for 2 weeks from the current date or setting the expiration of a season pass to 1 year from today or 6 months from the beginning of the year:

Important note

There is no `subtractDays` or `subtractYears` (or any other `subtract`) function. In order to "subtract" a particular unit of measure from a date, you need to indicate it by a "negative" number. See the second example in *Figure 9.15* for more detail.

Example	Returns
addDays(dateTime(2020, 1, 3), 4)	2020-01-07
addDays(dateTime(2020, 1, 3), -4)	2019-12-30
addYears(dateTime(2020, 1, 3), 2)	2022-01-03

Figure 9.15 – Example of addDays and addYears

Between functions

These useful functions calculate the given unit between two given dates. The available units range from milliseconds all the way up to weeks (`millisecondsBetween`, `secondsBetween`, `minutesBetween`, `hoursBetween`, `daysBetween`, `weeksBetween`):

Example	Returns
daysBetween(dateTime(2020, 1, 3),dateTime(2020, 1, 7))	4
daysBetween(dateTime(2003, 1, 3),[%CurrentDateTime%])	Varies but at the time of writing this 6395.938025

Figure 9.16 – Examples of daysBetween

Its possible use cases are determining how long a book was checked out before it was returned and calculating how long a given process took to execute.

Enumeration function calls

Enumeration functions allow your application to interact with enumerations and their respective values. Enumerations are essentially strings that can only contain predefined values that are determined in the database. At times it becomes important to interact with these values and it's important to be aware of the functions that allow you to do so. In the following sections, we will look at one of the functions that are commonly used.

getCaption

This function returns the string caption of the enumeration. Its possible use cases are displaying the caption value to an end user or writing a selection made to a log. The following figure shows the property window for the ENU_Example enumeration:

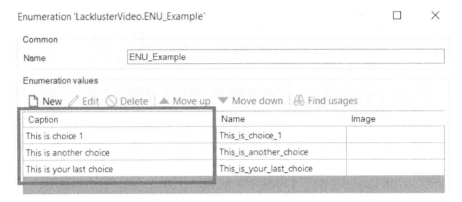

Figure 9.17 – Enumeration property window highlighting the caption of the enumeration values

The highlighted column shows the **Caption** value that would be returned on an attribute that used the ENU_Example enumeration.

Relational expressions

There are a number of relational expressions that can be used across various attributes and data types. They are useful in performing a wide variety of tasks to compare two data points. The following list shows the different types of relational expressions:

- \> Greater than
- \< Less than
- <= Less than or equal to
- \>= Greater than or equal to
- = Equal
- != Not equal

Relational expressions are used to compare two values with each other. They can be used with numeric values, strings, or date times.

Its possible use cases are to check whether one date happened earlier in time than another date or to see whether two strings are equal to each other.

Note that no matter what data type you use, the expression always returns a Boolean:

Example	Returns
dateTime(2003, 1, 3) < dateTime(2003, 1, 5)	True
'MyString' = 'MyString'	True
4 != 5	True

Figure 9.18 – Example of relational expressions (< = !=)

In this section, we discussed a wide range of various function calls. We discussed commonly used functions for strings, integers, enumerations, and DateTime attributes. We also discussed how to begin comparing values with relational expressions. These various functions and expressions will become extremely important as you begin working with data and needing to perform various levels of business logic. It's good to get a handle on how to comfortably use these early on in your learning path. It's also good to keep in mind that you won't become an expert overnight and memorize every single function and the proper syntax of each of them. It's most important that you are aware that these functions exist and are able to use them when appropriate; even if it means referring to documentation, that's OK!

In the next section, we will take a closer look at another very important core function of Studio Pro, the sub-microflow. Understanding what a sub-microflow is, how to use it, and why we use them will be a very important lesson as you continue learning more about Mendix and best practices in Studio Pro and as your project begins to expand in scope.

Understanding sub-microflows – when and why?

A **sub-microflow** is basically just a term for a microflow called from within another microflow. You will no doubt need to implement this type of logic in your application as it grows and you have the requirement for more complex business rules and validations. With that in mind, it's really important that you become familiar and comfortable with the concept and easily identify when and where it makes sense to harness the "power of the sub."

It might be easiest to think of sub-microflows as reusable code. That concept is not something new in the world of coding and software development; however, depending on your level of experience or knowledge in other languages, it could be somewhat of a new idea. No matter where on the spectrum you may fall, don't worry, we've got you covered!

As you are most likely discovering (hopefully with the help of this book!), one of the great benefits of Mendix is that it's relatively easy to jump in and just start building. And pretty much anyone, regardless of their background, can do that! In a matter of minutes, you can build up an application and run it "locally" and in another couple of minutes, you can have a few microflows handling a few different pieces of application logic. However, left unchecked, it's also really easy for your simple, couple-of-actions microflow to become this behemoth, 185-action-long beast that handles 47 different pieces of logic and functionality all in one ridiculous, linear microflow. It happens *all the time*.

The problem with a massively complex microflow like the one described previously is that it becomes extremely difficult to read, understand, and maintain. This is true for the developer who creates it and especially true for the poor developer who comes in months or years later and has to unravel what is happening. Thankfully, there are a number of ways to help mitigate a situation like this. One of those ways is by leveraging sub-microflows.

Of course, like most things, there are a number of reasons and benefits to using sub-microflows. In this section, we will discuss a few of the main reasons and the benefits that result. We'll specifically talk about how it's important to group similar functions and logic and how that benefits the overall reusability of microflows across your application as it grows over time. And of course, as your application and business rules expand over time, from a readability standpoint, leveraging sub-microflows becomes really important.

Grouping similar functions or logic

One of the easiest ways to start creating sub-microflows is to take a look at your existing microflows. You may notice areas where you are performing similar functions or logic. It's a great idea to begin grouping these parts of the microflow. One really common example of this concept is when performing custom validations. For instance, you may have a user-facing input screen and you are requesting some basic information from your users. Most likely, you are going to end up building out some custom validation to ensure that users are entering valid data. Grouping these validations into a sub-microflow is definitely the way to go!

In a moment, we will take a look at the validations built out in the previous section and see what we can do to group them and put them into a sub-microflow or two.

Reusability across your application

Out of the three reasons to consider utilizing sub-microflows that are presented in this section, reusability is the easiest and the biggest "pro tip." As you begin building out your application, you'll quickly discover that you will often need to perform similar functions in different areas of the application. As mentioned, custom validation microflows is a big one. You might find there is a user entry form but there may also be an edit page that internal staff has access to. The staff may need to edit data from time to time, perhaps a spelling error or an updated piece of information for a customer. Depending on the staff and the data they are allowed to edit, you may want to ensure the same validations are performed when the staff member saves the record as were performed when the customer filled out the form initially. If you were not leveraging a sub-microflow to handle this, it would become extremely difficult to maintain and keep consistent. Maybe not at first, but what about when you add a new field? Or add six more fields? Or decide a field is no longer required? As you can see, it can get quite complicated fast.

There are countless other examples of when you may need to reuse sections of logic throughout your application. The idea here isn't to cover every single possible use case, but rather make you aware of the concept. It's important that this idea is ever-present in your mind as you are building your application. Ideally, you recognize these opportunities even before they're needed a second (or more) times. As you gain experience and understanding, you will group and create sub-microflows as you go.

Improving the readability of large, complex microflows

As discussed earlier, it's really easy for your microflows to get out of control. In fact, Mendix suggests in their documentation that you generally do not want a microflow to be larger than 25 elements. These would include action activities, exclusive splits, loops, and so on. Of course, this isn't a hard rule; like anything, it's situational. However, it's a really good starting point and something to file away in your subconscious as you're building out your application.

You guessed it, sub-microflows are here to help you with that! Looking for opportunities to group functionality in sub-microflows either retroactively, or, better yet, as you go, will keep your main microflows moderate in size and much more readable.

Your future self will thank you!

In addition to sub-microflows making your life as a developer easier, there are many other ways in which you can do that. One way is by learning how to properly and thoughtfully use configurable settings in the runtime. We will discuss that in detail in the next section.

Go (con)figure – configurable settings

Configurable settings are simply a way for configurations and settings in your application to be modified during runtime. In other words, your application doesn't need to be brought down to change the value of a constant or, worse yet, doesn't need to wait days or weeks (depending on your sprint schedule) for a developer to make a change to a hardcoded value; just have it go through a **Quality Assurance (QA)** process and release it in production.

As an example, imagine you have an application that handles students enrolling in various courses. The business team gives you a requirement that says something like, "Each student may only enroll in a maximum of three courses per semester." *Great! That's really easy to implement*, you might think to yourself. You quickly throw together some logic that grabs the semester, the student, and the courses the student has enrolled in that are the part of that semester. You count the number of courses and then check to see whether the number is greater than 3. The following figure shows what that basic validation would look like:

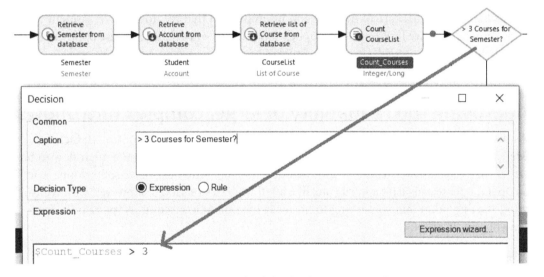

Figure 9.19 – Hardcoded value being compared

Done. The work passes QA, your product owner is happy, the business is happy, and the change is released to production with the sprint!

Now imagine a few weeks go by, and you've completely forgotten about the change and have been working on the next sprint. In blows an urgent request from your business team. They realize the request made a few weeks ago was wrong. They meant to request that four courses be the limit, not three. This change needs to happen immediately as the university is losing millions of dollars each week in enrollments. Sure, you can stop what you are doing, create a patch, and have it tested and released. All of this can certainly be done and probably with a fairly quick turnaround. But now, imagine they want to change it to five courses, then back to three, and then to six, and so on and so forth. You surely would not want to have to drop everything every couple of weeks just to continually be making this change.

In comes the concept of configurable settings. It would be nice if the maximum number of courses per semester could be changed on demand, by anyone with the proper access. There are a number of ways to accomplish this, but perhaps the simplest and easiest is to create some sort of Settings entity in your domain model. The following three steps show how you could accomplish this (but do not do this quite yet in your project):

1. Add an attribute to store the value(s) that you need:

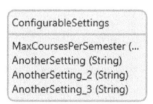

Figure 9.20 – Example of the ConfigurableSettings entity in the domain model

2. Retrieve the `Settings` entity during your microflow and use the new attribute to do the compare and validation, as shown in the following screenshot:

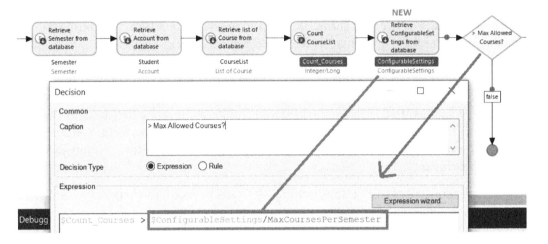

Figure 9.21 – Dynamic value being compared with the use of a configurable setting

3. Be sure to add an edit page so that your users can manipulate the attribute values. Have a look at the following screenshots for some ideas (we'll get more into this during the *Let's go make it!* portion later on):

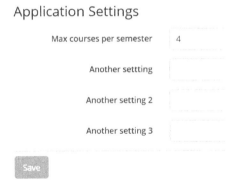

Figure 9.22 – Configurable setting being edited during runtime on the edit page

Now your logic will check the courses and compare them against whatever the value is for the particular setting. And a change to the max number of courses is as simple as a user logging in, making the adjustment, and clicking **Save**!

This, of course, is just one simple example of where you could apply the concept of configurable settings. There are several other ways too of implementing this idea. The example shown was not meant to be an exhaustive list of every way to accomplish this, rather just an opportunity to introduce the concept and provide a simple way of accomplishing it. No doubt, you'll find many use cases for this type of logic on pretty much every project you are involved with.

Beyond out-of-the-box Mendix functionality, you may run into scenarios where you need to extend the functionality of your application a bit further beyond what you can build in a microflow. But don't worry too much, you're not the first developer who has this desire. Thankfully, Mendix makes it really easy to extend your applications by leveraging Java. And they have some great modules available in the app store to help. In the next section, we will take a look at a couple of those modules.

Let's get some Java – Java actions

Java actions are a great way to extend your application's functionality by using Java code. Java actions generally handle logic and functionality that would be difficult, cumbersome, or even impossible to build directly in a microflow given standard Mendix functions and limitations. But basically, anything can be built out with Java actions. One drawback is, of course, you need to know Java to begin building out your own Java actions. However, you're not alone and Mendix has put out some excellent app store modules that you'll definitely want to include in most of your projects. Here's a brief look at a few of them:

Figure 9.23 – Community Commons Function library in the Mendix app store

You are definitely going to want this one! Just stop right now, go to the app store, and if you haven't already, add it to your project. The module contains *a ton* of useful Java actions that will help you with a wide array of use cases. Here's a few worth checking out:

- `EncryptString` and `DecryptString`: These actions complement each other well and are easy to use. You simply pass the Java action to the string you would like encrypted, along with an encryption key, and it will return an encrypted version of the passed string. Great for handling sensitive data especially when exposing in an API.

- `GetApplicationURL`: This action will return the runtime URL of the application.

- `DuplicateFileDocument`: This action clones the contents of one file document into another.

The ObjectHandling and FileHandling modules are both subsets of the Community Commons module mentioned previously. If you just need a few pieces from the Community Commons module and don't want or need to import the entire module into your project, these are definitely worth checking out!

Figure 9.24 – ObjectHandling and FileHandling modules in the Mendix app store

Let's go make it! Next, let's take the concepts and ideas we've discussed during this chapter for a spin! Over the last few chapters, you have been building out a place to create new members. In *Chapter 8, Getting to Know Microflows*, you built a Save microflow called Act_Member_Save and a basic validation microflow as a sub, called Val_Member. In the following sections, we will expand on the validation microflow and add some additional attributes to try out some of the concepts we discussed previously in the chapter.

Additional validations

Before we add some additional validations to our data, let's add some more data to work with. To add more data, follow these steps:

1. On the Member entity, add the following attributes:

*   Email (string)

*   Rating (enumeration with the following values: Platinum, Gold, Silver, and Sketchy)

*   Birthday (date and time)

2. In the Member validation microflow, add validations for the new attributes to ensure your users enter values for them and don't leave them blank or empty.

    Please note that the Member validation microflow (Val_Member) was an exercise mentioned in *Chapter 8, Getting to Know Microflows*, in the *Extracting a sub-microflow* section. If by chance you overlooked creating either of the microflows mentioned in *Figure 8.18* and *Figure 8.19*, please go back and create them now.

> **Important note**
>
> Leave the validations for first and last names as you created them in *Chapter 8, Getting to Know Microflows*. We will revisit these in the next chapter.

3. Once your validations are in place, add the new attributes (**Email**, **Rating**, and **Birthday**) to the `Member_NewEdit` page so that you can enter values and test out your new validations.

> **Important note**
>
> Please note that the `Member_NewEdit` page was created back in *Chapter 7, Understanding the Basics of Page Design*. See the steps associated with *Figure 7.7*. The page was then modified further with the steps associated with *Figure 7.19*.

You should now have a page where you can enter values for all the attributes on the `Members` entity. When you click **Save**, the validation microflow should be invoked and your validations should be ensuring that your users enter in data for all the required fields.

> **Important note**
>
> The preceding steps were intentionally left open to your interpretation. This is to test your understanding of the information presented during this chapter and previous chapters on adding simple validation checks and adding attributes to a page. If you are unsure at any point, please refer to the sample project of this chapter on `https://github.com/PacktPublishing/Building-Low-Code-Applications-with-Mendix`.

Great job! But don't get too excited. Requirements are constantly changing from your business users. Let's explore what that might look like with the functionality you just built.

Changing requirements

Now that your simple validations are in place, let's imagine that you are presented with a requirement from the business group you are supporting. The requirement now states, "Members must be a minimum of 18 years old to be enrolled in the application." What will you do?

When presented with a requirement, even as seemingly simple as the one mentioned previously, it's always good to pause and think through possible solutions, come up with questions, and get any needed clarification from the individual(s) making the request. Ultimately, going through that exercise, even if just in your head, will only make your life better in the future and will likely impact the solution you come up with. But for the moment, let's go through the steps needed to meet this requirement.

Unfortunately, up until Studio Pro version 8.15, Mendix did not have a native `yearsBetween` function. However, with the release of Studio Pro 8.15, a `calendarYearsBetween` function was introduced. For the years before 8.15 was released, Mendix developers leveraged a Java action found in the `CommunityCommons` module. For the next exercise, follow these steps to add a `CommunityCommons` Java action to your microflow and call the `YearsBetween` action:

1. Add a Java action after the exclusive split that checked for an empty birthday:

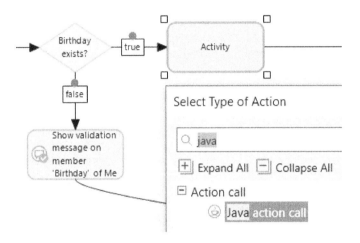

Figure 9.25 – Adding a Java action to a microflow

2. In the popup, click the **Select...** button and search for `YearsBetween`:

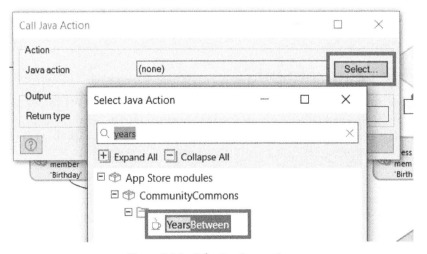

Figure 9.26 – Selecting Java action

3.   In the popup, enter the values as shown in the following screenshot:

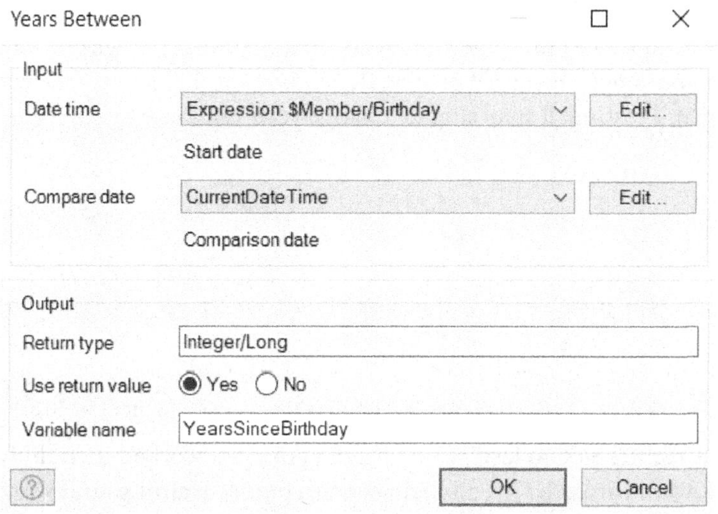

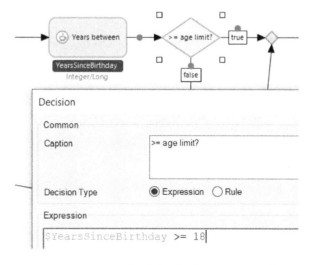

Figure 9.27 – Setting input parameters for a Java action

4.   Click **OK** once all the settings have been configured for the `YearsBetween` Java action

5.   Now add an exclusive split that checks whether the result of the `YearsBetween` Java action is greater than or equal to `18`:

Figure 9.28 – Hardcoded value being compared

6.   Add the validation message and be sure to change the `isValid` variable to `False`.

Now, your validation microflow should validate that the member is 18 or older upon saving the member. Go give it a try!

You should see a validation message similar to what is shown in *Figure 9.29* when you attempt this on your application. Of course, depending on the date you select and the date you are reading and testing, it may slightly change your outcome:

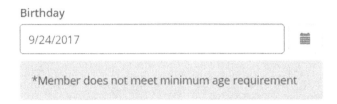

Figure 9.29 – Validation message (Note: this book was written in 2020)

Pretty awesome, right?! Not so fast! Now, let's imagine you worked incredibly hard on this development, it went through QA, passed user acceptance training, and was deployed into production only to find out 3 weeks later that the new VP of member experience wants to allow members to be 16 years old! Well, you could create a quick patch and change the hardcoded check to 16. Done. But, you're smarter than that, because you know the VP of member experience is going to change her mind in 6 months and then again next year and so on and so forth. So, in comes a configurable setting to save the day!

Let's set that up by following these steps:

1. In the project, add a new module and name it Configuration:

Figure 9.30 – Adding a new module

2. In the new module, go to the domain model and add a new entity also named
    `Configuration`.

3. Add an integer attribute named `MemberMinimumAge`:

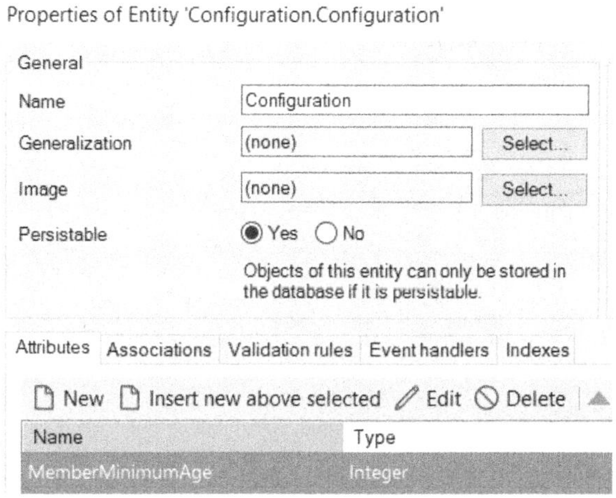

Properties of Entity 'Configuration.Configuration'

General

Name	Configuration
Generalization	(none) Select...
Image	(none) Select...
Persistable	● Yes ○ No
	Objects of this entity can only be stored in the database if it is persistable.

Attributes | Associations | Validation rules | Event handlers | Indexes

📄 New 📄 Insert new above selected ✏ Edit ⊘ Delete ▲

Name	Type
MemberMinimumAge	Integer

Figure 9.31 – Configuration entity with the MemberMinimumAge attribute

4. In the new `Configuration` module, add a new page to view the
    `Configuration` entity.

    See *Figure 9.32* for guidance on what elements the page should include. When
    adding the new page, feel free to try different templates and layouts. This is your
    app, see which layouts and template you like the best!

At a minimum, your page should contain a `Data View` of the Configuration entity as shown in *Figure 9.32*.

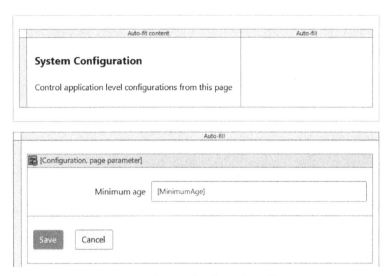

Figure 9.32 – System Configuration edit page

5. Next, add a modifying" microflow to the new module called `SUB_Configuration_GetCreate`.

    Note: `GetCreate` is a very useful pattern. Sometimes it's referred to as `Retrieve or Create` or `Create or Retrieve if Exists`. Either way, the pattern does the following, as outlined in *Figure 9.33*:

*   The microflow should attempt to retrieve the first `Configuration` record from the database. To accomplish this, add a new `Retrieve` action activity type to the microflow (see *A* in *Figure 9.33*).

*   Next, add a `Decision` to check that the configuration is not empty. If a record is found (true path), the retrieved `Configuration` record should be returned (see *B* in *Figure 9.33*).

*   If a record is not found (false path), a new one should be created. To accomplish this, add a `Create object` action activity to the microflow and create a new `Configuration` record. In the end event, be sure to return the `NewConfiguration` record (see *C* in *Figure 9.33*):

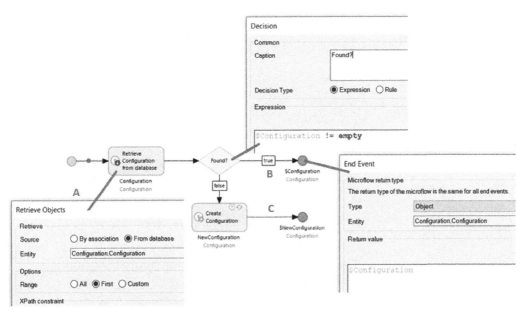

Figure 9.33 – The GetCreate sub-microflow method

6. Now add a microflow to the new module called `ACT_Configuration_View`.

    The microflow should call the sub-microflow you just created and then open the page you created:

Figure 9.34 – Retrieved or created configuration record being returned

7. Go to the project's navigation (*Ctrl + G)* and search for `Navigation`:

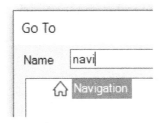

Figure 9.35 – Searching for the Navigation page

8. Click on **New item**.

9. The new menu item should call the `ACT_Configuration_View` microflow you just created:

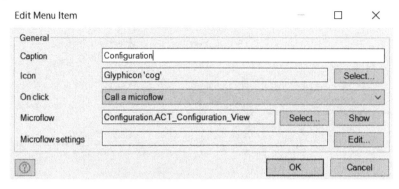

Figure 9.36 – Adding a new menu item

Now, you have a record that will be used as your runtime configurable settings across the entire system!

10. Next, recompile your project locally (press *F5*).

11. View your app and you should notice a new navigation option called **Configuration**:

Figure 9.37 – New menu item as seen in runtime

12. Click on the new **Configuration** navigation item.

13. Your new page should now be displayed. Enter in `16` for **Member minimum age**.

14. Click **Save**:

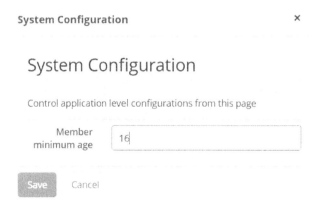

Figure 9.38 – Setting the System Configuration value

So, now that you have configured the setting, let's go use it in the validation microflow!

15. Go to your Member validation microflow and add a retrieve for the first Configuration record in the database between the Member/Birthday empty check and the YearsBetween Java action:

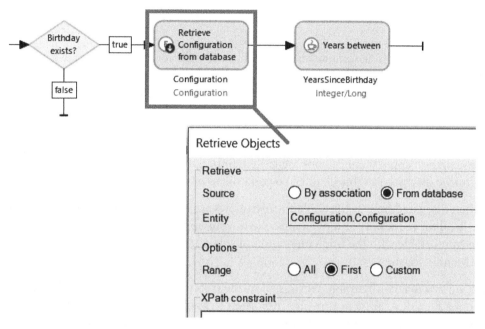

Figure 9.39 – Retrieve the first configuration from the database

16. Lastly, replace the hardcoded 18 with the MemberMinimimAge attribute from Configuration:

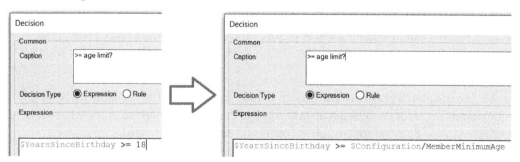

Figure 9.40 – Hardcoded comparison (before) and dynamic comparison using the Configuration record (after)

17. Recompile your project locally (*F5*) and give it a test!

You should now be able to change the `MemberMinimumAge` attribute to whatever you want as much as you want and your code will always work! Now, your VP of member experience can change her mind as many times as she wants and you will not need to spend any more development time coming up with a solution.

Don't forget to commit your changes!

Summary

In this chapter, we discussed many subjects that will help you customize your application to whatever requirements are thrown your way. It's important to remember that requirements from the business units you are supporting will likely change constantly. It's good to be familiar not only with the concepts we discussed but also with which concepts to implement and when. In this chapter, we first talked about a number of different functions and expressions that are commonly used. You learned how to implement and apply them in your logic. Remember, there are a lot more than just the handful we discussed in this chapter, so go familiarize yourself with them!

We then discussed how important sub-microflows are to every Mendix application. They are critical for reusability and hygienic code in your application. Becoming more and more comfortable with the implementation of sub-microflows will be an *essential* part of your Mendix journey.

Next, we saw that configurable settings allow the instant customization of your application without added development time. It's important to know when to leverage these sorts of configurations; most likely, any time you get the sense that a particular rule or input to a validation may change over time, it's probably a good idea to use a runtime configurable setting. Hence, in this section, you learned the benefits and how to use them in validations.

Lastly, we saw that Java actions really take your application to the next level. In this section, we touched briefly on a few app store modules that contain some really great Java actions. Consider getting acquainted with these modules so that you know what is available to you at any given time.

In the next chapter, we will discuss how to handle errors when they arise. It's crucial to understand that errors and issues always come up, so it's important to know what tools you have at your disposal for troubleshooting and resolving these issues.

Chapter 8 knowledge check answers

Here are the answers to *Chapter 8, Getting to Know Microflows* knowledge check:

1. b

2. c

3. a

4. a

5. b

6. c

7. a

8. a

Knowledge check

Test your understanding of the concepts that were discussed in this chapter. Answers will be provided at the beginning of the *Knowledge check* section in the next chapter:

1. What would the following function return as a value: `replaceAll('Hello World','World', '')`

   a. `'Hello'`

   b. `'Hello '`

   c. `'World'`

   d. `Error`

2. What should we expect the following to return?

   ```
   length(trim(replaceAll('This is my random string','random
   string','')))
   ```

   a. `10`

   b. `'This is my'`

   c. `11`

   d. `'This is my '`

3. What is a sub-microflow?

    a. It is a small microflow.

    b. It is a microflow called from another microflow that is made to be reusable.

    c. It is a type of sandwich ordered in the Netherlands.

    d. It is a type of microflow that performs a specific type of operation and returns a Boolean value.

4. What are two reasons (there are many more) that you might decide to leverage sub-microflows? (Pick two)

    a. Code reusability.

    b. Because it's super fun.

    c. It's what this book suggested to do.

    d. Grouping like functionality.

5. Why are configurable settings a good architecture idea?

    a. They complicate your implementation.

    b. They make you look super smart.

    c. They enable flexibility to your business rules and logic.

    d. They enhance your user experience.

10
Error Handling and Troubleshooting

Predicting the future can be a difficult task. But sometimes what's even harder is trying to go back in time and understand the past. In this chapter, we will take a look at how to do both; that is, how to handle anticipated issues in the future and how to best set up our future self to look back in time and understand what happened in the past.

To help get us there, we will cover the following topics and concepts:

- Defensive programming: This is the concept of trying to anticipate bad data coming into your application either from an integration or user entry. Once you've identified and anticipated where those entry points are, you need to find some ways to handle them gracefully.

- Custom error handling: Errors are always going to happen – it's just the nature of software development. But handling them in a way so as not to completely destroy your user experience is important. We will discuss ways to do this properly in Mendix.

- Logging: This is the practice of capturing important, useful information and writing it to your application's log. We'll explore how to accomplish that with Mendix.

- Debugging: The debugger will become your best friend. This incredibly helpful tool allows you to analyze your application at runtime and see exactly what is happening in a microflow.

- Developer pages: These types of pages are useful for displaying data all in one place, which is particularly helpful for developers or even support-level users. We'll talk about some dos and don'ts in this section.

By looking into the topics and concepts listed here, you will gain the following skills:

- Be able to understand and explain the core concepts of defensive programming

- Be able to set up and use custom error handling

- Be able to understand how to log useful information

- Be able to confidently use the debugger

- Be able to build developer-level pages to visualize your data

Let's get started!

Technical requirements

The sample project of this chapter can be found in `Chapter10` folder at `https://github.com/PacktPublishing/Building-Low-Code-Applications-with-Mendix`.

Being defensive with your programming

"Don't be so defensive!" or "Why do you get so defensive?" You may have been asked or told this over the years by a close friend or acquaintance for one reason or another. And, in most cases, this is sound advice. "Relax, don't take things so seriously." But is this the case with application and software development? Absolutely not! You need to be defensive, you need to expect the worst, and you definitely need to make it known!

The concept of "defensive programming" or being "defensive" is not new in the low-code space and certainly not a new concept in software development as a whole. This concept goes back as long as software development has been around. Since the time that the first lines of code were ever written, there have been bugs, there has been "bad data," and developers have had to find ways to handle them when they reared their ugly heads. But even better than trying to handle them *after* they happen, it's important to try and anticipate them and ensure your application takes note of them and then behaves in a predictable manner so that the user experience is not interrupted.

Mendix does provide some nice out-of-the-box "defensiveness" in the platform itself. For example, if a list is retrieved and it is empty, it will not create an error if you have an iterator attempting to iterate over each item in the list, even though it was empty. It may seem like a really minor piece of functionality the platform has to offer, but things like that make working with Mendix great!

This idea becomes even more important as you begin to interact with data outside of your control. For instance, consuming an API or some other form of external data can result in a whole plethora of garbage information that your application then has to try and handle. And, depending on how much "defensiveness" you put into play, it could wreak havoc on your application and the processes that you've built, thus quickly turning users away from using the application altogether.

There are a number of ways you can introduce a defensive mindset to your applications. This section is intended to provide a few ideas, but it's certainly a topic worth investing some additional research in and learning about outside of this book. It will only make you a better, stronger developer – which is a great thing! In this section, we will consider the following defensive strategies:

- Empty and ' ' (blank) checks
- Defensively minded `if` statements
- Manually checking your code
- Unit testing

Let's dive into each of them.

empty and '' (blank) checks

One of the simplest but most effective ways to add a dash of defensiveness to your application is to be rigorous and consistent in performing empty and '' (blank) checks on your data. And it's important to check for *both* of these conditions because they are different. An empty value, on either an object or an attribute, basically checks to see if it exists at all. Was the object ever created? Or was a value ever assigned to the attribute? You're essentially checking to see if any space in the database is allocated for this resource. A '' (blank) check, on the other hand, is looking to see if a value is *blank*. This check is for an object that has been created but the attributes contained in it were never assigned a value. To help solidify this concept, let's consider an example.

Think about the video rental application we are building. In *Chapter 12, Getting Some REST*, we will discuss connecting to an external API and consume some really interesting data. During this exercise, we will really put some of the concepts that will be discussed in this chapter into practice. However, just to highlight this concept, imagine you have pulled data down from another repository through an API. You have no way of knowing what sort of validation the other developers have put around the data entry that happens in their database. It might be designed really well or it could have been thrown together without any consistent checks and balances. Regardless, you are now working with the data in your application. One way to check on this data is by performing some empty and '' checks. Take a look at the following screenshot, which shows an example of one way to accomplish this:

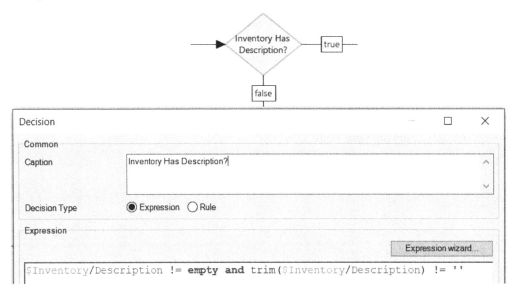

Figure 10.1 – Exclusive Split Decision property window checking empty and blank values

You'll notice that the first expression, `$Inventory/Description != empty`, is ensuring a value is present in this string attribute.

Then, the second expression, `trim($Inventory/Description) != ''`, is using the `trim` function that you learned about in the previous chapter. It removes all extra white space at the beginning and end of the string and makes sure what's left over isn't *blank* or ".

A variation of the second expression also uses the `length` function to make sure it's greater than 0. Have a look at the following screenshot to see how that is accomplished:

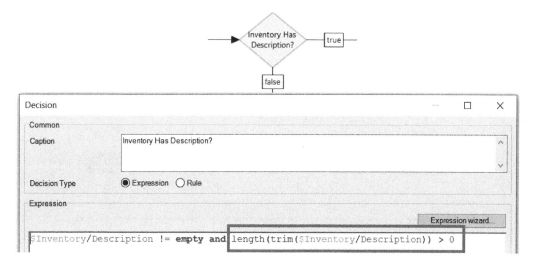

Figure 10.2 – Exclusive Split Decision property window checking empty and blank values variations

Another way to accomplish this is by using a "Rule" when selecting a **Decision Type**. Here, a Rule is essentially a reusable piece of logic that can be applied anywhere in your application. It is very similar to a sub-microflow. This can be seen in the following screenshot:

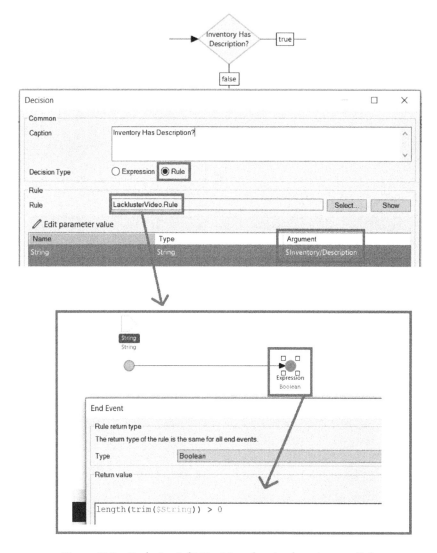

Figure 10.3 – Exclusive Split Decision showing how to use a Rule

Here, for **Decision Type**, you must select **Rule**. Then, you can either select or create a new Rule. The Rule looks and functions pretty much like a microflow. This is a really nice way to handle these sorts of validations since they are easily reusable and limit the chance of human error, or even forgetting to perform the empty and ' ' checks.

Additionally, note that the `empty` check was dropped in the preceding screenshot. A combination of the `length` and `trim` functions accomplishes essentially the same thing. This is just another variation of checking for good, valid data.

Defensively minded if statements

Another interesting way you can be defensive in your application is when you're handling string values that need to be converted into standardized enumeration values. The scenario might be that you are consuming some data from a third party (more on that in *Chapter 12, Getting Some REST*) and you need to map an incoming string value to an attribute in your database that is defined with an enumeration. Generally, this is a fairly straightforward sort of mapping exercise. However, as we mentioned in the previous sections, you have absolutely no way of knowing what sort of validations the other system performs regarding errant inputs or validations.

Let's consider a specific example. Perhaps you are integrating into a movie database and are working on a process to import movies. One of the requirements is that you gather all the movie ratings. So, you may receive some documentation that says the possible values for movie ratings are G, PG, PG-13, and R. So, with that in mind, you create some logic similar to what's shown in the following screenshot:

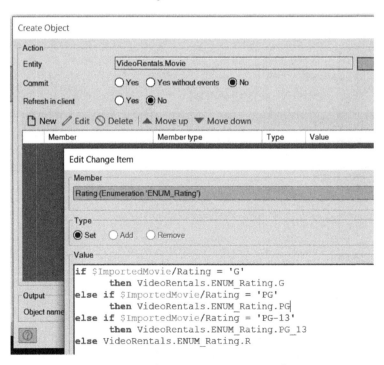

Figure 10.4 – Setting an enumeration value

This logic essentially says that if the `Rating` attribute of `ImportedMovie` is equal to the string value of G, then you will set the `Rating` attribute of your `Movie` record (to be stored in your database) to the enumeration value of `ENUM_Rating.G` – this logic is repeated for PG and PG-13. Then, you conclude that any other value that is present must be R because that's the only other possible option. So, you conclude your `if` statement with an `else` clause, mapping everything else to `ENUM_Rating.R`.

While this isn't *wrong*, it does present a number of potential problems. For instance, what if a new rating was introduced to the source system? Let's say they started adding "NC-17" movies. Now, your database will errantly be rating them all as "R" with the logic you added previously. Don't worry – there's a better way to do this!

Let's take a few steps to improve the logic. First, let's stop errantly rating the imported movies. To do that, let's at least set unexpected values to `empty`:

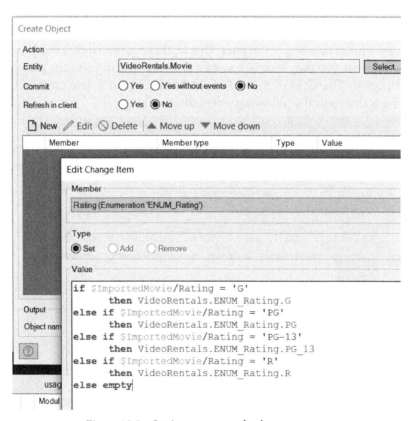

Figure 10.5 – Setting unexpected values to empty

Now, our application will at least be setting new values to `empty`. That's a step in the right direction. But we can get even more granular than that by adding a few more pieces here.

What we can't see in the preceding screenshot is the ability to find out if the `empty` value was a result of a brand-new rating, errant data, or `ImportedMovie` was retrieved with no rating at all. So, let's take care of that!

By adding two additional enumeration values, we can easily increase the visibility into what's happening, as shown here:

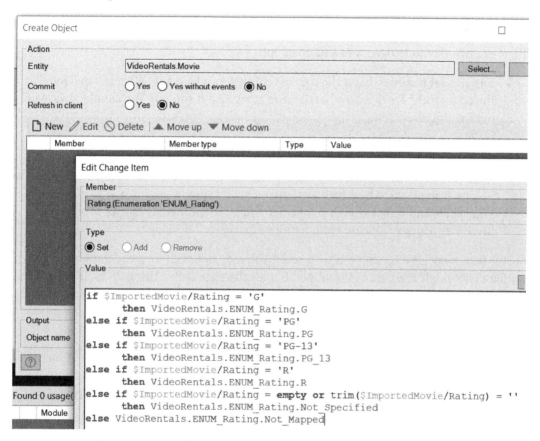

Figure 10.6 – Specifying empty or blank values from unexpected values

Now, by making this change, if the `Rating` attribute of `ImportedMovie` is actually *empty* or *blank*, then we map to the new `ENUM_Rating.Not_Specified`. This then makes it very clear that the imported value was missing. Then, if any other values come in on the imported record, we assign them `ENUM_Rating.Not_Mapped`. After that, if a new rating is added, such as "NC-17" or even an errant value such as "PG13," we would have clear visibility.

Manually checking your code

Now, this one might seem obvious, but so many developers – especially newer ones – often don't bother to test their own code. The rationale tends to be that QA is going to be looking at it anyway, so what's the point? That is a dangerous, irresponsible mindset to have. Granted, the change that you may be applying could be incredibly simple and require very little testing on your part, but it's *always* a good idea to test it out, even just once.

There are two methodologies you should adopt:

- **Functional testing**: This is the sort of testing your QA team will perform. Does the code work? Does it do what the user story said it should? You should always be performing these tests.

- **Technical testing/review**: This is sometimes referred to as the "4 eye principle" or simply peer review. Have another developer review your code. Yes, the code may work and do what the user story said it should, but is it built properly? Does what you built stand up to best practices and technical standards? It's best to grab one of your peers and walk through it together and have another set of eyes take a look! This is a great way to learn from a more experienced developer.

So, the take away here is, test your own code! You may not need to spend days upon days testing every single use case as QA might, but it's the responsible thing to do. If you make it a habit during your early days of development, then it's likely that those habits will stick with you throughout your career. It's much harder to retrain yourself after years of neglecting that exercise.

Unit tests

Just hearing the term "unit test" can bring even the most seasoned developer to a grinding halt. Not that unit tests are not valuable or worth the effort, but they are often very time-consuming to build, at least in the beginning. This section is not intended to cover the importance or theories of unit testing, but rather just bring the concept to your attention. It is highly recommended that you do some continued research on the subject outside of this book.

That being said, unit tests can play a very valuable role in your development life cycle – yes, even in a Mendix application. Often, developers will rationalize not building unit tests by saying, "well, of course I know my code works, I tested it, QA tested it, it's solid. And if I did build unit tests for it, I'm going to build the assertions in a way that they'll pass anyway, so what's the point?" So, while, yes, that statement may not be untrue, it's very shortsighted. The value of unit tests usually doesn't come immediately when you build them for the first time for a new piece of functionality, although they certainly can be. Most often, the real value comes from when you go back weeks or months later to that same functionality and modify something. You may not remember all the "gotchas" of the original implementation or integration you built. But, if you have well-designed unit tests, they will certainly remember! So, changing what appears to be a minor calculation or small piece of functionality may cause your unit test to fail – which is great! Because then you know it was working and you probably saved yourself a lot of time manually testing various combinations of inputs or calculations, trying to break your code. And maybe, just maybe, you prevented a bug from slipping through into production.

So, as we mentioned, please do some further reading on this subject. It's important enough to be aware of and have some experience with. Lastly, check out the UnitTesting module in the Mendix App Store. It will speed up the time it takes you to build your first unit tests with some great out-of-the-box functionality:

Figure 10.7 – UnitTesting module from Mendix

So, that's it! Being defensive. Simple, right? Don't worry if you're feeling a little overwhelmed or wondering how you are going to remember all of the things we've discussed here. Just keep in mind that these things take time and practice – lots and lots of practice. And do remember that this section was just intended to give you an idea of some defensively minded practices you can start putting in place. There is always more to learn and appreciate in this area of software. But keeping in mind *empty* and ' ' checks, defensively minded if statements, *always* manually checking your code, and even sprinkling in some unit testing will start you out on the right foot!

In the next section, we will discuss how to deal with the errors that will inevitably slip through all your defensive measures you put into place. Don't get discouraged when this happens – it happens to the best of us! Just get a handle on them!

Getting a handle on those errors – error handling

Even with your best efforts of trying to be predictive and defensive in your application, errors and issues will still arise – it's inevitable. And that's okay! There will always be situations and scenarios that you just are not able to account or plan for. You can try, but you will never release a single piece of functionality… ever. Generally, it's best to account for the most likely scenarios and then weigh up the likelihood of other possibilities, even perhaps performing some level of risk analysis. Ultimately, however you end up determining your functionality, you'll want some level of error handling on the most important or sensitive parts of your logic.

If you're not entirely sure of ALL the possible scenarios where something may go wrong in a particular process, you can always set the error handling on an entire process when it is called from a sub-microflow. That way, if an error is encountered at any point during the sub-microflow, the parent microflow will catch it and the behavior of the application can be specified. This, however, should not in any way replace specifically placed error handling inside the actual sub-microflow itself. Not doing this would lend to a casual approach to error handling by thinking, "well, the sub-microflow error handling will catch and handle ALL my potential errors in this process, so I'm good!" That's a potentially dangerous and, frankly, lazy approach to development. Think of error handling the sub-microflow as a security blanket if all else fails, not your first line of defense.

Error handling options

In this section, we will discuss the three main ways Mendix allows you to easily handle errors: **Rollback**, **Custom with Rollback**, and **Custom without Rollback**. We will also discuss one way that Mendix allows you to do things that's not advised but used very often: **Continue**. By the end of this section, you should be able to describe the differences between these error handling options and be able to identify when to use each one. Let's dive in!

Rollback (default)

By default, if an error occurs while a microflow is in the process of executing, Mendix rolls back all the changes up until that point and the process is terminated. The user (if there is one) is presented with an ugly "contact your system administrator" message like the one shown in the following screenshot and everyone is confused:

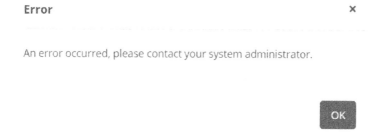

Error   ✕

An error occurred, please contact your system administrator.

OK

Figure 10.8 – Ugly error message

The **Rollback** option basically reverts all the changes that were made during the process. So, even entities that were modified, committed, and created do not persist in the database. Everything is restored to the state before the process was initiated.

The application logs (which we will discuss further in the next section) provide a general error message, but it's not really any more descriptive than "something went wrong in microflow X on process Y." It's left up to you to try and figure out what happened. And, depending on what process received the error, this can be a daunting and stressful task if it's in the production-level environment.

Rollback is the default behavior for any unhandled error. The next three options we'll discuss can be selected by right-clicking on any action in a microflow and clicking **Set error handling…**, as shown in the following screenshot:

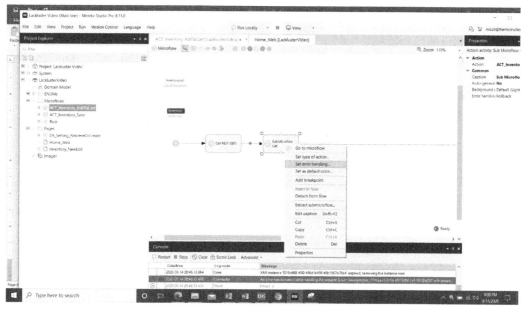

Figure 10.9 – Exclusive Split Decision property window checking empty and blank values

But what if you want to add some custom logic and roll back all the changes? Let's take a look at another error handling option and see how that's done.

Custom with Rollback

Custom with Rollback is similar to the **Rollback** option. Everything that has happened during the current "transaction" will be rolled back and reverted to its previous state. However, you also have the ability to continue the microflow to perform additional activities and business logic. This is great for creating useful logs (covered in the next section) or triggering alerts – maybe an email or text message to your Production Support team stating that a critical process encountered an error, for example, as shown in the following screenshot:

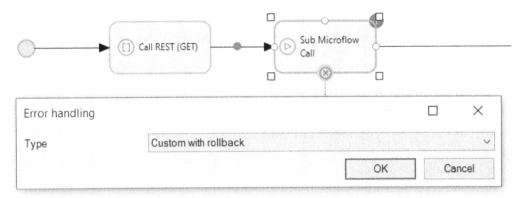

Figure 10.10 – Custom with Rollback error handling

It's also important to note that, in the preceding screenshot, because the error handling is set on the sub-microflow, everything that happened inside the sub-microflow will be rolled back. However, everything that happened before the sub-microflow won't be. This is just something to be mindful of and was worth mentioning alongside the example that was provided.

Once the error handling behavior has been selected, you have to create the logic you want to be executed. Then, you need to select **Set as error handler**, as shown in the following screenshot:

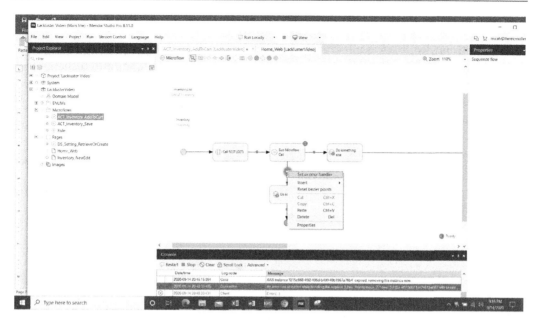

Figure 10.11 – Setting path as error handler

The end result will indicate which path is your error handler with an icon. With **Custom with Rollback**, you will see a red **x**, as shown in the following screenshot:

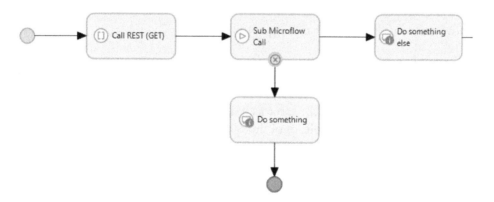

Figure 10.12 – Custom with Rollback path displayed with a red "x"

Now that we understand this error handling option, what if we do not want to roll back all the changes? Let's move on to our next error handling option and see how that is done.

Custom without Rollback

Custom without Rollback is a bit different than **Custom** with Rollback or the default Rollback option. This particular behavior will retain all successfully committed changes in the database that have already occurred up to the point of the error. This is helpful when you have a long-running microflow that manipulates several different records in the database. If an error occurs on the last activity, you don't necessarily want to lose everything that occurred up until that point... or maybe you do! It's up to you!

Here's what a **Custom without Rollback** handler looks like; notice the change in the icon:

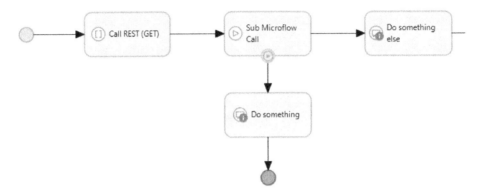

Figure 10.13 – Custom without Rollback path displayed with a blue triangle

Let's move on to our final error handling option.

Continue

The **Continue** option should be used as a last resort and sparingly in your applications. The microflow essentially treats the error as if it never happened. This might seem tempting without giving it a whole lot of thought, but generally, if an error occurs, you want to know about it! But, like everything, it's good to know that it's available and perhaps you will find some use case for it, but certainly be cautious when considering this as an option.

Here's what the **Continue** option looks like in a microflow:

Figure 10.14 – Continue error handling only displays one path but with the same icon as Custom without Rollback

It's important to note that because **Continue** is set on the sub-microflow, everything that happens inside the sub-microflow will still be rolled back, but everything before the sub-microflow will not be. This was similar to the behavior that we discussed regarding *Figure 10.10*.

In summary, be thoughtful about your error handling behavior and remember what each option's behavior will result in. Some areas to consider while implementing custom error handling are as follows:

- Integrations (REST calls)
- Processing external data
- Performing calculations on data
- Long-running, complex sub-microflows

In the next section, we will discuss log messages. Log messages serve a very valuable purpose in every application but can very easily become useless if the wrong information is captured, too little information is captured, or you go too log crazy and spam the logs with every piece of data imaginable, rendering them useless. Let's take a look at some good practices to keep in mind while creating log messages.

Channeling your inner lumberjack – logging

Log messages are a critical piece of every application that should not go overlooked. If you are not familiar with what a "log message" is, then let's first understand its meaning. A log message is a simple way of thinking about a piece or collection of pieces of information that indicate what is happening in your application, either through direct user interaction or system processes running behind the scenes. This contextual information is written to the application log as a "message" that is stored and can be accessed at any time either in real time or historically by downloading archived log files.

Log messages are helpful in so many different areas of your application. They are especially helpful when you're working with error handling, as we discussed in the previous section. If your application experiences an error, it's very important to write a message to the log describing what happened. This will be useful when you're trying to go back in time and determine what caused a user to receive an error, or perhaps trying to understand why an overnight integration failed to process some new data. Properly logging events, especially when errors occur, is critical in every good application.

There are, of course, incorrect ways of writing log messages. Two common areas that seem to be problematic for developers (especially Citizen developers) in Mendix apps is always writing to the Info log level and not providing enough useful information in a log message. The Info log level is the default level when you're creating a log message in the project, and many new developers do not change this appropriately. Ask yourself questions such as, what sort of information is being captured here? How often will this log level be triggered when my application is running in a production environment? If I opened the live log, would this message be "spamming" the entire log, making everything else unreadable? For example, if you had a process that needed to iterate over hundreds or thousands of records and in the iterator, you had an Info-level log message, it would be almost impossible to read anything else that was going on in the log at that time. In a situation like that, it would be wise to use the Debug level or even the Trace level. It's also important to consider the information provided in the log message. A message that reads "The record was saved" or "A user began the process" tells you absolutely nothing when you're looking at your live or historic log.

To create a log message, simply add a new activity to a microflow and select **Log Message** from the list of available actions. When the **Log Message** box opens, note the three sections: **Log level**, **Log node name**, and **Template**. **Log node name** is meant to indicate the source of the log message. You may choose to indicate this at the module level or perhaps get as specific as naming the process or microflow that triggered the log message. Mendix encourages developers to leverage a system constant here for the log node, but at a minimum, you should put the log node in a variable or use a microflow parameter to log all the messages in a process or microflow and use the same node name.

The following are three examples of leveraging log levels. The screenshots are of Info, Error, and Critical, respectively. All these screenshots represent the same logging message, just with a different level (of severity).

The following screenshot displays what an Info log level looks like in the console:

Console		
🖳 Restart ■ Stop ⊘ Clear 🔒 Scroll Lock Advanced ▾		
Date/time	Log node	Message
2020-09-20 21:08:01.333	Core	Initialized license.
2020-09-20 21:08:03.871	Core	Mendix Runtime successfully started, the application is now available.
2020-09-20 21:08:14.290	Log Node Testing	This is a log message

Stories (0)   Changes (7)   Errors (0)   Console   Find Results 1

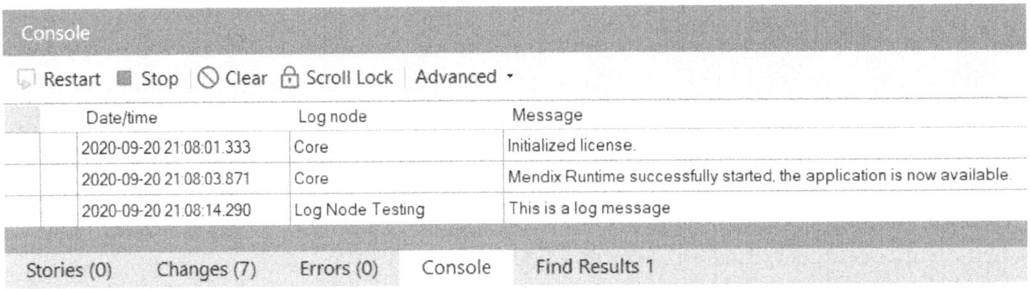

Figure 10.15 – Info log level

The following screenshot displays what an Error log level looks like in the console:

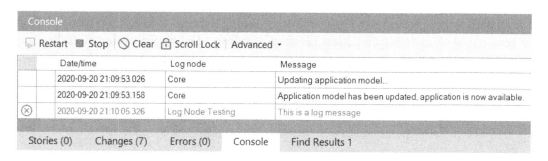

Figure 10.16 – Error log level

Finally, the following screenshot displays what a Critical log level looks like in the console:

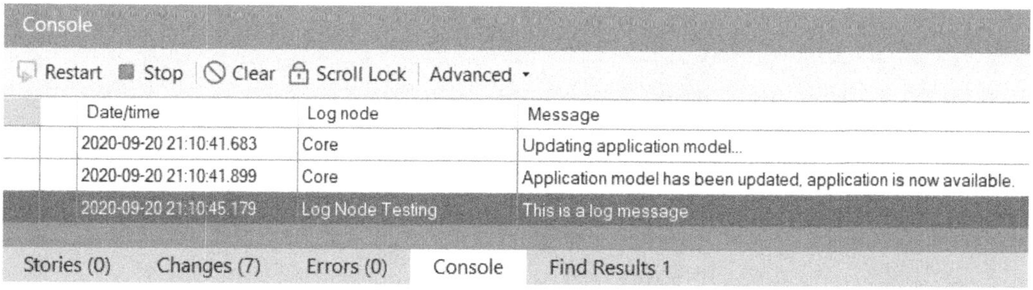

Figure 10.17 – Critical log level

Mendix offers some additional information on log messages on its documentation page. If you're interested in reading more, have a look here: `https://docs.mendix.com/refguide/log-message`.

We will discuss logging in the *Let's go make it!* section of this chapter. In the meantime, in the next section, we will talk about utilizing the Debugger tool. Inevitably, no matter what defensive programming, logging, and error handling you put in place in your application, errors will still occur and you'll still have to fix them. Being able to confidently pinpoint where the error is occurring and why it's occurring is incredibly important. The Debugger tool will be instrumental in you understanding just that! Let's take a look at how to use it.

Stepping through it – the Debugger

The Debugger is an essential tool in any Mendix developer's tool box. This will become your best friend when you are in development mode and inevitably tracking down those elusive bugs that will no doubt find their way into your application.

If your **Debugger** window is not already visible among the other windows in Studio Pro, be sure to add it! To do so, click **View | Debug Windows | Debugger**, as shown in the following screenshot:

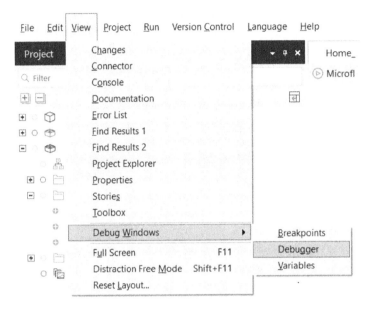

Figure 10.18 – Displaying the Debugger

The debugger is incredibly helpful during the development phase if you are trying to determine if a new piece of functionality works as intended. To begin using the Debugger, simply add a breakpoint anywhere in the microflow you wish to take a closer look at.

Right-click on any action and select **Add breakpoint**. You will know a breakpoint has been added to the microflow because you will see a red circle in the bottom-right corner of the action, as shown in the following screenshot:

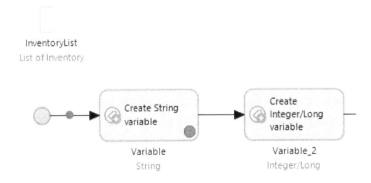

Figure 10.19 – Microflow with a breakpoint added

Once a breakpoint has been added to a microflow, you can begin testing the microflow, action by action. To do this, start by invoking the microflow. Once the breakpoint has been encountered, the application will stop on that activity. The activity will have a red outline and you will also see the microflow's name listed in your **Debugger** window. The following screenshot shows what this will actually look like in Studio Pro:

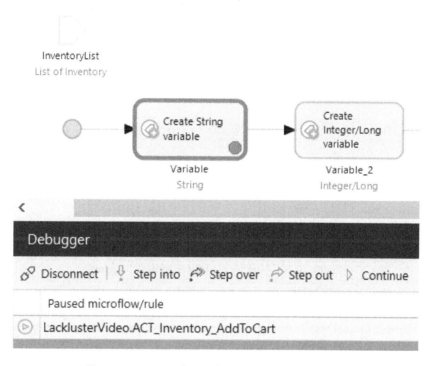

Figure 10.20 – Breakpoint hit and Debugger window

In the **Debugger** window, there are several options you can implement in order to proceed. These are as follows:

- **Step into**: This option will move you forward, action to action. It will also dive into sub-microflows and iterators.

- **Step over**: This option will essentially do the same as **Step into**, except it will skip over sub-microflows and iterators.

- **Step out**: This option will get you out of one level of the Debugger. For example, if you are in a sub-microflow and click **Step out**, the entire sub-microflow will be executed and you will be brought back to the parent microflow to resume stepping through. If there is no parent microflow, for example, clicking **Step out** will execute the rest of the process and end the debugging session.

- **Continue**: This option will execute the rest of the process until another breakpoint is encountered. This is helpful if you wish to step through the process until you reach the piece you wish to view or test. Once you are satisfied, simply click **Continue** for the rest of the process to run.

Another thing to take note of while debugging is the **Variables** window. Variables provide a great deal of contextual information about the user, the session, and anything that's happening during the current microflow. Armed with the Debugger and these variables, you will become an expert Mendix developer in no time! The following screenshot shows what your variables will look like when you're looking at the **Variables** window while debugging:

Variables		
Name	**Type**	**Value**
currentDeviceType	Enumeration 'System.Device...	Desktop
currentSession	System.Session	(id: 6473924464346189, state: normal)
currentUser	System.User	(id: 281474976711757, state: normal)
InventoryList	List	(size: 1)
TestVariable	String	'This is a variable'
TestVariableLength	Long	18

Figure 10.21 – Variables you'll see while debugging

In the next section, we will briefly discuss how building pages so that you can easily see all your data in one place is extremely helpful for developers and even support-level users. However, before you just wildly dump all your data onto a page, there are some things to keep in mind. Let's take a look!

Seeing it – developer pages

It's often important to have a complete and unobstructed view of the data within your application. This statement sounds simple and obvious, but sometimes, it isn't quite that easy. Many times, the core pages and data grids you will be asked to add to your application will constrain your data over certain criteria. Perhaps an XPath over a certain attribute or combination of attributes, for example. And, depending on that data and application, it could become difficult to get a complete picture of your entire dataset. The concept of a "developer page" is just that complete, unobstructed view of a particular dataset. Think of a data grid without any XPath applied to it where all (or almost all) attributes are visible.

Sounds like a great idea, right? In many scenarios it is, yes. But, like all things, it's important to always keep the *context* in mind. For example, what data are you making available to be viewed? Is it personal, financial, or medical information? Or is it just basic, nondescript inventory information? The *context* is very important. Use good judgement here!

Overview pages

If you decide to build pages that display all (or most) of the data on a particular entity, there is a nice shortcut that Mendix has that can help you with this. Mendix allows you to, with just a couple clicks, create overview pages for your entity or entities. It's a lot quicker than building the page yourself and manually adding all the attributes. Here's how to do this:

1. Navigate to the desired entity you wish to expose.

2. Right-click on the entity and select **Generate overview pages…**, as shown in the following screenshot:

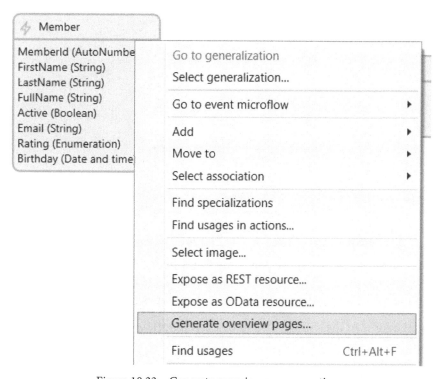

Figure 10.22 – Generate overview pages… option

3. From the pop-up menu, choose the entity or entities you wish to generate overview pages for and click **OK**:

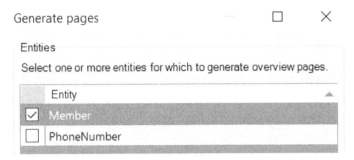

Figure 10.23 – Generating overview pages

Notice that, in the **Project Explorer** window, you now have a folder named `OverviewPages` with some new pages added:

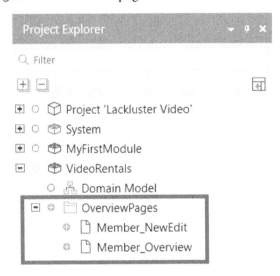

Figure 10.24 – Newly created overview pages in the Project Explorer window

You can, of course, customize those pages any way you like. You just have to connect them up to some navigation or call them from a microflow so that you can display them. This is a really simple (often overlooked) way to create these types of pages!

Now, let's take some of the concepts we've discussed during this chapter and add them to our project!

Let's go make it!

Let's take the concepts and ideas we've discussed in this chapter and take them for a spin! In this section, we will run our application, fix a reported bug by applying some better validation, turn the validation into a rule, and utilize the Debugger to identify exactly what is happening. These small changes will move us closer to an excellent, functioning application!

To begin, we will remove the validation rule that was set up on `Member/FirstName`:

1. Navigate to the `VideoRentals` Domain Model, like so:

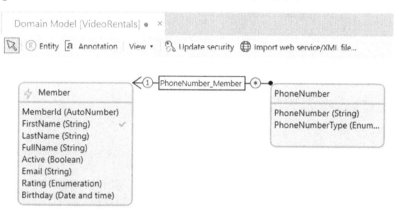

Figure 10.25 – VideoRentals domain model

2. Next, open the **Member properties** window by double-clicking on the **Member** entity.

3. Click the **Validation rules** tab:

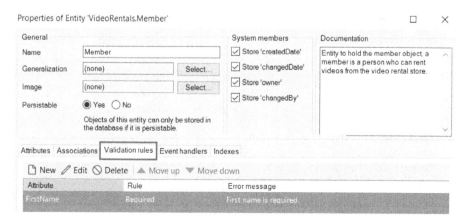

Figure 10.26 – Member properties window – Validation rules

4. Select the **FirstName** validation rule and click **Delete**:

    This validation rule was created in *Chapter 6, Understanding Domain Model Basics* in the steps associated with *Figure 6.18*. If, for some reason, you are missing the validation rule as shown in *Figure 10.28*, that is okay because we are just removing it at this point. But it may be worth going back to *Chapter 6, Understanding Domain Model Basics* and reviewing the steps to create the validation rule so that you understand the concept.

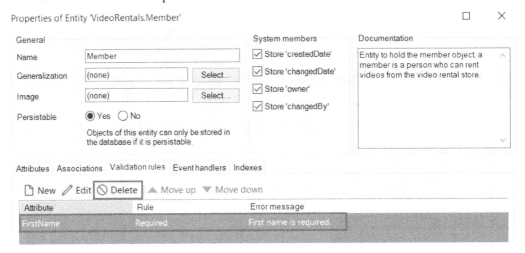

Figure 10.27 – Deleting the FirstName validation rule

5. Click **OK**.

    Confirm that the green checkbox has been removed from being next to the `FirstName` attribute on the entity in the domain model view, as shown in the following screenshot:

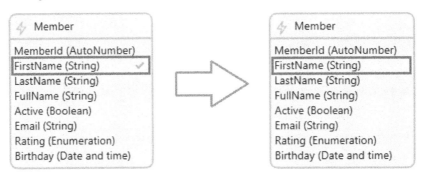

Figure 10.28 – Before and after removing the validation rule

Next, let's put our knowledge of the debugger to use!

Debugger

Probably the most important piece of functionality we covered during this chapter was the use and understanding of how the Debugger works. In this section, we are going to investigate a bug that's been reported by the QA team on our project and leverage the Debugger to find out exactly what is happening in the project.

The bug the QA team is reporting is as follows: "While testing the functionality to create a new member, we noticed that, by entering *spaces* one or more times in the **First name** and **Last name** fields, we were still able to save the member. As a result, the application allows members to be created without a first name and a last name. This should not be allowed."

Generally, the first thing you must do when investigating such a bug is to see if you can replicate it. So, let's go ahead and see if we can do that by following these steps:

1. Go to your project and click the **Run Locally** button:

Figure 10.29: Run Locally button

2. Once the project is done compiling, click the **View** button:

Figure 10.30 – View application button

3. From the user interface of the application, click the side navigation and select the **Members Overview** navigation item in order to view the overview page:

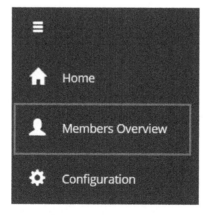

Figure 10.31 – Members Overview navigation item

4. From the **Members Overview** page, click the **New** button.

5. In the pop-up page that appears, enter a single space in the **First name** and **Last name** fields.

6. Enter valid values for the remainder of the fields and click **Save**. Your page should look something similar to the following:

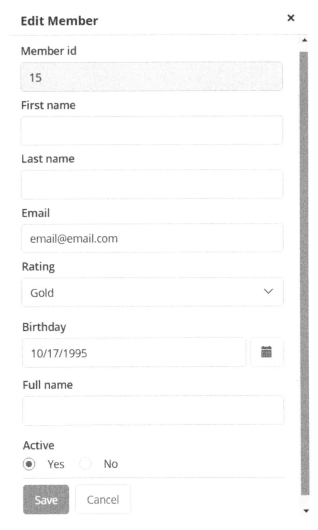

Figure 10.32 – Edit Member page

Your application should have allowed you to save the new member with some missing data in the **First name** and **Last name** fields. Confirm you have something similar to the following:

Member id	First name	Last name	Full name	Email	Rating	Active	Birthday
15				email@email.com	Gold	Yes	10/17/1995

Figure 10.33 – New record without First name and Last name field values

You may be questioning some of the validation that was built in the previous chapter and wondering how this bug was able to slip through. You added a check for empty values, right? You tested it, right? So, how is this possible? Let's find out by taking a closer look.

7. Press *Ctrl + G* and enter `Val_Member`:

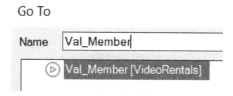

Figure 10.34 – Go To page and searching for Val_Member

8. Select the microflow and click **Go to**.

9. On the first action, right-click and select **Add breakpoint** from the available options:

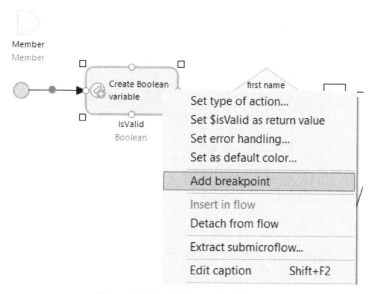

Figure 10.35 – Adding a breakpoint

Confirm that the action now has a breakpoint, as shown in the following screenshot:

Figure 10.36 – Action with a breakpoint added

10. From the user interface of the application, repeat steps *4-6* to create a Member with errant data in the **First name** and **Last name** fields.

At this point, once you click the **Save** button, the breakpoint in your application should be hit. You may notice that the Mendix Studio Pro icon starts flashing in your taskbar:

Figure 10.37 – Studio Pro icon flashing in the taskbar

11. Go back to Studio Pro. You should notice that the breakpoint has been hit and that the first action is highlighted in red, as shown in the following screenshot:

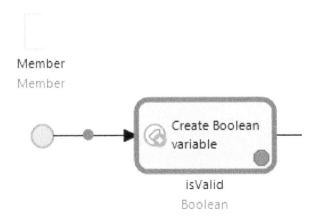

Figure 10.38 – Action when the breakpoint is activated ("hit")

Before we begin stepping through the microflow and the logic, take note of the **Variables** window. You will notice that the values you entered are shown in the Member variable. In particular, you can see the `FirstName` and `LastName` attributes and the single space that was entered, as shown in the following screenshot:

Variables		
Name	**Type**	**Value**
currentDeviceType	Enumeration 'System.Device...	Desktop
currentSession	System.Session	(id: 6755399441056445, state: normal)
currentUser	System.User	(id: 281474976711357, state: normal)
Member	VideoRentals.Member	(id: 3659174697239031, state: instantiated)
id	Long	3659174697239031
Active	Boolean	true
Birthday	Date and Time	UTC time: 1955-07-08 00:00:00.000 Session time: 1955-07-...
changedDate	Date and Time	UTC time: 2020-10-15 01:30:11.868 Session time: 2020-10-...
createdDate	Date and Time	UTC time: 2020-10-15 01:29:58.715 Session time: 2020-10-...
Email	String	'email@email.org'
FirstName	String	' '
FullName	String	(empty)
LastName	String	' '
MemberId	AutoNumber	17
Rating	Enumeration 'VideoRentals.E...	Platinum
System.changed ...	Reference	System.User (ID: 281474976711357)
System.owner	Reference	System.User (ID: 281474976711357)

Figure 10.39 – Variables, as shown in the variables window

12. To begin stepping through the microflow, open the **Debugger** window and click **Step over**:

Figure 10.40 – Debugger window showing the microflow that has been paused due to a breakpoint

When you click on **Step over**, you will notice that the next action in the microflow is highlighted in red. This is always an indicator of where the microflow has stopped. The logic, actions, or decision regarding an action are not executed until the breakpoint has moved to the next action:

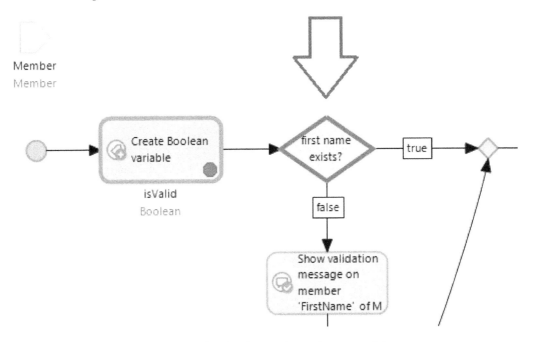

Figure 10.41 – Breakpoint moving to the next activity

At this point, the breakpoint has stopped on the first Exclusive Split, which is checking the first name and whether it exists. We *should* anticipate the expression to evaluate to *false*, if it was written correctly.

13. Let's click **Step over** one more time and see what happens. You will notice your breakpoint move to the next action in the microflow. But which one? Take a look at the following screenshot and see if it matches what is happening in your project:

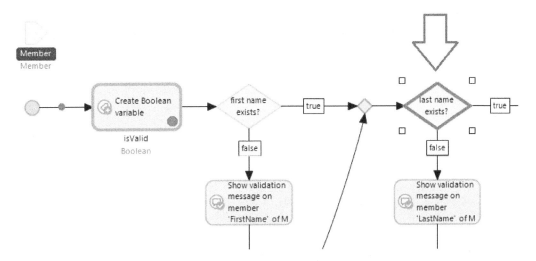

Figure 10.42 – Breakpoint moving to the next activity errantly

So, unfortunately, the validation wasn't written properly, the expression evaluated to *true*, and we were brought to the next Exclusive Split instead of to the *Show validation message* action. But this means we're seeing where the issue is and where the bug resides. Go ahead and either step through the rest of the microflow or click **Continue** so that the entire microflow is executed.

14. Double-click the **first name exists?** Exclusive Split so that the expression can be analyzed.

You will notice that something with the expression isn't quite right. Any ideas? Hint: maybe we're missing a function to wrap the ' ' check? Take a look at the following screenshot and see what you think:

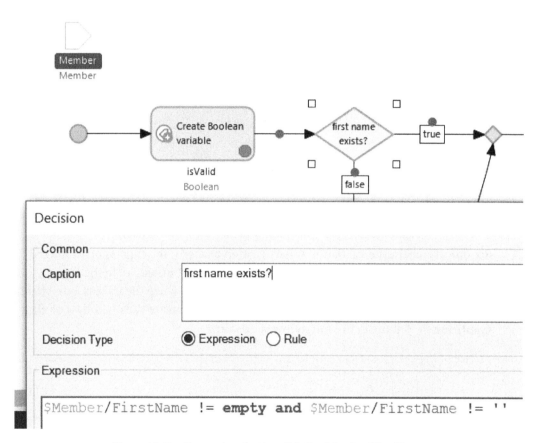

Figure 10.43 – Expression that is validating Member/FirstName

Let's try wrapping the second expression with the `trim` function and see what happens. (Recall that the `trim` function, as described in the previous chapter, will remove white space from before and after any text value in an attribute. This should help with our spaces. We also discussed `trim` briefly at the beginning of this chapter.) Your new expression should look something like the following:

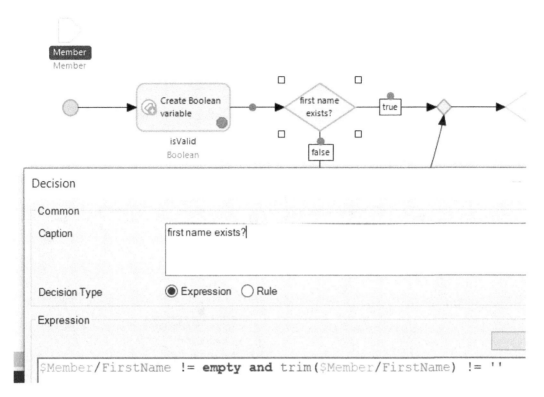

Figure 10.44 – Updated expression with trim

15. Repeat steps *1-6* to create a new Member with errant data in the **First name** and **Last name** fields.

Your breakpoint should still be enabled and, as previously mentioned, you'll notice the Mendix icon flashing again, indicating that the breakpoint has been hit.

16. Jump back over to Studio Pro and go back to the **Debugger** window.

17. Click **Step over** until you are able to see how adding the `trim` function impacts the logic in the Exclusive Split.

You should now be validating properly, and the breakpoint should be moving down to the false path, as shown in the following screenshot:

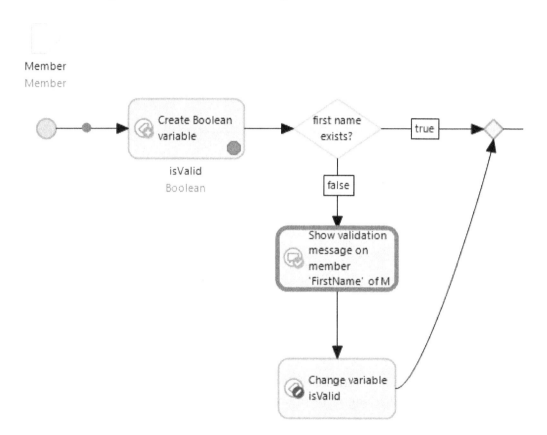

Figure 10.45 – Breakpoint moving to the false path, as expected, with the updated expression

18. Continue stepping through the microflow or click **Continue** to allow the entire microflow to execute.

19. Navigate back to the user interface and confirm that the application did not allow you to save the new Member. Your screen should look similar to the following:

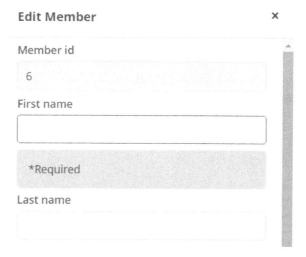

Figure 10.46 – Validation message displayed under the First name field, as expected

20. Apply the same adjustment to the LastName validation and confirm that you can produce a screen similar to the following:

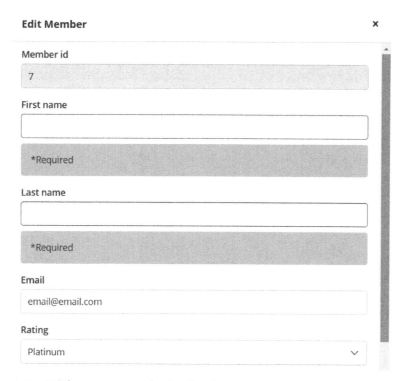

Figure 10.47 – Validation messages displayed under both the First name and Last name fields

Congratulations! The bug QA you've found is now technically fixed. However, don't stop there. There is an even better way to implement this functionality. Remember that we previously discussed creating *Rules* for similar validations. Let's do that next:

1. In Studio Pro, navigate back to Val_Member and double-click on the first Exclusive Split for the **First name** field's validation.

2. Click the **Rule** radio button to set a **Decision Type** value and then click **Select**, as shown in the following screenshot

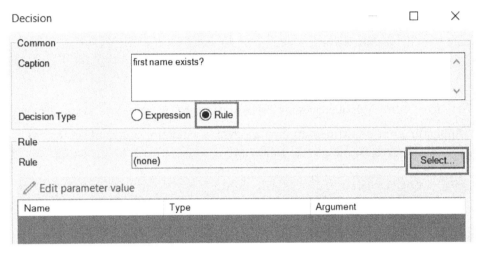

Figure 10.48 – Selecting Rule in the Decision window

3. In the **Select Rule** popup, click **New**:

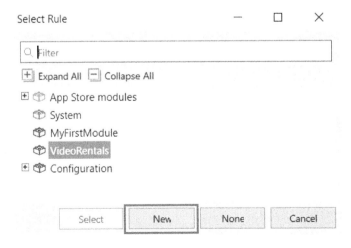

Figure 10.49 – Selecting New in the Select Rule pop-up window

4. Name your new Rule VAL_String_IsNotEmpty and click **OK**.

5. Click **Show**:

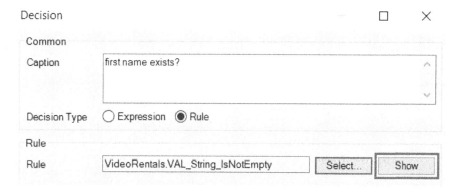

Figure 10.50 – Selecting Show in the Decision window

6. Add an input parameter of the String type and name it String. Change the endpoint expression so that it matches what's shown in the following screenshot:

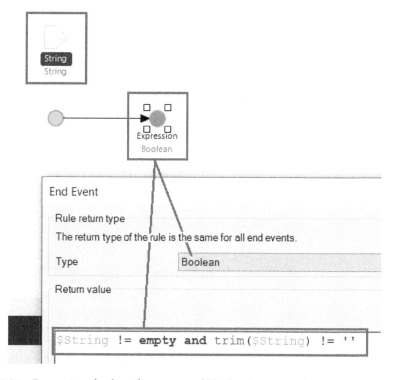

Figure 10.51 – Expression checking for empty and blank values using the String input parameter

7. Save the new Rule and navigate back to `Val_Member`.

8. Open the **Properties** window for the Exclusive Split that we've connected to the new Rule.

9. Select the `String` parameter, click **Edit parameter value,** and enter the text shown in the following screenshot:

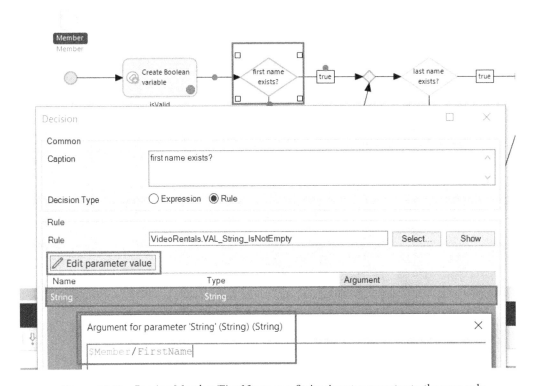

Figure 10.52 – Passing Member/FirstName as a String input parameter to the new rule

10. Click **OK** and ensure that it now looks as follows:

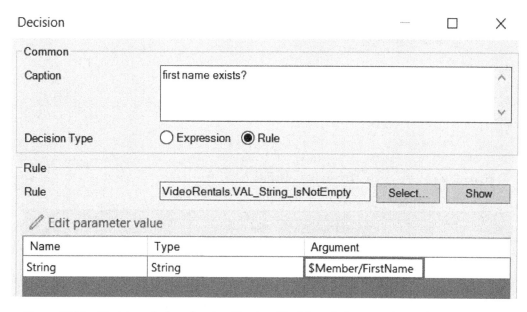

Figure 10.53 – Decision window showing Member/FirstName being passed as an input parameter

11. Once confirmed, click **OK**.

12. Open the **Properties** window of the Exclusive Split for the **Last name** field's validation.

13. Select **Rule** as **Decision type** and click **Select**.

14. Instead of creating a new Rule, select the Rule we just created and click **Select**:

Select Rule

Q Filter

⊞ Expand All   ⊟ Collapse All

⊞ 🗊 App Store modules

🗊 System

🗊 MyFirstModule

⊟ 🗊 VideoRentals

◈ VAL_String_IsNotEmpty

⊞ 🗊 Configuration

Figure 10.54 – Selecting a new Rule

15. Indicate the Member's `LastName` value as the **Argument** value, as shown in the following screenshot:

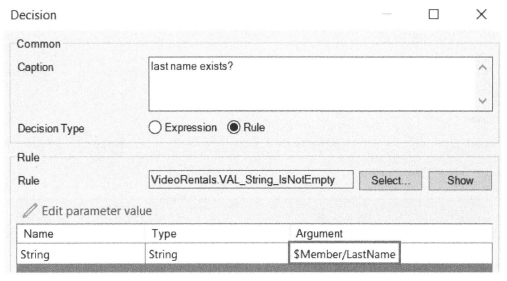

Figure 10.55 – Decision window showing Member/LastName being passed as an input parameter

16. Once confirmed, click **OK**.

Rerun your project locally and test everything to make sure all the validations still work as expected.

This new Rule can be applied to any other `string` attribute that has a validation check like this one.

Summary

In this chapter, we covered a number of subjects that will help you tackle issues when they arise. The concepts we discussed will also help you become a better developer in Mendix (and beyond). It's important to also remember that issues will come up and bugs will occur! It happens to the best developers and the best applications – it's just part of development. However, it's often how the application handles them and how the development team reacts that will set you (and your app) apart.

In the *Defensive programming* section, we discussed trying to anticipate bad data. There are many ways to do with this, but we mainly discussed empty and blank checks, as well as writing defensively minded `if` statements. This is especially important when dealing with third-party data such as when you're consuming an API, for example.

After this, we saw that no matter how well you write your code, errors will occur. Due to this, we discussed the importance of gracefully handling errors and leveraging error handling. In Mendix, there are four ways to handle errors: **Rollback** (default function), **Custom with Rollback, Customer without Rollback**, and **Continue** (avoid if possible).

Because errors and issues are inevitably going to occur, it's important to not only handle them well but to make records of them. This can primarily be done by writing useful log messages to the application log. Thus, we discussed various log levels, how they can be used, and what sort of information is useful to write to the log.

Then, we saw how useful the Debugger tool is and that it will, over time, become your best friend. Undoubtedly, as you begin to create more and more complicated applications or consume third-party data from REST APIs and so on, you will be leveraging the Debugger on a daily basis. The Debugger, as we discussed, is a means to pause a microflow and step through the logic and processes action by action. This is an incredibly powerful tool that you have at your fingertips.

Developer pages are another way to view your data. We discussed the importance of being able to see all the attributes of an entity without XPath constraints or any filtering. This will help you or any support team members see what may be happening behind the scenes. Remember to exercise caution with these sorts of views, depending on the data you are exposing. Keep your target audience in mind when you're contemplating whether sensitive data should be exposed.

In the next chapter, we will build off of a lot of the subjects we covered in *Chapter 6, Understanding Domain Model Basics*, regarding domain models. We will take a deeper dive into attributes and associations and talk about a number of best practices to keep in mind as your application grows over time.

Knowledge check

The following are the answers to *Chapter 9, Customizing Your App* knowledge check:

1. b
2. a
3. b
4. a, d
5. c

Chapter 10 knowledge check

1. What is the best way to reuse an expression?

    a. Sub-microflow

    b. Attribute

    c. Rule

    d. Nanoflow

2. What is an attribute called that contains a list of specific values?

    a. String

    b. Enumeration

    c. Integer

    d. Datetime

3. Which error handling method will revert the changes you've made and allow you to create custom behavior once an error is encountered?

    a. Rollback

    b. Custom with Rollback

    c. **Customer without Rollback**

    d. Continue

4. Which error handling method should be avoided unless absolutely necessary?

    a. Rollback

    b. Custom with Rollback

    c. **Customer without Rollback**

    d. Continue

5. Which developer feature will allow you to pause a microflow?

    a. Breakpoint

    b. Stop point

    c. Pause point

    d. All of the above

11
Storing Data

Data data data! What is an application without data? It would be like a pizza without cheese and sauce, a movie without actors and a plot, or a book without words! Every application needs some amount of data in order to be useful and needed. In this chapter, we will discuss how to make the best use of the Mendix domain model for data storage and retrieval. We will build off the information presented in *Chapter 6, Understanding Domain Model Basics*, of this book and continue to build out the project you have been creating throughout the book. Specifically, we will discuss the following topics:

- Creating associations for your data – Associating your data with various entities is a core concept of any Mendix project. In this section, we will cover the different types of associations you can choose from.

- Building functional modules – Modules are the cornerstone of every Mendix project. In this section, you will learn what a module is and how to build one with reusability in mind.

- Understanding generalizations and specializations – This can be a tricky concept for some to master. In this section, we will discuss the generalization and specialization of entities and understand what they can help you accomplish.

- Let's go make it – As we've done in the last few chapters, we will take the concepts we've learned in this chapter and apply them to the project you have been building out.

After considering the topics listed, you will be able to confidently perform the following:

- Determine which association type is best for linking your entities

- Understand when to add a new module instead of adding more entities or other artifacts to a currency module

- Understand some pros and cons of inheritance

Technical requirements

The sample project of this chapter can be found in `Chapter11` folder at `https://github.com/PacktPublishing/Building-Low-Code-Applications-with-Mendix`.

Creating associations for your data

In *Chapter 6, Understanding Domain Model Basics*, we briefly discussed the different types of associations between entities. In this section, we will dive a little deeper into that subject and discuss each of the different types of associations, as well as know when to apply each one.

The first thing to know about setting up your domain models is that each project is going to be different. Of course, the principles remain the same, but the data you will be working with will differ from project to project. It's important to have a firm understanding of what's possible and what's preferred when starting to define your application's data layer. At the heart of all your data in a Mendix project is your entities and the associations between those entities. No architect and no domain model are perfect, it's just not possible, but the closer you are to getting your data structure correct the first time around, the easier it will be to build on your project over time.

Often times, asking clarifying questions from your product owner or business users helps build your understanding of how they envision the project and the data being used over the long term. For example, in *Chapter 6, Understanding Domain Model Basics*, you built an association between the `Member` entity and the `PhoneNumber` entity. This was a simple association between the two core entities of the project. However, setting up the type of association between those two entities changes the project drastically. Take a look at the following figure and see how it differs from the association in your project:

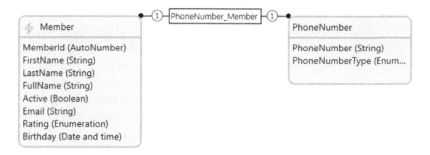

Figure 11.1 – One-to-one association between Member and PhoneNumber

Now compare *Figure 11.1* to *Figure 11.2*:

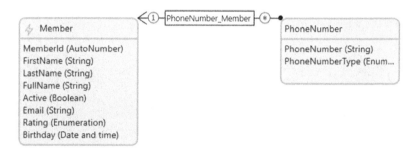

Figure 11.2 – One-to-many association between Member and PhoneNumber

Figure 11.2 should be closer to what you have in your project. So, what's the difference between the two figures?

Visually, they look different, right? But what about functionally? What's the difference between the types of associations? Let's take a closer look.

One-to-one association

As its name would suggest, a **one-to-one** association is fairly limiting. One record can only be associated with one other single record and vice versa. So, in our example from *Figure 11.1*, one Member could only be associated with one PhoneNumber, and one PhoneNumber could only be associated with one Member. While this may appear to be limiting, there are very good use cases for one-to-one associations! Take, for example, some of these entity examples (not a part of the example project):

- **Customer** and **Account** (one customer only has one account. One account only has one customer)

- **Employee** and **Cubicle** (one employee only has one cubicle. One cubicle only has one employee)

Like our example from the project we have been building, it may have been easy to mistakenly create an association between Member and PhoneNumber as a one-to-one association. However, asking questions during your requirements gathering and refinement stages, such as "Will a member only be asked to provide one phone number?" or "Can a member have more than one phone number saved?" would have helped you picture the domain model more clearly as you began to plan it out. Asking questions such as these does come with some time and practice but it's a very important skill to start building. Like a lot of the concepts we've discussed over the course of this book, questions lead to clarifying information, which leads to better solutions.

In addition to associations appearing differently, visually, in the domain model, they also behave differently when you interact with them at the microflow level. For example, take a look at *Figure 11.3*. This is a retrieval of PhoneNumber through the association with Member when the association is set to one-to-one:

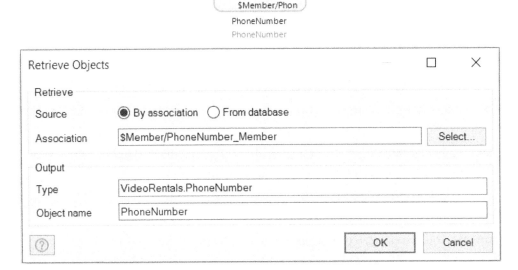

Figure 11.3 – Retrieval of PhoneNumber through Member association when set to the one-to-one association type

The biggest thing to note here is that this retrieval only returns one record. It makes sense when you think about it because the association itself indicates only one PhoneNumber record would be associated with Member. This is a simple concept but important to keep in mind.

One-to-many (or many-to-one) associations

The concept here, similar to the one-to-one association type, is fairly straightforward. This indicates that one record of entity *X* will be (or could be) associated with one or more (many) records of entity *Z*. But inversely, records of entity *Z* will only be associated with one record of entity *X*. Consider the following examples:

- Student to School (one student will only be associated with one school but one school will be associated with many students)

- Team to Player (one team will be associated with many players but one player will only be associated with one team)

To make it a little clearer, let's refer back to the `Member` and `PhoneNumber` example. Look back at *Figure 11.2* and remember that this association between `Member` and `PhoneNumber` (the one you should still have configured in your project) indicates one `Member` will be (or could be) associated with one or more (many) `PhoneNumber` records. But one `PhoneNumber` record will only be associated with one `Member`. And this makes sense even in the real world. You probably have a cell phone or a direct office line… those phone numbers don't belong to anyone else, right? They are "associated" just with you. And you may or may not have multiple phone numbers. You may have a cell phone or you may not. You may have a direct office line or you may not. But the possibility exists that you have both. And that's exactly what this association type indicates.

Just as the one-to-one association type has a direct correlation to how you will interact with associated records on the microflow level, so does one-to-many. Have a look at the following figure and see how it differs from *Figure 11.3*:

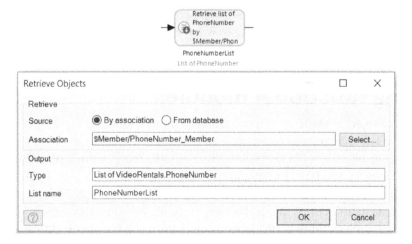

Figure 11.4 – Retrieval of PhoneNumber through Member association when set to the one-to-many association type

The big difference here is now you are returning a list of `PhoneNumber`. It doesn't matter if you only have one `PhoneNumber` record associated with `Member`, it will always be represented in the form of a list when retrieving over the association.

That may seem simple in concept but it does tend to trip up new developers. The association type has a direct correlation to the type of result you are able to work with in a microflow.

Many-to-many associations

This type of association basically just indicates that records on both sides of the association can be associated with multiple records. Consider the following examples:

- Students to Courses (one student can be associated with multiple courses and one course can be associated with multiple students)

- Candidate to Job (one candidate can be associated with multiple jobs and one job can be associated with multiple candidates)

Many-to-many associations behave similarly to how the one-to-many association does at the microflow level. Expect to see a list returned with performing a retrieve activity over association.

This is by no means meant to be an exhaustive description of associations and their behavior. Mendix has some great documentation of its own. For further reading, you may consider starting here: `https://docs.mendix.com/refguide/associations`.

The information we discussed in this section lays the groundwork for your project and domain models as your application begins to expand. How does this begin to take shape as you start working with different types of data centered around different functional areas of your application? In the next section, we will see where the type of data you plan on storing in your application should be broken out into different modules.

Building functional modules

Each Mendix project is made up of a collection of **modules**. When you first create a project, it will contain a `System` module and a module named `MyFirstModule`. As the project grows, you will likely add more modules. You can think of modules as groupings of similar or related functionality. For example, you may have an application that is an online shop. Perhaps one module handles everything related to inventory, another module handles ordering, and another module handles customers and their data. The number of modules really depends on the project, how many different areas of functionality it has, and often times on the development team, as well as the guidelines and governance put in place at the company.

Notably, each module will contain its own domain model. As you are now aware of from the previous chapters and building out the example project, the domain model is your database (or data model) for the project. So far in the project, we have built out a very simple domain model with `Member` and `PhoneNumber`. As you can imagine, it will take a lot more than just these two entities to build out an entire video rental application! Additionally, the data that is stored in each entity in any given domain model can be passed to functions and actions contained in different domain models. The main concept here is that by breaking down your app into various domain models, it simply groups the functionality. The data contained in all the various domain models is accessible and reachable throughout the project. This will make more sense as we dive deeper into this chapter and the example project.

Another consideration when adding more modules is that each module contains its own set of user roles and permissions. The user role in each module will need to be assigned to a user role at the project level. This sounds a little confusing but it's a fairly simple concept. Mendix has some nice documentation on the subject that is worth reading up on as diving deep into the matter is out of scope for the sample project we are building. The documentation can be found here: `https://docs.mendix.com/refguide/user-roles#1-introduction`.

In the next section, we will discuss associating entities across modules, why you may do that, and a few pitfalls of doing so.

Cross-module associations

As you add more and more modules to your project, it will likely become important to associate entities across different modules. This isn't necessarily a bad thing or even considered fully against best practices but it's something to really be thought out and planned. Modules are supposed to be designed in such a way that there is as little dependency on other modules as possible. This includes artifacts such as entities, pages, microflows, constants, enumerations, images, rules, and anything else you see listed in the **Project Explorer** window of the project. If there is minimal or no dependency on other modules, you can easily export a module from a project and import it into another project. Or better yet, export it from a project and make it available in the Mendix public app store or your private Mendix company app store. Either way, the concept here is trying to design your modules in such a way that they can be reusable. Of course, this isn't appropriate for all modules because they may be very specific to your application and the functionality it serves up.

Some examples of exportable and reusable modules are as follows:

- A scripts module that handles common logic for running and executing scripts
- A notifications module that generates emails or is integrated with a third-party solution for sending text messages
- A payment processing module that is integrated with a payment solution provider such as Stripe or PayPal

These modules could be used in any application and would likely need to be built in a way that they have minimal dependency on other modules within the project. Of course, these were just some ideas; no doubt you could think of many others!

The process to actually create a **cross-module association** is a bit different than how you would associate two entities within the same module. Let's consider the steps to create that association, but don't worry about performing this anywhere in your project quite yet, let's just get an understanding of what is happening first. We will have an opportunity to do this in the sample project at the end of the chapter:

1. Double-click on the entity you wish to serve as the parent entity to open the **Properties** window.

2. In the **Properties** window, click the **Associations** tab and then the **New** button. See *Figure 11.5* for a visual aid for this step:

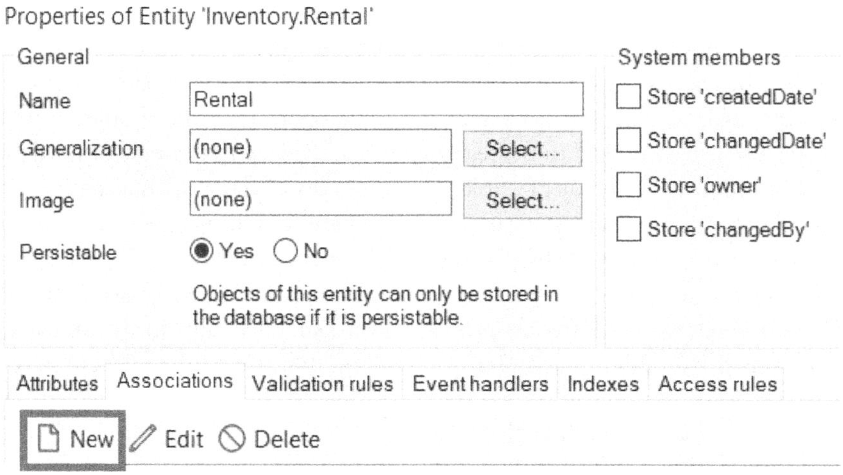

Figure 11.5 – Entity properties window

3. In the **Select Entity** window, choose the entity you wish to associate by single-clicking:

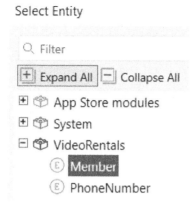

Figure 11.6 – Selecting the desired entity to associate to in the Select Entity window

4. Click **Select**.

You will now see a new association listed in the **Properties** window, as seen in the following figure:

Properties of Entity 'Inventory.Rental'   □   ✕

General

Name	Rental
Generalization	(none) Select...
Image	(none) Select...
Persistable	● Yes ○ No

Objects of this entity can only be stored in the database if it is persistable.

System members

☐ Store 'createdDate'
☐ Store 'changedDate'
☐ Store 'owner'
☐ Store 'changedBy'

Documentation

Attributes | Associations | Validation rules | Event handlers | Indexes | Access rules

📄 New   ✏ Edit   ⊘ Delete

Name	▲	Type		Owner		Parent	Child
Rental_Member		Reference	∨	Default	∨	Inventory.Rental	VideoRentals.Member

Figure 11.7 – New association details in the Properties window

In the domain module, the visual representation of the association is represented slightly differently as well. Notice in *Figure 11.8* that the association runs off the screen, signifying the association is to an entity that is in another module:

Figure 11.8 – Association to an entity in another module

To quickly be able to view the entity on the other side of the association, you can right-click on the line representing the association and note **Go to other side (Inventory. Rental)**, as seen in the following figure:

Figure 11.9 – Right-clicking on the cross-module association

By clicking on **Go to other side (Inventory.Rental)**, you will be brought to the other entity in the other module. This is a nice shortcut to jump to entities across modules.

> **Important note**
>
> Steps *1–4* were just discussed for explanation purpose only. You are not suppose to perform these steps in your project quiet yet. We will get into that later in this chapter.

In the next section, we will continue considering entities, specifically discussing specializations and generalizations.

Understanding generalizations and specializations of entities

The concept of **generalization** and **specialization** (or **inheritance** as it is often referred to) can be a little tricky to wrap your head around if you don't already have experience with it. The basic concept is that generalization entities sit at the top of the hierarchy and specializations are customizations of the generalization entity. *Figure 11.10* shows what this would look like in the domain model:

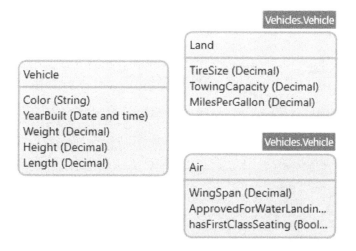

Figure 11.10 – Domain model with generalization and specialization entities

As shown in *Figure 11.10*, one example to help better explain this would be if you had a domain model with an entity called `Vehicle`. `Vehicle` contains attributes that would be common for any vehicle, such as `Color`, `YearBuilt`, and `Weight`. However, the application deals with very specific classes of vehicles: vehicles that travel on land and vehicles that travel through the air. In this case, you decide to create specialization entities to represent vehicles that travel on land and those that travel through the air because each of those vehicles would have specific attributes you would want to capture. Also, the attributes you would be specifically interested in for land vehicles don't really make sense to store with those about air travel. A truck is likely never going to need `WingSpan` stored because it doesn't have wings.

You also may notice in *Figure 11.10* that the generalization is represented by a blue label above the specialized entity. This indicates the module name and the entity name of the generalization.

The relationship between the generalized and specialized entities is set on the specialized entity. To do this, follow these steps:

1. Open the **Properties** window of the entity.

2. Click the **Select** button next to **Generalization**.

3. Select the entity you wish to be the generalization of the entity.

   See *Figure 11.11* for reference:

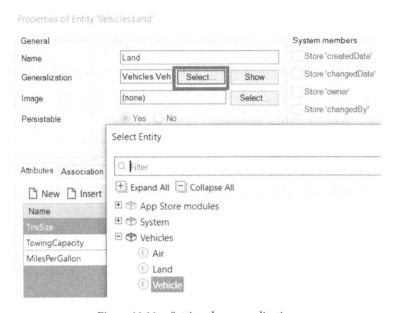

Figure 11.11 – Setting the generalization

Just like anything you do, there are pros and cons of opting to use generalization and specialization. Let's take a brief look at some of them.

Pros

Without an actual association between the two entities, Mendix doesn't need to store an association table like it would for a one-to-one association between two entities.

If both the generalized and specialized components are always modified together, your microflows become easier to maintain. No additional retrieve or commit activities are required.

Cons

Because Mendix uses the concept of transactions (`https://en.wikipedia.org/wiki/Database_transaction`) when performing activities on the database, if you are committing a specialized entity, the project will potentially put all generalizations of that entity in a lock status. Basically, it means that no other process can read or modify that record. This may not be an issue for an application with low transaction volume, but it's something certainly worth considering as it could become a major performance concern. Each entity may have its own event handlers and could result in conflicting results. On that note, it's not really advised to use any more than one level of specializations. This means to try and avoid something such as what's shown in *Figure 11.12*:

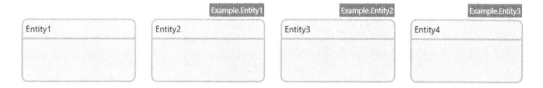

Figure 11.12 – Multi-level specialization

Figure 11.12 shows a multi-level specialization pattern, where `Entity3` is a generalization of `Entity4`, `Entity2` is a generalization of `Entity3`, and `Entity1` is a generalization of `Entity2`. This isn't wrong and Mendix will allow you to do it, but it could result in some serious performance concerns down the road for your project, so it's advised to try and avoid a situation like this.

Conclusion about inheritance

In the end, it's important to know all the pros and cons of, well, everything you are attempting to do! This requires thoughtful planning, a firm understanding of what the end product (your application) will be expected to do, and sometimes a conversation with a trusted colleague or two to weigh out the pros and cons. Generalization and specialization (inheritance) are often misused in projects and create a world of headaches for developers and users. This section was not intended to cover every aspect of this functionality but rather to provide an overview and introduce you to the topic. Mendix has some nice documentation on the subject. Here is a good resource to get you started: `https://docs.mendix.com/refguide/generalization-and-association`.

In the next section, we will take a few of the concepts we have discussed during this chapter and start applying them to our sample project to help build out our domain models in anticipation of the next chapter. Let's dive in!

Let's go make it!

In this section, we are going to put into practice a few of the topics we discussed in this chapter. We will add a few more entities to the project with various association types, add a new module or two, and create some cross-module associations. Let's get started:

1. Create a new module and name it `Inventory`. To do so, take the following steps:

    a) Right-click in the white space of **Project Explorer** and select **Add Module**, as seen in *Figure 11.13*:

    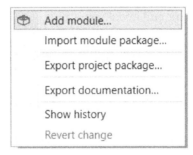

    Figure 11.13 – Adding a new module

    b) Type `Inventory` and click **OK**.

2. Open the domain model of your new module by double-clicking on it in **Project Explorer**:

    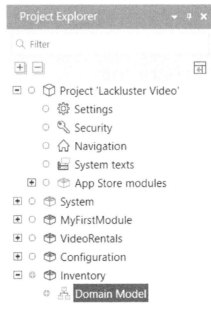

    Figure 11.14 – New domain model

3. Click the **Entity** button and drag the new entity anywhere on the white space in the domain model, as you can see in the following figure:

Figure 11.15 – Adding a new entity

4. Change the name of the entity to Movie.

5. Add the following attributes to the entity (see *Figure 11.16*):

- Title (type = String)

- Description (type = String)

- Rating (type = Decimal)

- ReleaseDate (type = Date and time)

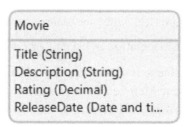

Figure 11.16 – Movie entity with attributes

6. Add a new entity and name it Rental.

7. Add the following attributes to it:

- RentedDate (type = Date and time)

- DueDate (type = Date and time)

8. Add an association to `Movie` where a rental can be associated with one movie and a movie can be associated with many rentals.

9. Check whether your domain model now looks similar to the following figure:

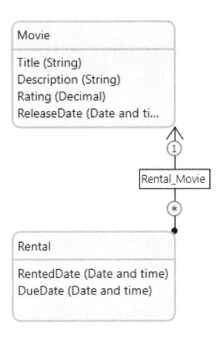

Figure 11.17 – Inventory domain model

10. Now, add a cross-module association between `Rental` and `Member`.

One member should be able to have multiple rentals and a rental should only be associated associated to one Member. For a reminder on how to add this type of association, see the *Cross Module Associations* section of this chapter.

11. Check whether your domain model now looks similar to the following:

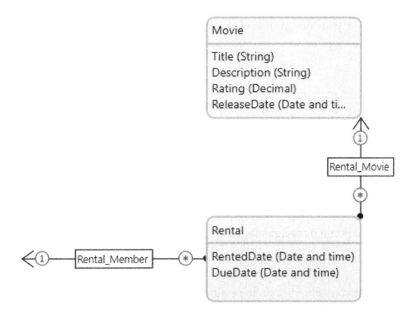

Figure 11.18 – Inventory domain model with updated cross-module association

12. Add another module and name it `Payment`.

13. In the new `Payment` module, add a new entity and name it `Fee`, and add the following attributes:

- `RentalFee` (type = `Decimal`)

- `LateFee` (type = `Decimal`)

- `TotalAmountDue` (type = `Decimal`)

- `Discount` (type = `Decimal`)

14. Add cross-module associations to Member and Rental. Both associations should be one-to-many from Fee.

15. Check whether your domain module looks similar to the following figure:

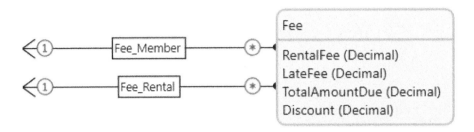

Figure 11.19 – Fee entity with cross-module associations

16. Now, let's add some overview pages for all of the entities we just added:

> **Tip**
>
> Recall that if you right-click on the entity, you can choose to have Studio Pro generate the overview page(s) for you! See *Figure 11.20*.

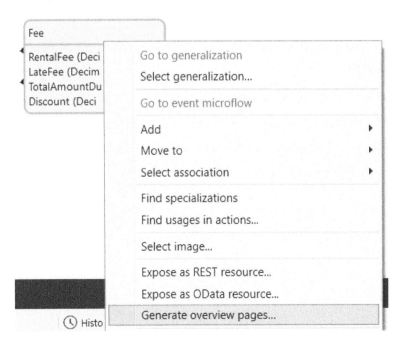

Figure 11.20 – Generate overview pages

Now that you have overview pages for all the new entities, let's add some access to them from the home page!

17. From **Project Explorer**, open **Navigation**:

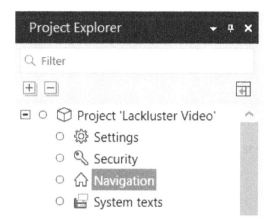

Figure 11.21 – Navigation in the Project Explorer window

18. From the **Navigation** window, add a new item by clicking **New item**.

19. Set the **Caption**, **Icon**, **On click**, and **Page** properties, as shown in *Figure 11.22*:

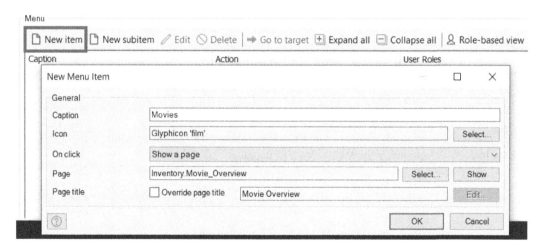

Figure 11.22 – New "Movies" menu item

20. Add another menu item for `Rentals`. See *Figure 11.23* for how to set the values:

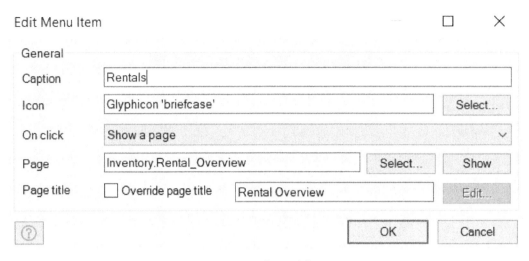

Figure 11.23 – New "Rentals" menu item

21. Add another menu item for `Fees`. See *Figure 11.24* for how to set the values:

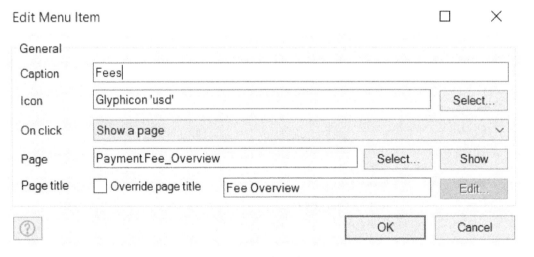

Figure 11.24 – New "Fees" menu item

22. Run your application locally and check out the new pages and navigation you just added!

23. Add a few member records and a few movies.

24. Then, try adding a few rental records and associating them to a movie and a member. See *Figure 11.25* for an example:

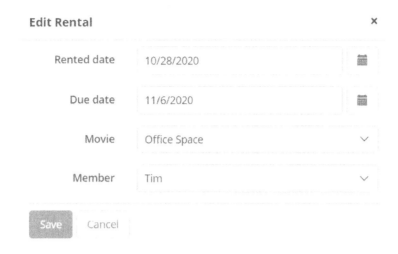

Figure 11.25 – Example of adding a rental record

That concludes the *Let's go make it!* section of this chapter! With the simple few additions we just made to the sample project, we've laid the groundwork for the next chapter to integrate with a real external database and pull in data for our app!

Summary

In this chapter, we covered a few topics that were briefly discussed earlier in the book. Each of these subjects helped us better understand our domain models and how to extend them as we require more and more data to be present in our application. No matter what type of application you build, the data will be the heart of it. The more you know about setting up entities, modules, and associations, the better decisions you will likely make and the better your application will scale over time.

We began the chapter with a discussion on various association types. Understanding the correct association to use to connect your entities will be crucial as you build applications. While you can always change the association type down the road, it can create a number of issues. For example, going from a one-to-many association to a many-to-many will change all the retrieve actions in all your microflows to now return a list rather than one single record. This will include having to add iterators and a means to identify records properly. The point is, it is a major headache if you have to do this. It's best to get the association type correct when first implementing your domain!

Next, we discussed modules and how to associate data across them. Depending on the size of your application, you will likely end up with numerous modules. It's important to endeavor to keep your modules small with only a few entities in each domain model. Sometimes, that's easier said than done but it's a good practice to try and keep. It's also a good idea to try and think of each module as a potentially exportable chunk of your application, something that could be imported and reused in other applications.

Lastly, we discussed generalizations and specializations, or inheritance as they're often referred to. Inheritance offers some great upsides but should be used very thoughtfully and carefully. Remember to try and avoid more than two layers of inheritance as this can cause major performance issues in your application.

In the next chapter, we will use the new modules and entities that were added during the *Let's go make it!* section of this chapter. We will connect to a third-party database with the RESTful API and see what it's like to deal with external data in our application!

Knowledge check

The following are the answers to the *Chapter 10, Error Handling and Troubleshooting,* knowledge check:

1. c

2. b

3. b

4. d

5. a

Chapter 11 knowledge check

1. Generalization and specialization are also known as:

   a. Inheritance

   b. Heritage

   c. A co-modular relationship

   d. Interdependence

2. True or False: Associating entities across modules is not possible?

   a. True

   b. False

3. What are two types of associations? (Choose two)

    a. One-to-many

    b. One-to-two

    c. One-to-one

    d. Many-to-none

4. True or False: Choosing inheritance over one-to-one association is always the best and preferred method of linking to entities?

    a. True

    b. False

5. True or False: A module must always contain at least one entity in the domain model?

    a. True

    b. False

12
Getting Some REST

It is a massively huge world out there! You are going to want your application to connect to it. In the modern era, almost every application connects to or integrates with some other database or application in some manner. There are many methods for exchanging data through some form of web service; **SOAP** (**Simple Object Access Protocol**), **REST** (**Representational State Transfer**), and **GraphQL** are just three common ways. In this chapter, we will discuss one form of integration: the REST API. Specifically, we will discuss third-party REST APIs, what a third-party API is, how to interact with it, and understand the crucial artifacts in Studio Pro that will get you up and connected in no time. We will briefly take a look at how to publish your own REST API from Studio Pro and discuss some of the artifacts important for making that happen. We will also discuss the importance of security and authentication as well as a few native ways provided by Mendix to ensure that your APIs keep your data safe and secure.

In this chapter, we will also take a look at Postman as an API testing tool. Of course, there are dozens of, if not more, tools for performing testing with APIs, but this is just one easy-to-use example that we will take a quick look at. The following are the topics that we are going to cover:

- Understanding REST
- Testing your integration
- Consuming REST
- Publishing REST
- Understanding basic security and authorization

After considering these topics, you will be able to confidently perform the following:

- Consume a REST API within your Mendix project

- Publish a REST API from your Mendix project

- Explain basic security and authorization methods for the APIs you publish in your Mendix project

Technical requirements

The sample project of this chapter can be found in `Chapter12` folder at `https://github.com/PacktPublishing/Building-Low-Code-Applications-with-Mendix`.

Understanding REST

As mentioned in the introduction, REST is a type of web service that leverages HTTP(S) protocols. It is a great integration method because it is easy to implement and has a lot of flexibility. While working with REST, clients can make various types of calls, including the following:

- `Get`: This is the equivalent of a **read** request or a query request with the intention of returning one or more records.

- `Post`: A client would submit a post request to **create** a record or records.

- `Put`: This call is used to **update** or **replace** a record or records in the target application.

- `Delete`: This call would be used by a client to, you guessed it, **delete** a record or records. (Use caution when allowing this method.)

Clients can also request the response to their call to be in a variety of formats, such as these:

- **XML**: eXtensible Markup Language: `https://en.wikipedia.org/wiki/XML`

- **JSON**: JavaScript Object Notation: `https://en.wikipedia.org/wiki/JSON`

- **YAML**: "YAML Ain't Markup Language": `https://en.wikipedia.org/wiki/YAML`

There are countless resources on the internet to help you better understand REST and the ways in which to implement it. In this chapter, we will primarily focus on consuming a `Get` request from a third-party service in JSON format, and then we will also publish a REST service in our sample application to see how that is done.

First, let's talk about how to get connected to a third-party service and how to run some preliminary tests on the API.

Testing your integration

During the remainder of this chapter, we will be working with a third-party website that allows developers to use their API for free. The website is https://www.themoviedb.org. We will create an account with them and connect to one of their APIs so that we can begin pulling in some information about movies into our sample project with a few simple REST Get calls. Let's begin!

1. Fill in all the details on the following web page to create an account with The Movie DB: https://www.themoviedb.org/signup.

2. Once you have created an account and are logged in, navigate to your account settings and select the API option and request a new API key.

3. Follow the instructions to create an API key.

4. Once your API key has been created, you should be able to find it by navigating to your account settings and selecting **API**. Refer to the following screenshot as an example:

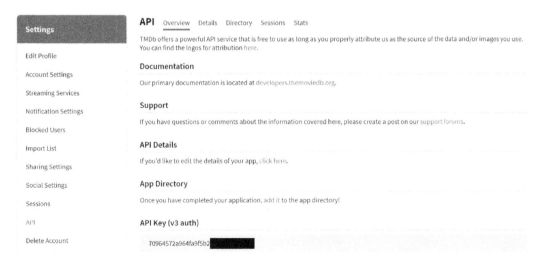

Figure 12.1 – Account settings showing the API key

Now that you have an API key, let's test out the Search Movies API method by navigating to `https://developers.themoviedb.org/3/search/search-movies`.

The documentation here indicates that there are a number of possible parameters to add to our request, but we will keep it simple by just focusing on `query` and `API_key`. The following screenshot shows various request parameters:

Query String

api_key	string	default: <<api_key>>	**required**
language	string	Pass a ISO 639-1 value to display translated data for the fields that support it. **minLength:** 2 **pattern:** ([a-z]{2})-([A-Z]{2}) **default:** en-US	optional
query	string	Pass a text query to search. This value should be URI encoded. **minLength:** 1	**required**
page	integer	Specify which page to query. **minimum:** 1 **maximum:** 1000 **default:** 1	optional
include_adult	boolean	Choose whether to inlcude adult (pornography) content in the results. **default**	optional
region	string	Specify a ISO 3166-1 code to filter release dates. Must be uppercase. **pattern:** ^[A-Z]{2}$	optional
year	integer		optional
primary_release_year	integer		optional

Figure 12.2 – Request parameters for the Search Movies method

The developer portion of the website has some nice features that allow you to test API requests directly from the browser. To do so, perform the following steps:

1. Navigate to the **Try it out** tab. See *Figure 12.3* for help:

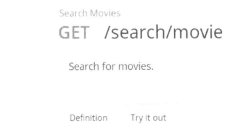

Figure 12.3 – Try it out tab of the Search Movies method

2. Fill in the values for the variables and query options as seen in *Figure 12.4*:

Figure 12.4 – Variables and Query String options

3. Once values are entered as shown in *Figure 12.4*, click the **SEND REQUEST** button and note that the request string is being built as you enter values in the **Query String** options:

Figure 12.5 – The SEND REQUEST button and request string

If your request was built properly, you should see something similar to the results shown in the following screenshot:

Response 200

Body   17 Headers   0 Cookies

Pretty   JSON Explorer   Raw

```
 1  {
 2      "page": 1,
 3      "total_results": 21,
 4      "total_pages": 2,
 5      "results": [
 6          {
 7              "popularity": 83.214,
 8              "vote_count": 5400,
 9              "video": false,
10              "poster_path": "/AkJQpZp9WoNdj7pLYSjiL0RcMMN.jpg",
11              "id": 353081,
12              "adult": false,
13              "backdrop_path": "/aw4FOsWr2FY373nKSxbpNi3fz4F.jpg",
14              "original_language": "en",
15              "original_title": "Mission: Impossible - Fallout",
16              "genre_ids": [
17                  28,
18                  12
19              ],
20              "title": "Mission: Impossible - Fallout",
21              "vote_average": 7.4,
22              "overview": "When an IMF mission ends badly, the world is faced with dire consequences. As Etha
23              "release_date": "2018-07-13"
24          },
25          {
26              "popularity": 35.285,
27              "id": 954,
```

Figure 12.6 – Response from the API request

So, from the response we received with this simple built-in test on the website, we were able to simulate making a request to the server for specific information. Let's now take this one step further and test it outside of the tools provided by The Movie DB.

There are many software packages that provide resources for API testing. We will take a quick look at one of those tools, that is, Postman, and test the API with it before moving forward with any requests in our Mendix project. The following steps will instruct you on how to download the application and make a simple request using some of the information obtained from The Movie DB a few moments ago:

1. Download the Postman desktop app by following the steps at https://www.postman.com/downloads/.

2. Once the application is downloaded, create a new request by clicking the + button.

Important note

There are two + buttons. Make sure not to create a new collection but rather a new request by using the + button in the center tabs pane.

---

3. Set the call type to **GET** and the request URL to `https://API.themoviedb.org/3/search/movie`, as shown in *Figure 12.7*:

Figure 12.7 – The GET call type and request URL provided in the Postman interface

4. Next, on the **Params** tab, add the following **Key** and **Value** pairs. See *Figure 12.8* for the reference:

- **Key**: `api_key`
- **Value**: Your API key from your account
- **Key**: `query`
- **Value**: `Mission Impossible`
- **Key**: `page`
- **Value**: `1`:

Figure 12.8 – Request and parameters configured

5.   On the **Authorization** tab, set **TYPE** to **No Auth**:

Figure 12.9 – Authorization tab with No Auth set

6.   Once all the values have been configured as described in steps *3-5*, click the **Send** button.

You should receive a response from The Movie DB API as shown in *Figure 12.10*. It should look really similar to the response that was received while testing the API directly on the website during the steps associated with *Figure 12.6*:

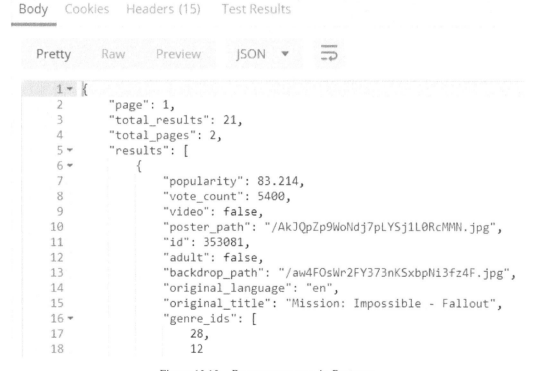

Figure 12.10 – Response as seen in Postman

Great! It looks like our request is configured properly and we are receiving a response from the third party successfully.

> **Important note**
> Postman is a great API testing tool. As mentioned previously, it's one of the many tools that are available to developers. If you are comfortable with another tool for testing APIs, go ahead and use whichever tool you prefer. This tutorial was simply intended to give you an idea of how to test an API and one possible tool option for doing so. The great thing about software development in modern times is that there are so many tools available to developers that you can often find one that works for you!

It's also worth noting that testing an API with a tool such as Postman isn't required before testing it in your Mendix project. Depending on your familiarity with API requests, you may opt to jump right into Studio Pro and start testing. Many have found, however, that using a testing tool outside of Studio Pro just to understand the request syntax and response payloads is helpful. Either way, it's up to you!

Now that we are confident in the API and the way we have built our request, we will connect it all up inside our sample project in Mendix. Let's take a look at how to do that in the next section!

Consuming REST

Consuming a REST API is simply a way to indicate that your application is using that REST API or making a call to it. That call may be a GET, POST, or any of the call types that are available for that API that *another* application has made available and you are connected to. In this section, we will discuss what some of the Mendix native artifacts are for helping you connect your application to a REST API and start consuming it. Later, in the *Let's go make it!* section, we will put into practice some of the things mentioned in this section.

JSON structure

The first artifact we will discuss is called a **JSON structure**. This allows us to store a JSON string to help define how it is constructed. This then allows Studio Pro to create a structure of the schema and ultimately define what the Mendix objects will be.

The JSON structure is made up of two main components: the **JSON snippet** and the **Structure**. The JSON snippet is simply the JSON string, and the structure helps to define the schema and the Mendix objects. Refer to *Figure 12.11* to see a sample of this:

Figure 12.11 – Sample JSON structure

The JSON structure will become one of the core functions for the integration we are building in this chapter and also for future integrations. In addition to the JSON structure, Mendix also offers another way to define the structure of an inbound or outbound message. A **message definition** allows you to define the structure of the message, create import and export mappings, and can be used with JSON or XML. For more information on message definitions, visit the following link: `https://docs.mendix.com/refguide/message-definitions`.

Import mapping

Another important artifact to become familiar with when consuming an API is **import mapping**. The import mapping defines the schema of the data you anticipate to receive in your response payload. It is made up of the following components:

- **Schema source**: This is where you can select where the schema is sourced from. As you can see in *Figure 12.12*, there are a few options here. You can select **XML schema**, **Web service operation**, **JSON structure**, or **Message definition**. In this example, we're using the JSON structure that was set up in the previous subsection.

- **Schema elements**: Once you select a source of the schema, Studio Pro will convert that into selectable elements, as shown in *Figure 12.12*. The schema elements define the attribute names, types, how often they would expect to occur (one time or many times), and whether or not the attribute is nillable:

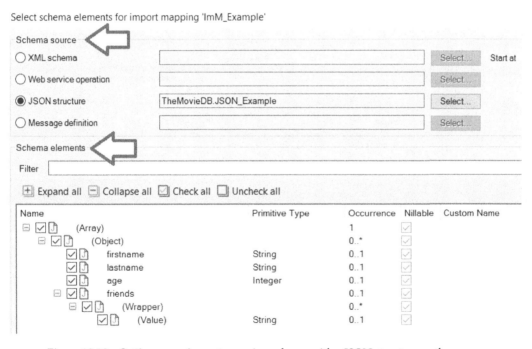

Figure 12.12 – Setting up an import mapping schema with a JSON structure as the source

Once **Schema source** is selected and the schema elements chosen, Studio Pro can automatically define and generate the Mendix entities that the incoming data will get mapped to. Refer to the following screenshot to see how this is visually represented in the import mapping:

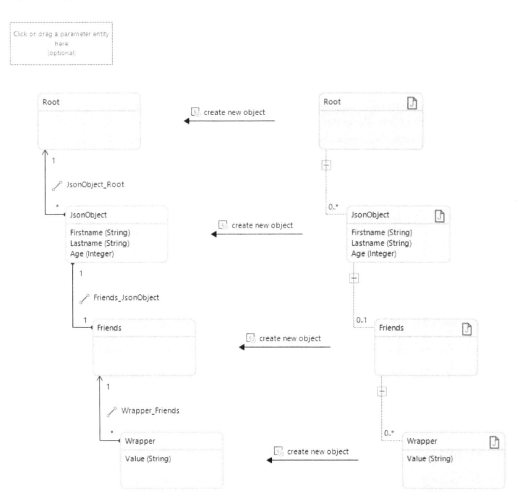

Figure 12.13 – Example import mapping with defined JSON objects and Mendix objects

Of course, you may want to clean up some of the default naming conventions to make more sense in your domain model, as `Root` or `JsonObject` may not mean a whole lot outside of the context of the import mapping shown in *Figure 12.13*. However, that is totally up to how you want to implement each integration. *Figure 12.13* is simply showing the default behavior of Studio Pro.

Message definition

The last artifact we will discuss in this section is **message definition**. Message definition makes provision for an additional means to define the structure of the message(s) that are being consumed (or produced) by your application. Similar to the JSON structure, the message definition is composed of the following main components:

- **General**: This is where you define the name and select the entity that the message definition is composed of.

- **Structure**: This is where you can choose the specific attributes and associated entities of the base entity chosen in the general settings area. Whatever is selected in this area has a direct correlation to what is available in the import mapping.

The following shows an example of a message definition that has **Name** and **Entity** selected, along with a handful of other attributes:

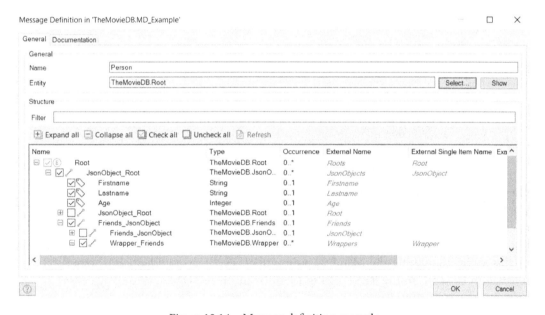

Figure 12.14 – Message definition example

Message definition can then be selected as the schema source of an import mapping. Recall *Figure 12.12*, which showed a JSON structure being selected as the schema source. Now, look at *Figure 12.15*, and see that a message definition has now been selected as the schema source:

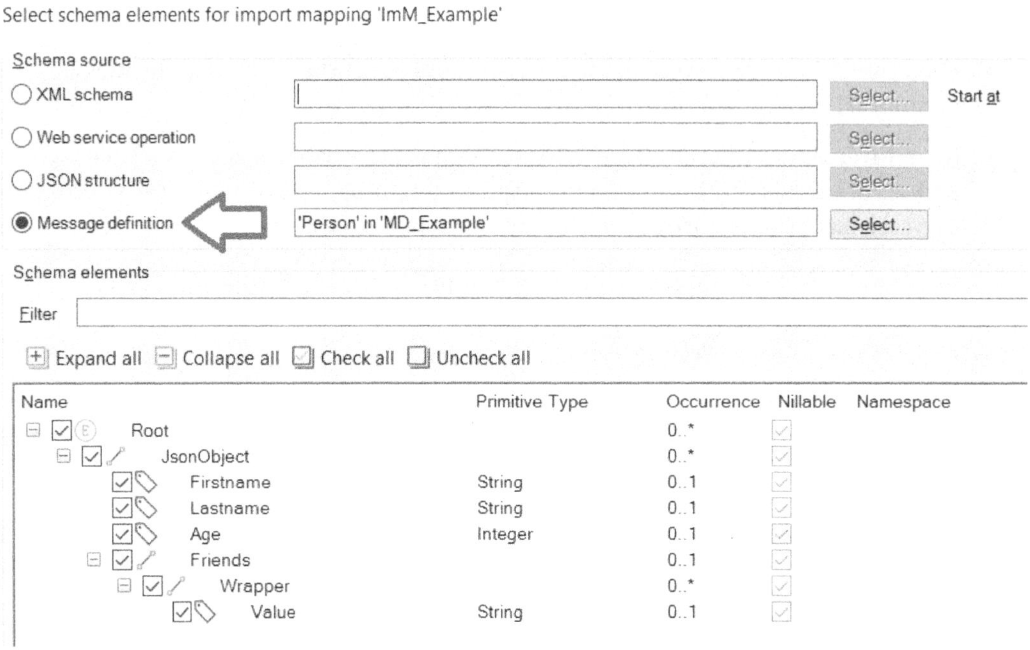

Figure 12.15 – Setting up an import mapping schema with Message definition as the source

These are a few of the most important artifacts that Mendix provides out of the box for working with REST APIs. The section was not intended to describe every single detail of each artifact, but rather give an overview of what they are, what they do, and how to use them. Additionally, there are many other helpful resources available on the web on this topic. Thankfully, the Mendix community is ever growing! Here is a helpful tutorial for the consuming REST API in Mendix: `https://www.youtube.com/watch?v=NJD4DS0Rv3o`.

In the next section, we will consider a few others that enable you to publish a REST API from your own application so that others may consume it. Let's take a look!

Publishing REST

In the previous section, we discussed the concept of consuming a REST API and some of the artifacts that are native to Mendix to help accomplish that. In this section, we will look at the other side of that, that is, publishing a REST API for others to consume.

Eventually, you will wish to make some of your data available to other applications or services. One way to accomplish this is to publish a REST API, which other applications or services can consume. Thankfully, Mendix makes it really easy to accomplish this in a few simple steps. In this section, we will discuss export mapping and the published REST service as two key components of building your published API.

Export mapping

Similar to import mapping, **export mapping** defines the schema of the data. But instead of it being the data you are anticipating on receiving, it is the data you will be sending to other applications that request it. Export mapping is composed of the same key elements as import mapping: **Schema source** and **Scheme elements**. Both function exactly as they do for import mapping. In fact, one of the only real differences you will notice between export and import mappings is how the data is directionally represented to flow. Notice in *Figure 12.15* that the data is visually shown to flow left to right, from a Mendix entity to a JSON object, symbolizing that it is leaving the application, whereas in *Figure 12.13*, we saw the opposite; the data was depicted as flowing right to left, or coming into the application:

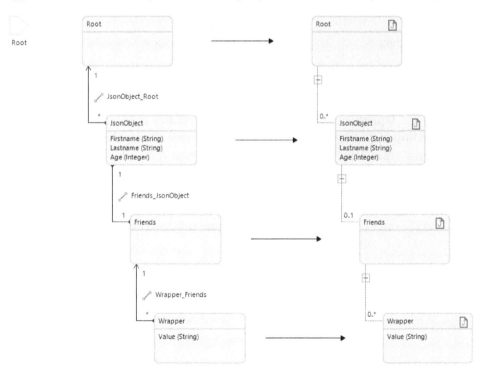

Figure 12.16 – Export mapping example

This is a subtle difference but an important one to note.

Published REST service

The **published REST service** allows you to publish a REST web service, which is a single API or collection of API methods. What's nice is that this is all native functionality from within your Mendix project and configured all right within Studio Pro. The published REST service is composed of several components. Let's discuss a few of them next:

- In the **General** settings area, you will be able to define the service name, along with the version of the service and its location. Note in *Figure 12.17* that the location's base URL is defined as `http://localhost:8081/`. This is because the app is running locally in Studio Pro. Once you deploy to a cloud node, the base URL is automatically updated to whatever the base URL of the cloud node is. You will be able to define the endpoint, but generally, the suggested naming convention is suitable:

Figure 12.17 – General settings of the published REST service

- The other main components of the published REST service are the **Resources** section and **Operations for the resource**. The resource is generally the entity or operation in which the service is acting on. So, for example, you may have a resource called `Course`, if you had a collection of API calls all centered around a `Course` entity, perhaps a `GET` operation to query for courses and a `POST` operation for other services to create new courses; either way, all the operations performing a **CRUD** (**Create**, **Read**, **Update**, **Delete**) action on the base entity of `Course`. Notice in *Figure 12.18* a resource named `Course` and a `GET` operation for the `Course` resource:

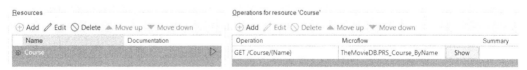

Figure 12.18 – Resource and operation example

Operation is where you define many of the specific options and functionality of the API. There, you can define the following:

- **Method**: GET, POST, PUT, PATCH, DELETE, HEAD, OPTIONS.

- **Operation path**: Including an operation path value allows the REST service to be called with that value in the URL that acts as a path parameter type of the request.

- **Example location**: What the full URL of the API is.

- **Microflow**: Which microflow is actually executed when another service makes a request to your service.

- **Parameters**: Just as a microflow accepts input parameters, so will many APIs. You may need to pass an ID or name of a record. Defining those parameters in the microflow will allow them to be connected in the **Operation** settings:

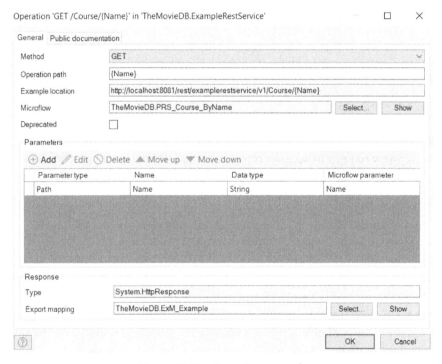

Figure 12.19 – Operation example

These are the main artifacts used when publishing a REST API from Studio Pro. Using and becoming familiar with these native pieces of functionality will allow you to create robust, easy-to-use REST APIs for others to begin consuming.

In the next section, we will briefly discuss some basic security and authorization methods to keep your data safe.

Understanding basic security and authorization

In any application, security should always be at the forefront when designing and building. This is true when considering which users should be able to access which data and becomes even more important when you begin to expose certain data to the outside world. Thankfully, Mendix makes it really easy to wrap your web services with security. Natively, Mendix offers a few choices when it comes to security. These are as follows:

- **None**: Just as the name indicates, no security or authentication is needed. This method should be used very sparingly and perhaps only during the testing phase of development.

- **Username and password**: This is often referred to as "basic authorization." This requires the other application or client to pass a valid username and password in the **Authorization** header of the request.

- **Active session**: This is another layer of security that requires the requesting client to have an active session and pass an X-Csrf-Token in the header of the request. This can be a bit confusing if you are just getting started with this sort of security, but Mendix has some nice detailed documentation available here: `https://docs.mendix.com/refguide/published-rest-service#1-introduction`.

- **Custom**: This authentication method calls a microflow every time a user or client makes a new request to access a resource. This can be used if you choose to have the user pass an encrypted authentication token, for example.

> **Important note**
>
> These security and authentication methods are only visible on the published REST service if the project level security is set to **Production**.

Notice in *Figure 12.20* the various methods that are selectable for authentication. Because there are different methods of authentication, it's a good idea to come up with a best practice for your company. It is a good idea to have all your applications authenticate in the same manner. This will help all your teams, developers, and users be on the same page and take the guesswork out of the equation when setting up a new service:

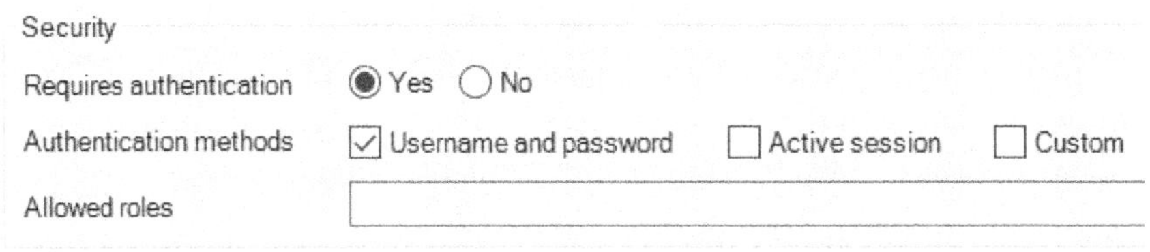

Figure 12.20 – Security options for the published REST service

You are now armed with pretty much everything that you need to start consuming a REST API, publish your own API from your application, and apply security! Now, let's take some of the concepts we've discussed during this chapter and add them to your project!

Let's go make it!

In this section, we will take what we've already learned about the GET request API call from Postman and begin building the request in Studio Pro. We will need to set up a new module and a few artifacts in the project first before actually connecting to the API. Let's get started!

1. Add a new module to your project and name it TheMovieDB:

Figure 12.21 – New module

2. Add a new JSON structure by right-clicking on the new module and selecting **Add other** and then **JSON structure**:

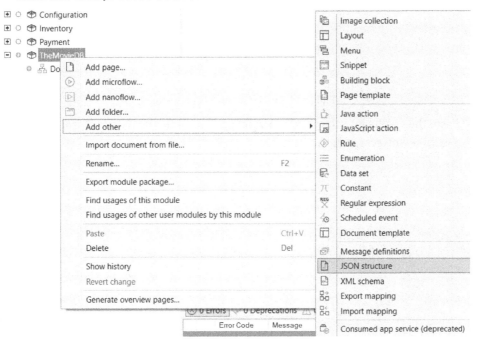

Figure 12.22 – Adding a JSON structure

3. Name it `JSON_Movie`.

4. In Postman, make the same request to `MovieDB` that we made during the steps associated with *Figure 12.10* in the *Testing your integration* section of this chapter.

5. Once you have a made a successful request to `MovieDB`, copy the results:

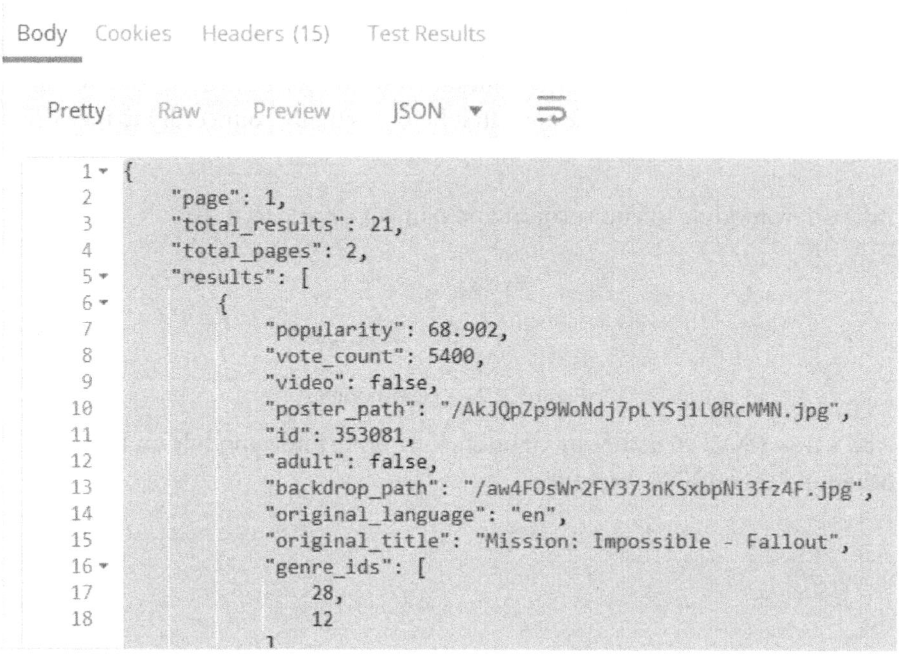

Figure 12.23 – JSON results in Postman

6. Paste the results into the **JSON snippet** section of the JSON structure, as shown in the following screenshot:

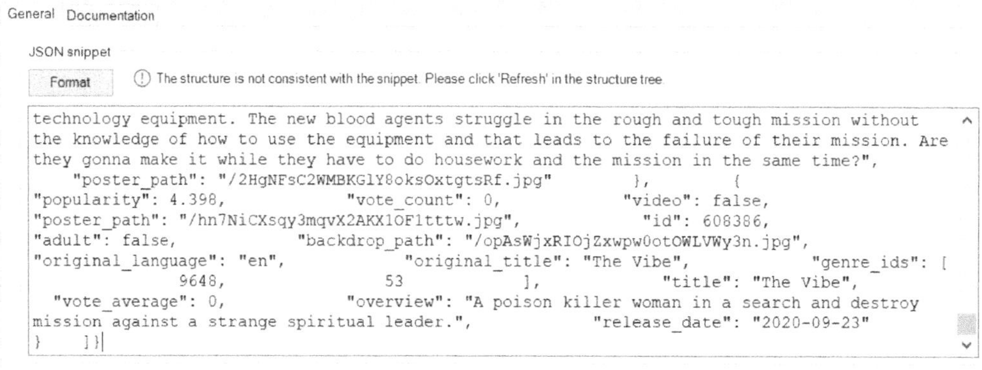

Figure 12.24 – An unformatted JSON string in the JSON snippet section of the JSON structure

7. Then, click the **Format** button to clean up the formatting of the JSON snippet to make it more readable:

Figure 12.25 – A formatted JSON string in the JSON snippet section of the JSON structure

An optional but recommended step here is to clean up the JSON snippet. Because you are showing actual results from a real request, there is real data being stored in the example snippet. And because we pasted the entire JSON string into the snippet, we have a lot of unnecessary iterations of the result, so let's trim the results and then generalize what's left.

Since `results` is a list (as denoted in the JSON by the `[` (open square bracket)), we can remove all of the results except the first one. Your JSON snippet should now look like the following:

```
{
    "page": 1,
    "total_results": 21,
    "total_pages": 2,
    "results": [
        {
            "popularity": 68.902,
            "vote_count": 5400,
            "video": false,
```

```
    "poster_path": "/AkJQpZp9WoNdj7pLYSj1L0RcMMN.
        jpg",
    "id": 353081,
    "adult": false,
    "backdrop_path": "/
        aw4FOsWr2FY373nKSxbpNi3fz4F.jpg",
    "original_language": "en",
    "original_title": "Mission: Impossible -
        Fallout",
    "genre_ids": [
        28,
        12
    ],
    "title": "Mission: Impossible - Fallout",
    "vote_average": 7.4,
    "overview": "When an IMF mission ends badly,
        the world is faced with dire consequences.
        As Ethan Hunt takes it upon himself to
        fulfill his original briefing, the CIA
        begin to question his loyalty and his
        motives. The IMF team find themselves in
        a race against time, hunted by assassins
        while trying to prevent a global
        catastrophe.",
    "release_date": "2018-07-13"
        }
    ]
}
```

But let's not stop there! Let's now generalize the results that are stored in the snippet.

Simply change any string value by removing the text between the quotes. For example, `"Remove Me"` would now read `""`. And for any integer or decimal value, change the number to either `1` or `1.0`. For example, `"vote_count": 5400` now reads `"vote_count": 1`. Once completed, your JSON snippet should read something like the following:

```
{
    "page": 1,
```

```json
    "total_results": 1,
    "total_pages": 1,
    "results": [
        {
            "popularity": 1.0,
            "vote_count": 1,
            "video": false,
            "poster_path": "",
            "id": 1,
            "adult": false,
            "backdrop_path": "",
            "original_language": "",
            "original_title": "",
            "genre_ids": [
                1,
                2
            ],
            "title": "",
            "vote_average": 1.0,
            "overview": "",
            "release_date": "2018-07-13"
        }
    ]
}
```

Cleaning up your JSON snippet in this manner makes it much more readable and easier to maintain. It also removes any potentially sensitive data from being stored in the project directly.

8. In the **Structure** section of the JSON structure window, click the **Refresh** button to sync the snippet to the structure, as shown in the following screenshot:

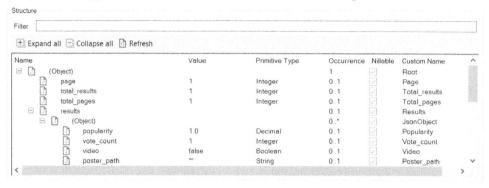

Figure 12.26 – Refreshed structure

9. Once completed, click **OK** to save and close the new JSON structure.

10. Now, add a new import mapping by right-clicking on the module and selecting **Add other** followed by **Import mapping**:

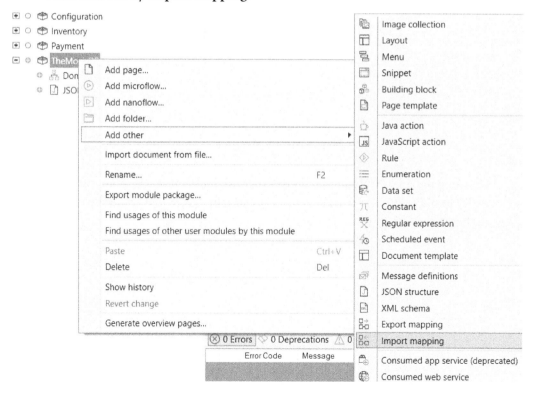

Figure 12.27 – Adding import mapping

11. Name the import mapping `ImM_Movie`.

12. Set the JSON structure that was just created in steps *2-9* as the schema source. See *Figure 12.28*:

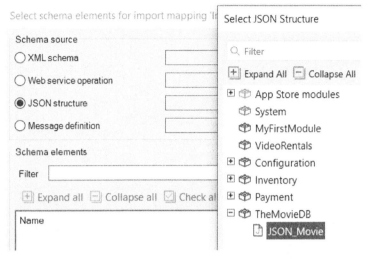

Figure 12.28 – Selecting the JSON structure as the schema source

13. Once your schema source is selected, in the **Schema elements** section, click on **Expand all** and then click **Check all** option to select all the elements from the schema. Your **Schema elements** section should now look as follows:

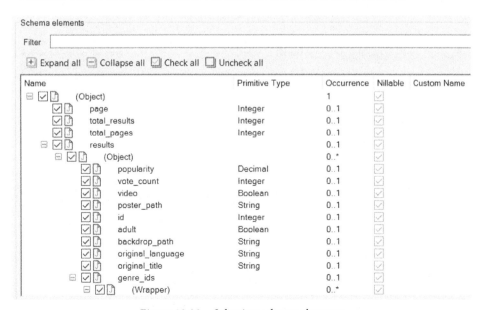

Figure 12.29 – Selecting schema elements

14. Once everything looks similar to *Figure 12.29*, click the **OK** button.

Your import mapping will now begin to take shape. You should see something similar to *Figure 12.30*, where you have a few JSON objects on the right-hand side, but nothing mapped on the left… yet:

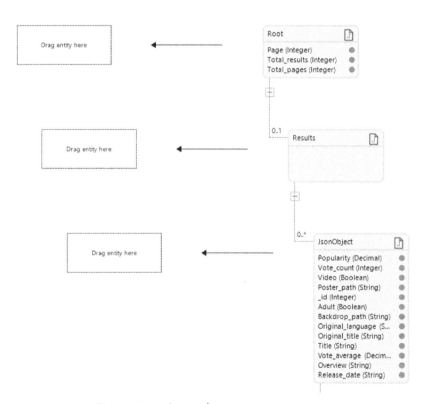

Figure 12.30 – Incomplete import mapping

15. Next, click the **Map automatically...** button in the top ribbon of the import mapping window:

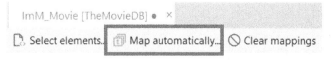

Figure 12.31 – The Map automatically... button

Now, your import mapping looks a little different because Studio Pro is automatically generating several Mendix entities and mapping them to the JSON objects. Your import mapping should look something like this:

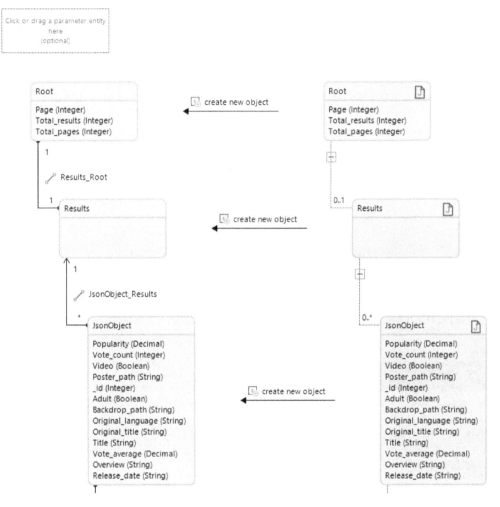

Figure 12.32 – Completed import mapping showing JSON objects (right) and Mendix entities (left)

With these steps completed, we now have the foundational pieces in place to set up the REST call to pull some data into our project! Next, we just need to build a microflow that makes the REST call and some logic to save the results. Let's dive in!

1. In the Domain Model of `TheMovieDB` module, create a new non-persistent entity and name it `Request`.

    In order to make an entity non-persistent, select **No** for the **Persistable** option in the properties window the entity you are creating.

2. Add a string attribute named `MovieName`. Your entity should look like this:

Figure 12.33 – New request; non-persistent entity

3. Add a new page to `TheMovieDB` module and name it `Request_NewEdit`.

4. Select **Form Horizontal** as the page layout and choose **PopupLayout** as the **Navigation Layout**. Refer to the following screenshot for reference:

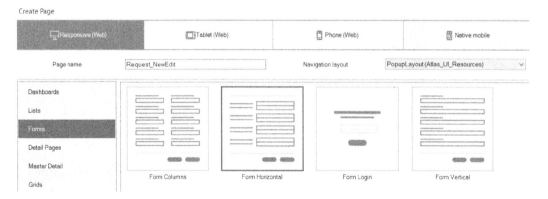

Figure 12.34 – Adding a new page

5. Replace the **Data view** source with the `Request` entity we just created in steps *1* and *2*, as shown in *Figure 12.35*:

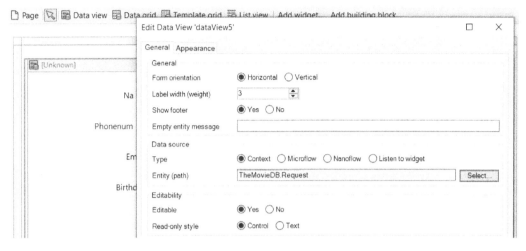

Figure 12.35 – The Data View option

6. Click **OK** on the **Edit Data View** window.

7. Click **Yes** when the popup shown in *Figure 12.36* displays:

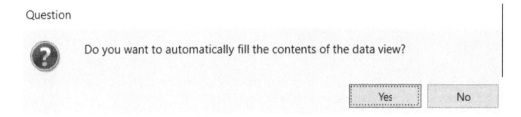

Figure 12.36 – Automatically filling the contents popup

Studio Pro will automatically grab the `MovieName` attribute and create an input field on the page. Your new page should now look like this:

Figure 12.37 – New page with an input box

8.   Add a new microflow to `TheMovieDB` module and name it `ACT_Request_New`.

9.   Add a **Create Object** action to create a new request (the entity we created in steps *1* and *2*).

10. Add a **Show Page** action to open the page we just created in steps *3* and *4*. See *Figure 12.38* for reference:

Figure 12.38 – The Show Page action setting

11. Once the new page is selected and `NewRequest` is selected under **Object to pass**, click **OK**.

Your microflow should look something similar to this:

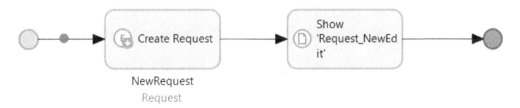

Figure 12.39 – Microflow example

12. Add a **Constant** in the `TheMovieDB` module and name it `APIKey`.

13. As the default value, use your API key that you received from The Movie DB and that was used with your Postman testing:

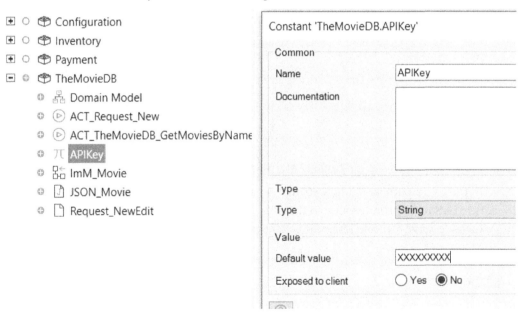

Figure 12.40 – Adding a constant and setting the default value

14. Create a new microflow in `TheMovieDB` module and name it `ACT_TheMovieDB_GetMoviesByName`.

15. Add an input parameter to the microflow where the **Data** type is **Object** and choose the `Request` entity that was created in steps *1* and *2*.

16. Add an exclusive split to the microflow that checks to make sure that the `MovieName` field of `Member` is not empty (hint: use the rule we created previously to make this validation easier and consistent with other similar validations).

17. In the `false` path, add a validation message indicating that `MovieName` is required.

18. Confirm that your microflow looks like this:

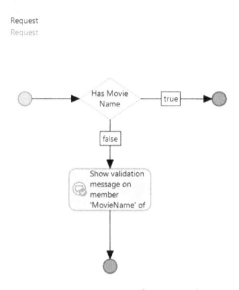

Figure 12.41 – Microflow example

19. In the `true` path, add a new string variable so that we can URL encode the `MovieName` attribute value so that it is safe to pass in the request. Name the variable `MovieName_Encoded`. Refer to the following screenshot:

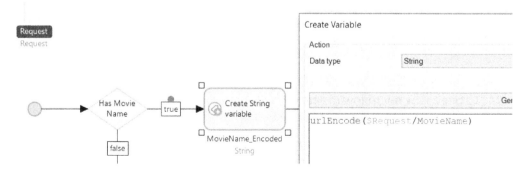

Figure 12.42 – Adding a urlEncode function to a string variable

20. Next, add a **Call REST Service** action as shown in *Figure 12.43*:

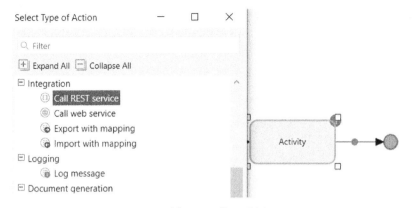

Figure 12.43 – Adding a Call REST Service action

21. Set the location of the REST call to the following: `https://API.themoviedb.org/3/search/movie?API_key={1}&query={2}`.

The {1} and {2} values will be replaced with values we specify in the **Parameters** section of the **Location** settings window. Set yours up as shown:

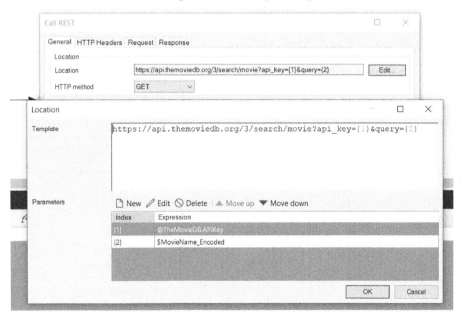

Figure 12.44 – Setting the location and parameters

22. Once your location is configured as shown in *Figure 12.44*, click the **OK** button to close the window.

23. In the **Call REST** window, go to the **Response** tab and set the values as shown in the following screenshot:

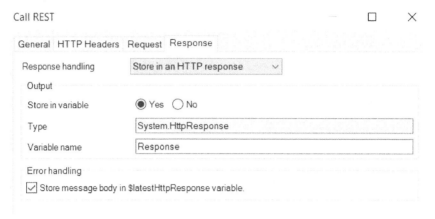

Figure 12.45 – The Call REST Response tab

24. Once all the values are configured as shown in *Figure 12.45*, click the **OK** button to close the window and return to the microflow.

Next, let's add an **Import With Mapping** action.

25. Configure the new action as shown in the following screenshot:

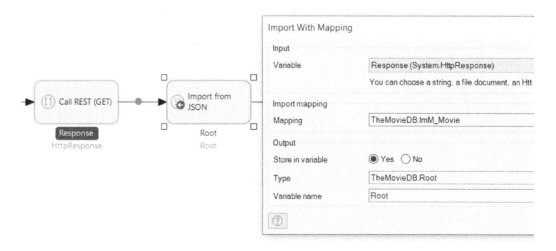

Figure 12.46 – Adding imports with a mapping action

> **Important note**
>
> You may also choose to apply the import mapping directly in the **Call REST** action by selecting **Apply import mapping** in the **Response** handling drop-down box. See *Figure 12.45*, where it shows **Store in an HTTP response** selected.

26. Either response method is correct. We've found that by handling the import mapping separate from the **Call REST** action makes it a little easier to debug if something goes wrong. But you will find what works best for you! Next, we will add a **Retrieve** action to retrieve the `Result` record that is associated with `Root`. Refer to the following screenshot to see how to configure the **Retrieve** action:

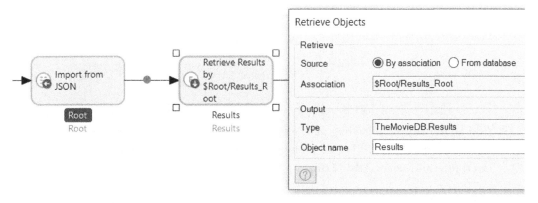

Figure 12.47 – Adding Retrieve

Now we will need to retrieve the list of the movies that were actually returned from the request to `TheMovieDB`.

27. Add another **Retrieve** action to retrieve a list of `JsonObject` over the `Results` association:

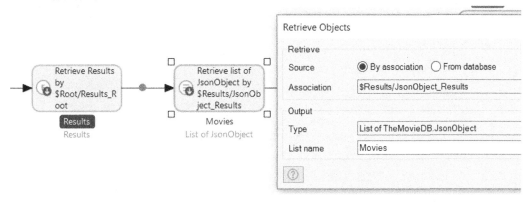

Figure 12.48 – Adding a second retrieve

Now let's add a **Create List** action

28. Set the **Entity** to `Inventory.Movie`. This list will initially be empty, but we will be adding records to it momentarily. See *Figure 12.49*:

Figure 12.49 – Adding a Create List action

29. Add an **iterator** next in the microflow. Iterate over the list of `JsonObject` that we retrieved in step *27*. To add an iterator, right click on any white space in the microflow and select **Add | Loop**:

Figure 12.50 – Adding an iterator

30. Inside the Iterator, add a **Create Object** action to create a new `Inventory.Movie` record. Set the values as shown in *Figure 12.51*:

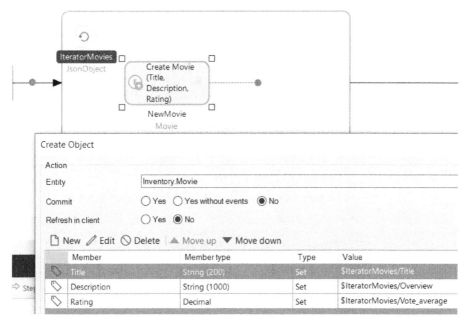

Figure 12.51 – Adding Create Object and setting the attribute values

31. Still inside the iterator, add a **Change List** action to add the new `Movie` record to the list we created in step *28*:

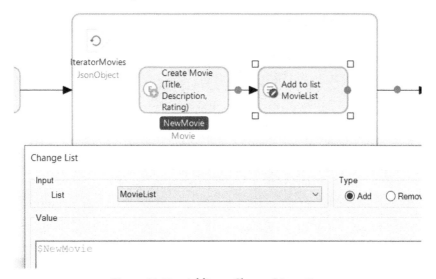

Figure 12.52 – Adding a Change List action

32. Now, outside of the iterator, add a **Commit Object(s)** action to commit the list we created in step *28*:

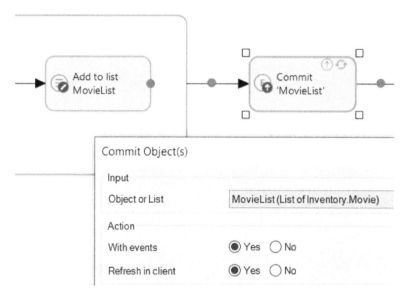

Figure 12.53 – Adding a Commit Object(s) action

33. Finally, add a **Close Page** action as the last action of the microflow:

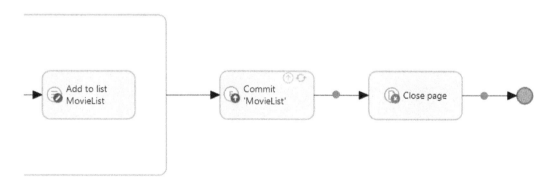

Figure 12.54 – Adding a Close Page action

34. Navigate to the domain model in the Inventory module and change the Description attribute in the Movie entity to allow for 1000 characters:

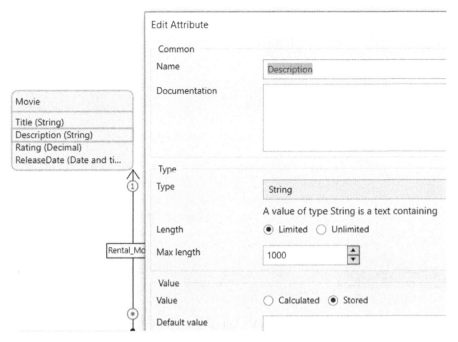

Figure 12.55 – Changing Max length of the string attribute

Now that we have all the logic in place to make the GET call, let's connect it up to some buttons in the user interface so that we can test it out!

35. Navigate to the Request_NewEdit page that was created in steps 3 and 4.

36. Change the **On click** action to **Call a Microflow** and select the microflow that we created in step *14* (ACT_TheMovieDB_GetMoviesByName). See *Figure 12.56* for reference:

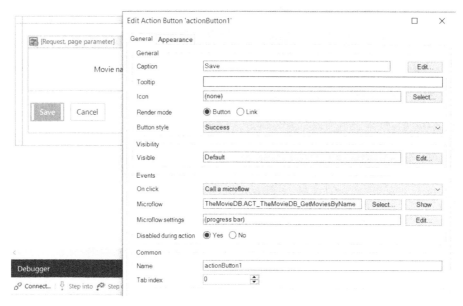

Figure 12.56 – Changing the On click action of the Save button

37. In the **Microflow settings** option, click **Edit** to open the **Microflow Settings** page.

38. Configure the settings as shown in the following screenshot:

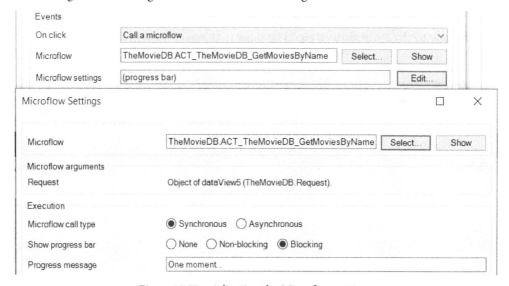

Figure 12.57 – Adjusting the Microflow settings

39. Navigate to the `Movie_Overview` page.

40. Add a new **Action** button to the data grid:

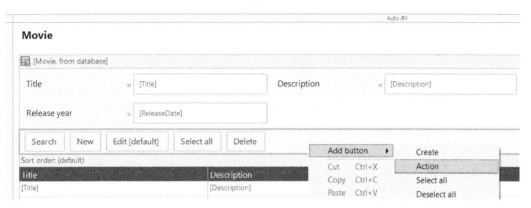

Figure 12.58 – Adding the Action button to the data grid

41. Edit the new action as shown in *Figure 12.59*:

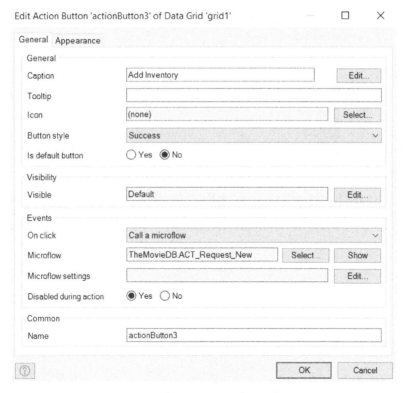

Figure 12.59 – The new Action button's settings

Now we have everything we need to test it all out and add some movies to our project!

42. Recompile your project by clicking the **Run Locally** button in Studio Pro.

43. Once the project has finished compiling, click the **View** button in Studio Pro to view the project in a browser.

44. Navigate to the **Movie** page and you should see the new button we just created in steps *40* and *41*:

Figure 12.60 – Movie overview page as seen in the user interface (UI)

45. Click the **Add Inventory** button and then type `Mission Impossible`:

Figure 12.61 – Popup prompting the name of the movie

46. Click the **Save** button to invoke your REST request microflow.

You should see the **One moment…** blocking popup for a few seconds while the request is executing in the background:

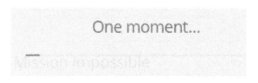

Figure 12.62 – The One moment… popup while actions are executing in the background

If the request is successful, you should see a list of movies now present on your page:

Movie

| Search | New | Edit | Select all | Delete | Add Inventory |

Title	Description	Rating
Mission: Impossible - Fallout	When an IMF mission ends badly, the world is faced with dire consequences. As Ethan ...	7.40
Mission: Impossible	When Ethan Hunt, the leader of a crack espionage team whose perilous operation has ...	6.90
Mission: Impossible - Ghost Protocol	Ethan Hunt and his team are racing against time to track down a dangerous terrorist n...	7.00
Mission: Impossible - Rogue Nation	Ethan and team take on their most impossible mission yet—eradicating The Syndicate...	7.20
Mission: Impossible III	Retired from active duty to train new IMF agents, Ethan Hunt is called back into action ...	6.70
Mission: Impossible II	With computer genius Luther Stickell at his side and a beautiful thief on his mind, agen...	6.10

Figure 12.63 – A successfully updated movie list following the GET call to MovieDB

Congratulations! You have now connected your project up to a third-party REST service and are able to query movies by name and save them to your local database!

> **Important note**
> If you experience any errors when making the request in steps *45* and *46*, add a breakpoint on the `ACT_TheMovieDB_GetMoviesByName` microflow and step through it action by action.

During this section, we have added what would be considered the minimal amount of functionality to our app that will allow us to connect to a REST service. We added a JSON structure, import mapping, a page to allow the user to enter a movie name as a query parameter, and a few microflows to connect everything together. By way of some stretch assignment ideas, you may also consider extending the functionality we just added with some of the following:

- Error handling
- Checking whether the REST action actually returned any results
- Adding logic to ensure that duplicate movies are not imported into your database

Those, of course, are just a few suggestions! Have some fun with the new functionality and see what great things you can come up with!

Summary

In this chapter, we covered a few topics specifically geared toward connecting to the outside world. Consuming data or posting data into other application is increasingly common in this integrated, connected world in which we live. Although we didn't cover every scenario and every method to connect to another application, we hopefully gave you some helpful tips to get started. Integration is one of those areas where you can spend quite a long time building knowledge and skills over years of practice and research. And what's really interesting about this space is that it is ever evolving, ever changing and adapting to the world.

The biggest concept we covered in this chapter was that of consuming data from a third-party service. Of course, The Movie Database was just one example of thousands of websites and systems that have REST service capabilities. This example made the most sense because we were building a video rental application. Feel free to add to the sample project and do some research of your own and see what other free APIs are out there that you can experiment with. A quick Google search returns a very extensive list of options!

In the next chapter, we will do a brief review of each of the chapters outlined in this book. We've covered a lot of awesome topics and a wide variety of information. We will also touch on the next steps in your Mendix journey!

Knowledge check

The following are the answers to the knowledge check from *Chapter 11*, *Storing Data*:

1. a
2. b
3. a and c
4. False
5. False

Chapter 12 knowledge check

1. What are two examples of REST call types?

    a. GET

    b. GRAB

    c. POST

    d. READ

2. What are the two types of mapping artifacts in Studio Pro?

   a. Import

   b. Expansion

   c. Integration

   d. Export

3. What are two types of schema sources that Studio Pro supports natively?

   a. Import mappings

   b. JSON structure

   c. Message definitions

   d. Sub-microflow

4. How important is security and authentication when publishing a web service?

   a. Not very

   b. Moderately important

   c. Extremely important

   d. Don't worry about it all

5. If your application is calling out to a third-party REST API, you are:

   a. Publishing a REST API

   b. Consuming a REST API

   c. Accomplishing a REST API

   d. Dominating a REST API

13
A Review and What's Next

Congratulations! You have completed the whole of this book and have built a functioning, running application in Mendix. Take a moment and let that sink in. In addition to being in possession of a working application, you are, more importantly, in possession of some incredible knowledge! This knowledge has built your Mendix foundation and will push you forward along your journey.

In this chapter, we will take a brief look back at the topics and information that we covered along the way. From the introduction to low-code in *Chapter 1, Introducing Mendix*, all the way through to integrating with a third-party service using a REST API. It's been a great journey so far! The following are the topics that we are going to cover:

- Reviewing the material
- Preparing for the next steps

Reviewing the material

In the following subsections, we will take a brief look back over all 12 chapters of this book. We will review the core concepts and ideas that were presented and highlighted in each chapter. It's been a fun ride, and we hope you enjoyed it!

Chapter 1

In *Chapter 1, Introducing Mendix*, we introduced you to the authors as well as to what to expect in the book. We then dived into what low-code is, and how it differs from traditional programming, as well as low-code platforms. We then explained what Mendix is, the low-code platform that we will be using and discussing further as we move through the book. We provided some details regarding its history, as well as what makes Mendix different from the other low-code platforms.

Chapter 2

In *Chapter 2, Getting to Know the Mendix Platform*, we walked through the account creation process. Once registered and once you had landed on the home page, we started breaking down the features that a user receives once registered. We went over the basic home page layout and the navigation links at the top of the page.

Through the navigation, we explored the App Store, where you can connect with and download apps and widgets directly into your project. We also explored the forum and docs pages. These pages provide a connection with the Mendix community where you can ask and explore answers to any questions you may have.

Chapter 3

In *Chapter 3, Getting to Know Mendix Studio*, we learned all there is to know about Mendix Studio. We walked through where to find and launch Mendix Studio. Once launched, we dissected the many features that Mendix Studio has to offer. We browsed through the UI and provided details on what each button and option does, along with all the different features and the reasons why you should use Mendix Studio.

Chapter 4

In *Chapter 4, Getting to Know Studio Pro*, we provided details on learning what Studio Pro is. We also took a look at how to launch Studio Pro, as well as where to download the platform.

Once downloaded, we explored the UI and pointed out some important functionality and where to find it. After exploring the UI, we explored why you should use Studio, as well as Studio Pro, and what the advantages are of using Studio Pro.

Chapter 5

In *Chapter 5, Getting Started with Your Baseline App*, we learned how to create a project from the Developer Portal and open your project in Mendix Studio Pro to access the full features of the Mendix platform. We used the App Store to add common functions to our app so that we could easily deliver ready-made features to our app's users. For the cases where App Store content is not available, we learned how to create our own modules so that we can create custom features in our Mendix app. We also learned how to find project security, settings, and preferences in Mendix Studio Pro so that we can gain full control of the development environment.

Chapter 6

In *Chapter 6, Understanding Domain Model Basics*, we learned the basics of a Mendix domain model. We learned about entities and how they are data objects to be used in the application to store data for later retrieval in business logic and user interfaces. We also learned about attributes and data types and how different data types can be stored in an entity. The pieces of data themselves are like cells in an Excel table, the columns are attributes, the worksheets are the entities, and each row is an object, or a record of data. Last but not least, we learned about associations and how to relate objects to one another, along with learning about a few use cases for relating objects.

Chapter 7

In *Chapter 7, Understanding the Basics of Page Design*, we learned how to create robust user interfaces. Studio Pro provides the construct of the page for us to display information to end users. The user interface is designed using pages, layouts, widgets, and Atlas UI building blocks in Mendix Studio Pro. We also learned how to call pages from the app's main navigation, directly from page widgets, and with microflows. The exercises showed you how to apply these concepts to the example video store application.

Chapter 8

In *Chapter 8, Getting to Know Microflows*, we learned how to create custom logic with microflows in our Mendix app. We explored some common microflow activities and created a custom microflow with decision logic to validate our object on save. We also learned about annotations and how to add clarity to your microflows. Mendix Assist is a great tool for learning how to build microflows and ensure that you are choosing the right actions in the right order.

Chapter 9

In *Chapter 9, Customizing Your App*, we discussed a few different topics that all centered around creating custom business logic and functionality for your ever-expanding application and business requirements. Specifically, we talked about functions for various attribute types: strings. integers, enumerations, and date times. These functions will undoubtedly be used day in and day out as you build out custom logic in Mendix. As mentioned in the chapter, it's a good idea to become familiar with what functions Mendix provides natively and become familiar with the documentation that Mendix provides. Remember, it's not about memorizing every possible function that could be used, but rather knowing they exist and where to go for information about them. The rest will come with time!

We then talked about sub-microflows at length. The big takeaway from this section was knowing how to appropriately use sub-microflows and understanding why we use them. The biggest reason is reusability. As your application grows, it's very likely you will need to perform the same calculation, make the same REST call, or retrieve the same type of record over and over again. Maintaining this logic in one place, a sub-microflow, rather than having it spread all over your application in various locations, will make ongoing maintenance and the predictability of your application so much easier. Hone this skill from the beginning; your future self will thank you!

In the next portion of the chapter, we discussed the concept of configurable settings. Settings like these are nothing more than user-defined settings that control some aspect of the application's functionality. Generally, the idea is that a particular setting may be adjusted by a user and that setting is pulled into some business logic somewhere in the application rather than hardcoding a value. This is a simple, yet important, concept to understand. Understanding when it's appropriate to implement a solution like this will really help as your application scales and rules may evolve over time.

Lastly, we briefly discussed the power of custom Java actions. Mendix provides an extensive list of native functionality that can all be accomplished without any traditional coding. However, there are limitations as to what Studio Pro has to offer. When you begin to hit those boundaries, custom Java actions can be a real lifeline. We discussed the Community Commons App Store module and how it contains several useful Java actions that you may consider incorporating in your applications.

Chapter 10

The theme of *Chapter 10, Error Handling and Troubleshooting*, was anticipating, handling, and documenting errors in your data and processes. We discussed several ways in which to approach these subjects with the tools Studio Pro offers. The first subject we covered was the concept of defensive programming. As mentioned in the chapter, defensive programming is not a new concept for low-code or Mendix. However, there are some specific ways in which to implement defensive programming concepts within your Mendix project. We first discussed defensively minded IF statements. These statements, when written as discussed in the chapter, allow for visibility of your data when things go wrong. This is a simple concept but one that quite often gets overlooked.

The next concept we discussed in the chapter was building out empty checks properly. This becomes really important especially when you start pulling in data from outside sources as you never know what you will come across. One of the main takeaways from this chapter was leveraging rules when performing validations on your data. Rules allow for reusability with your validation. Think sub-microflow for validation!

The last big concept we discussed in this chapter concerned error handling. One of the themes we tried to make sure was understood is that errors are going to happen; that's just part of application development. Because errors are inevitably going to happen, implementing proper error handling is crucial. We discussed the different types of error handling: custom with rollback, custom without rollback, and continue (which should be avoided if possible). Hand in hand with encountering errors is the debugger tool. Throughout your development life cycle, the debugger is a very important tool in your tool bag. Understanding how to set breakpoints and step through a microflow is a foundational skill in Studio Pro!

Chapter 11

Chapter 11, Storing Data, consolidated some of the topics first presented in *Chapter 6, Understanding Domain Model Basics*. As with anything, there are always deeper layers of understanding to be had. The same is true of understanding associations, the first topic covered in this chapter. We discussed the various types of association: one-to-one, one-to-many, and many-to-many. The key takeaway from this section was understanding the difference between the different types of associations and knowing when to use each one.

Next, we discussed how and why to implement modules in your project. Like a lot of the concepts discussed up to this point, the underlying idea is reusability. Adding a module to your project that handles very specific boundaries of functionality allows the module to be exportable to other projects and reused. This could apply to sharing functionality internally among various applications that you and your team are developing or even extending the module to be made available publicly on the Mendix App Store.

Lastly, we discussed the generalization and specialization of entities. This is also known as inheritance. Leveraging inheritance in your project can be a great thing to do but understanding the pros and cons of doing so was part of the key information presented in this chapter. It's best to fully understand a request and need for a particular piece of functionality before jumping straight to inheritance as a solution. It's best to weigh out inheritance versus a one-to-one association, and vice versa.

Chapter 12

In *Chapter 12, Getting Some REST*, we focused on connecting to the outside world. Almost every application is now connected to some other system in one way, shape, or form. If you don't understand how to build simple integrations between your applications, you will quickly be left in the dust! Thankfully, Mendix makes it really easy to build integrations with some great native tools.

Before we jumped into Studio Pro, we first discussed the basic concept of the REST API. That section was by no means meant to be an exhaustive discussion about REST and integrations as a whole. We would strongly encourage you to continue your learning on this subject as there is an incredible amount of information to take in! We also touched on one tool to help with integration testing. Postman makes it incredibly easy to test out any API before you bring it into Studio Pro. It's certainly not a required step in the development life cycle, but we have often found it very helpful and useful to first work out the integration in Postman (or a similar tool) and then jump into Studio Pro with the integration.

Next in the chapter, we discussed at some length the various tools for consuming a REST API that Mendix offers in Studio Pro. We discussed JSON structures, message definitions, and import mappings. These were just three of the tools offered, and probably the most commonly used ones. It's important to feel comfortable with these and use them in a correct manner while building your connection to a REST API.

In addition to consuming an API, we also discussed how to publish your own from your Mendix project. Even though we didn't actually build this out in our sample project, you should have all the information you need to do so if you so desire. The export mapping and published REST service artifacts were discussed in quite some detail and are the foundational pieces when it comes to publishing your own API from your Mendix project.

Preparing for the next steps

Now that you have a foundation in low-code and Mendix, where will you go with it? The great thing is that this is totally up to you! You can choose to file it away and move on to the next thing or you can choose to dig deeper and turn it in to an entire career path; the choice is yours. Either way, there are a number of steps you may choose to take in the coming weeks, months, and years!

Rapid Developer Certification (and beyond)

The first thing you may want to consider is getting your Rapid Developer Certification from Mendix. The certification exam is a series of multiple choice questions. The topics covered in the exam are largely the same material covered in this book. In fact, the content of this book was designed specifically to be a stepping stone to passing the Rapid Developer Certification.

When you are ready to take the exam, head over to the following link and sign up:

```
https://academy.mendix.com/link/certification/rapid
```

Once you pass the exam and receive your Rapid Developer Certification, you will join the growing community of certified Mendix developers!

Advanced Certification

The next certification step is to get your Advanced Developer Certification. This exam differs significantly from the rapid exam. Instead of a multiple choice exam that can be completed at your leisure, the advanced exam is a practical exam that drops you into a Mendix project. You have 3 hours to complete a number of user stories and fix a handful of bugs reported by users. The solutions you come up with are then graded according to a number of different criteria, including usability and overall impression. Mendix suggests that you should have 6 – 9 months of practical, hands-on experience with Studio Pro before taking the exam. But when you are ready, head over to the following link and sign up: `https://academy.mendix.com/link/classroom/6/Advanced/Exam`.

Expert Certification

The next certification again differs from the one before it. Expert Certification doesn't include any exam or project. Rather, these are replaced with an extensive package of documents you need to put together. These include things such as a project portfolio, references, and an essay. In addition to the documents you need to submit, you will also have an interview that you should prepare for. The concept behind Expert Certification is that Mendix is confirming that you have extensive experience using the platform and can prove it. When you're ready, head on over and sign up: `https://academyportalcloud.mendixcloud.com/index.html`.

Mendix MVP

Lastly, the Mendix MVP program is a bit different to any of the certifications. The MVP program is designed to give recognition to the **Most Valuable Professionals** (**MVPs**) for their devotion in giving back to the Mendix community in various ways. Developers can be nominated for the MVP program or can apply themselves. If accepted, the status of MVP is valid for 1 year. For more information on the program, visit the following link: `https://docs.mendix.com/developerportal/community-tools/mendix-mvp-program`.

For information on current MVPs, visit the following link: `https://developer.mendixcloud.com/link/mvp`.

Additional experience and resources

Mendix has also done a great job in adding additional training resources in recent times. They offer a wide array of learning paths that focus on specific areas of the platform. They vary from beginner, introductory concepts all the way up to expert-level concepts and ideas. We strongly encourage you to check out some of the great resources over at Mendix Academy. Visit the following link for more information: `https://academy.mendix.com/link/path`.

Summary

We hope you enjoyed your time going through the lessons and information presented in this book! No doubt you felt that there were some topics that could have benefitted from their own books by themselves! Even though this book presented a fairly brief look at some of the core features and functions of Mendix Studio and Studio Pro, hopefully you feel confident and excited to continue your learning and journey.

Cheers!

Chapter 12 knowledge check answers

The following are the answers to the knowledge check in *Chapter 12, Getting Some REST*:

1. a, c
2. a, d
3. b, c
4. c
5. b

Packt.com

Subscribe to our online digital library for full access to over 7,000 books and videos, as well as industry leading tools to help you plan your personal development and advance your career. For more information, please visit our website.

Why subscribe?

- Spend less time learning and more time coding with practical eBooks and Videos from over 4,000 industry professionals

- Improve your learning with Skill Plans built especially for you

- Get a free eBook or video every month

- Fully searchable for easy access to vital information

- Copy and paste, print, and bookmark content

Did you know that Packt offers eBook versions of every book published, with PDF and ePub files available? You can upgrade to the eBook version at packt.com and as a print book customer, you are entitled to a discount on the eBook copy. Get in touch with us at customercare@packtpub.com for more details.

At www.packt.com, you can also read a collection of free technical articles, sign up for a range of free newsletters, and receive exclusive discounts and offers on Packt books and eBooks.

Other Books You May Enjoy

If you enjoyed this book, you may be interested in these other books by Packt:

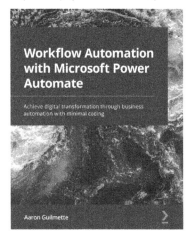

Workflow Automation with Microsoft Power Automate

Aaron Guilmette

ISBN: 978-1-83921-379-3

- Get to grips with the building blocks of Power Automate, its services, and core capabilities

- Explore connectors in Power Automate to automate email workflows

- Discover how to create a flow for copying files between two cloud services

- Understand the business process, connectors, and actions for creating approval flows

- Use flows to save responses submitted to a database through Microsoft Forms

- Find out how to integrate Power Automate with Microsoft Teams

Hands-On Low-Code Application Development with Salesforce

Enrico Murru

ISBN: 978-1-80020-977-0

- Get to grips with the fundamentals of data modeling to enhance data quality

- Deliver dynamic configuration capabilities using custom settings and metadata types

- Secure your data by implementing the Salesforce security model

- Customize Salesforce applications with Lightning App Builder

- Create impressive pages for your community using Experience Builder

- Use Data Loader to import and export data without writing any code

- Embrace the Salesforce Ohana culture to share knowledge and learn from the global Salesforce community

Packt is searching for authors like you

If you're interested in becoming an author for Packt, please visit `authors.packtpub.com` and apply today. We have worked with thousands of developers and tech professionals, just like you, to help them share their insight with the global tech community. You can make a general application, apply for a specific hot topic that we are recruiting an author for, or submit your own idea.

Leave a review - let other readers know what you think

Please share your thoughts on this book with others by leaving a review on the site that you bought it from. If you purchased the book from Amazon, please leave us an honest review on this book's Amazon page. This is vital so that other potential readers can see and use your unbiased opinion to make purchasing decisions, we can understand what our customers think about our products, and our authors can see your feedback on the title that they have worked with Packt to create. It will only take a few minutes of your time, but is valuable to other potential customers, our authors, and Packt. Thank you!

Index

Made in United States
North Haven, CT
23 February 2022

16415029R00183